Mastering Real-Time Analytics with Apache Flink
Comprehensive Techniques for Stream and Batch Processing

Nova Trex

Published by Wang Press

For permissions and other inquiries, write to:
P.O. Box 3132, Framingham, MA 01701, USA

Contents

Introduction

In today's digital age, the paradigm of data processing has dramatically shifted from traditional batch processing to a more dynamic, responsive form of computation capable of handling real-time data streams. Apache Flink stands at the forefront of this transformation, offering comprehensive tools and techniques for tackling both streaming and batch processing challenges. The book, "Mastering Real-Time Analytics with Apache Flink: Comprehensive Techniques for Stream and Batch Processing," charts a path through the complex landscape of Flink's capabilities, equipping data engineers, architects, and researchers with the skills to unleash the full potential of real-time analytics.

Apache Flink is renowned for its powerful stream processing capabilities, which are complemented by its robust support for batch processing. Flink's architecture is purpose-built to address the demands of modern data-driven applications, emphasizing scalability, resilience, and low-latency processing. In a world where data is generated at unprecedented volumes and speeds, Flink empowers organizations to ingest, analyze, and act on data in real-time, thereby ensuring that insights are timely and actionable.

This book guides readers through the intricacies of Flink, starting with the core concepts and advancing towards more specialized topics. It begins with an introduction to Flink's architecture and its dual capabilities in streaming and batch processing. Readers will learn how to set up a Flink environment and become familiar with its programming interfaces for handling both data streams and datasets. As the journey progresses, the reader is introduced to Flink's sophisticated state management and fault tolerance mechanisms, which are essential for preserving data consistency and ensuring the reliability of processing workflows even in the face of failures.

The book further explores Flink's advanced windowing systems and time-based operations, which are pivotal in executing complex stream processing logic. A dedicated chapter on integration discusses how Flink can seamlessly connect with a myriad of data sources and sinks, showcasing its versatility in diverse computing environments and real-world applications.

Advanced features such as Flink's Complex Event Processing (CEP) library and SQL integration are covered in detail. These features allow users to implement pattern matching and complex querying over streaming data, providing the tools necessary for advanced data analytics and real-time event detection. The integration of SQL enables users familiar with relational queries to leverage Flink's processing power without a steep learning curve.

In the concluding chapters, the focus shifts to performance optimization and best practices for deploying Flink applications at scale. Readers will gain valuable insights into tuning Flink jobs for performance efficiency, identifying and resolving bottlenecks, and applying best practices to ensure smooth operation in production environments. By learning how to circumvent common challenges and implement effective solutions, readers will be equipped to achieve optimal results from their Flink deployments.

"Mastering Real-Time Analytics with Apache Flink: Comprehensive Techniques for Stream and Batch Processing" targets a diverse audience, providing value to both newcomers and seasoned professionals in the field of data processing. Regardless of the readers' prior experience, this book is crafted to be an indispensable guide, offering in-depth understanding and practical knowledge in wielding one of the most powerful platforms available for modern real-time data processing. With comprehensive explanations and practical examples, the book is an essential resource for anyone aspiring to master Apache Flink and revolutionize their data processing strategies.

Chapter 1

Introduction to Apache Flink and Stream Processing

Apache Flink is a leading technology in the realm of data stream processing, providing a powerful infrastructure for processing large-scale, real-time data streams. This chapter explores the foundational concepts necessary for understanding how Flink operates within the broader context of stream processing. It covers the architecture of Flink, highlighting its unique capabilities and components such as Job-Manager and TaskManager, which offer robust solutions for managing data streams. Additionally, the chapter discusses Flink's evolution and compares it with other platforms to underscore its distinct features and advantages in real-time data applications, along with showcasing real-world use cases that demonstrate its versatility and effectiveness in various industry scenarios.

1.1 Understanding Data Streams and Real-Time Processing

The domain of data streams represents a dynamic and crucial area in modern computing, facilitating the continuous flow and processing of data in transit. Unlike traditional batch processing, which deals with static datasets, stream processing allows for the management of live data. This capability is indispensable for applications requiring instant feedback, such as monitoring systems, e-commerce platforms, and fintech applications.

Data Streams and Stream Processing

Data streams are sequences of digitally encoded signals used to convey information. They are characterized by their real-time nature, where data elements are generated continuously and processed incrementally. The core concept here revolves around processing data as it is produced, allowing systems to generate results concurrently rather than after-the-fact, like in batch processing.

In stream processing, the data system receives events in real time, processing them on the fly. This architecture fits well with operations that involve time-sensitive data or require live analytics. One can imagine a scenario where a stream processor is deployed to track sensor data from an industrial setup, allowing for immediate response to anomalies.

To enhance understanding, consider the following pseudocode exemplifying a stream processing operation:

```
while (dataStream.hasMoreData()) {
    Event event = dataStream.getNextEvent();
    ProcessedData processed = process(event);
    storeResult(processed);
    if (isAnomaly(processed)) {
        triggerAlarm(processed);
    }
}
```

The pseudocode demonstrates a basic operational framework where each event, fetched continuously from a data stream, is processed almost instantly. This real-time processing capability is pivotal in numerous modern applications, providing essential up-to-the-minute decision-making capacities.

Difference Between Stream and Batch Processing

Batch processing involves collecting data over a period and processing it in bulk, traditionally well-suited for non-urgent data operations. In contrast, stream processing centers around the live handling of data as it arrives, offering a perpetual pipeline that performs computations asynchronously and in parallel with data movement.

The critical distinction lies in the latency and the immediacy of the outputs produced. Batch processing can afford a comprehensive analysis with a latency that can extend from minutes to hours, while stream processing operates within a window of milliseconds to seconds.

Table 1.1 outlines the key differences between these two data processing paradigms:

Batch Processing	Stream Processing
Processes static data	Processes continuous data streams
High latency, potentially hours	Low latency, often sub-second
Suitable for complex analytics	Ideal for real-time analytics
Typically uses databases	Leverages event-based streams

Table 1.1: Comparative Analysis of Batch and Stream Processing

Importance of Real-Time Processing

The demand for real-time data processing has been accelerated by an increase in applications where decision latency affects business outcomes or user experience. Real-time processing systems provide insights at the speed required by markets characterized by rapid fluctuations, such as finance and online advertising, but also by environments requiring agility and precision, such as autonomous vehicles and smart grids.

Real-time processing is instigated by the exigency of acting on data at the moment it is available. Consider, for instance, an e-commerce recommendation engine that personalizes offers based on current user interactions and market trends. These adjustments in recommendations, effected in real time, can influence purchasing behavior substantially.

Further illustrating this concept is an example code snippet, which depicts how real-time processing can be implemented in a simplified model:

```
EventProcessor processor = new EventProcessor();
processor.connectStream(dataStreamSource);
processor.setListener(new EventListener() {
    @Override
    public void onEvent(Event event) {
        // Real-time processing logic
        Valuation valuation = computeRealTimeValuation(event);
        updateRecommendationEngine(valuation);
    }
});
processor.start();
```

In this code, an EventProcessor is configured to listen to a data stream source, performing real-time actions as each event is received. The logic signifies the computational transformations applied to enrich another system component—such as a recommendation engine—with fresh insights.

Applications of Data Stream Processing

Stream processing stands as an enabling force for numerous industry applications. In telecommunications, monitoring traffic patterns to optimize bandwidth allocation benefits directly from instantaneous data analysis. Similarly, financial institutions leverage stream processing for fraud detection systems that correlate complex patterns across data streams to identify suspicious activities swiftly.

In the Internet of Things (IoT), real-time analytics of sensor data allows for rapid responses in environments such as smart homes or industrial automation. The ability to process and act upon data as it streams in ensures that systems remain adaptive and responsive to the changing states of devices and the environment.

Challenges and Considerations

Despite its advantages, real-time processing of data streams introduces several complexities. These include dealing with the high velocity and volume of data, as well as ensuring messages are processed in the correct order and without loss. Additionally, systems need to maintain a balance between latency and throughput, often necessitating the use of distributed architectures such as those employed by Apache Flink or Apache Kafka.

Concerning fault tolerance, stream processing systems must ensure continuity despite potential failures in data sources or nodes within the processing pipeline. Modern frameworks address these concerns through state checkpointing and robust data flow management.

A straightforward example illustrating this implementation in Flink might look like:

```
StreamExecutionEnvironment env = StreamExecutionEnvironment.
    getExecutionEnvironment();
DataStream<String> dataStream = env.addSource(new FlinkKafkaConsumer<>("
    topic", new SimpleStringSchema(), properties));

dataStream
    .flatMap(new Tokenizer())
    .keyBy("word")
    .timeWindow(Time.seconds(5))
    .sum("count")
    .writeAsText("/path/to/output");

env.execute("Real-Time Word Count");
```

In this Flink job, a Kafka consumer streams text data into Flink, where it undergoes real-time processing to count occurrences of words within specific time windows. The example illustrates how Flink manages incoming data and applies transformations efficiently.

The implementation of real-time processing paradigms, while complex, continues to yield tremendous value. The ongoing evolution in this field brings opportunities to extract actionable insights swiftly, providing significant operational advantages in a competitive marketplace.

1.2   Overview of Apache Flink

Apache Flink is a powerful framework and distributed processing engine for stateful computations over unbounded and bounded data streams. It holds a significant position in the landscape of big data technologies due to its ability to process data streams in real-time with low latency and high throughput. Flink's architecture and design are deeply rooted in handling streaming data, distinguishing it from traditional batch processing frameworks in fundamental ways.

Historical Perspective and Evolution

Apache Flink originated as a research project, known as Stratosphere, co-founded by data management professors and researchers at numer-

13

ous academic institutions. This project aimed to address the limitations of batch-centric computation models prevalent in systems such as Apache Hadoop. Over time, it transformed into Apache Flink and incubated under the Apache Software Foundation, where it has gradually evolved into a leading real-time stream processing tool.

Flink's development has been guided by the need for a scalable, efficient, and extensible computation engine capable of handling data streaming operations robustly. With each release, the system has expanded its capabilities, introducing new features and integrations that leverage its core design principles.

Core Design and Features

At the heart of Flink is a native streaming engine, with a stream-first approach for data processing, enabling both batch and streaming applications. This capability stems from its ability to execute complex data transformations continuously and at scale, largely tuned toward minimizing latency while maximizing data throughput.

Flink excels in several key areas:

1. *Stateful Stream Processing*: Flink offers robust support for stateful computations necessary for applications like machine learning models, streaming analytics, and financial calculations. It achieves this by maintaining state consistency and fault tolerance through checkpointing.

2. *Event Time Processing*: Flink supports event time semantics, allowing for complex temporal analytics. This feature is crucial for applications where the timing of the events matters, permitting the handling of out-of-order data by using windows and triggers.

3. *High Throughput and Low Latency*: Flink's architecture is designed to handle terabytes of data per second with millisecond latency, achieved through its native support for distributed streaming processes.

4. *Scalability*: By supporting distributed processing, Flink can scale horizontally across hundreds and even thousands of nodes, making it suitable for enterprise-level tasks.

5. *Fault Tolerance*: Checkpointing and savepoints ensure that Flink jobs can recover with minimal data loss in the event of failures, bolstered by exactly-once state consistency guarantees.

Key Components of Apache Flink

To comprehend the efficacy of Apache Flink in handling tasks of varying complexity and scale, it's vital to understand its primary components:

- **JobManager**: This is a central component responsible for coordinating distributed execution. It controls job scheduling, resource allocation, failure recovery, and task coordination.

- **TaskManager**: This component executes tasks on data subsets, works closely with JobManager, and performs actual data transformations and computations.

- **DataStream API**: This provides developers with a high-level API to define complex data stream applications using an expressive programming model. It supports operations such as transformations, aggregations, and windowing.

- **State Backend**: Integral for storing state information; Flink supports multiple state backends, including in-memory, RocksDB, and file systems for managing state across checkpoints.

- **Flink Runtime**: The execution layer that facilitates task execution within the scope of distributed, parallelized systems tied closely with message-passing mechanisms.

Below is an example illustrating a simple Flink setup for streaming:

```
StreamExecutionEnvironment env = StreamExecutionEnvironment.
    getExecutionEnvironment();

DataStream<String> streamData = env.addSource(new SomeSourceFunction());

streamData
    .flatMap(new Tokenizer())
    .keyBy(value -> value.f0)
    .sum(1)
    .print();

env.execute("Flink Streaming Example");
```

15

This code fragment demonstrates how Flink access supports data ingestion, transformation, and aggregation. The operations are performed
over a data stream ingested through a custom source function, exemplifying Flink's fluent API design and operational model.

Flink's Role in Modern Data Ecosystems

Flink has established itself as an instrumental technology within data
ecosystems, readily integrated with other tools and platforms. Its connectors allow seamless synergy with a variety of data sources and sinks
such as Apache Kafka, Amazon Kinesis, Apache Cassandra, and Elasticsearch, facilitating smooth data flow across heterogeneous systems.

Moreover, Flink performs admirably within cloud-native environments. Deployed in Kubernetes clusters or serverless frameworks,
Flink's architecture capitalizes on cloud scalability features,
translating to optimal resource utilization in cost-effective ways.

Practical Applications and Use Cases

Flink showcases its utility across diverse sectors such as finance,
telecommunications, e-commerce, and entertainment:

- **Fraud Detection**: Banks and financial institutions use Flink for
  real-time analysis of transaction streams, identifying potentially
  suspicious activities through complex event processing patterns.

- **Network Optimization**: Telecommunications firms rely on
  Flink to monitor network load; rapid adjustments in network parameters optimize user experience dynamically.

- **Real-time Personalization**: Web and mobile services employ
  Flink to adapt content delivery instantaneously to user interactions, urging engagement and user satisfaction through personalized experiences.

- **IoT Solutions**: Environmental and industrial sensors generate
  real-time data processed through Flink, granting operational insight and facilitating automation responses.

Community and Continuous Development

Apache Flink's strengths are bolstered by an active community and
sustained contributions from a wide-ranging network of contributors.

This input from both individual developers and organizations guarantees continued innovation, improvement, and troubleshooting across its service spectrum. Flink's reputation is also maintained through its adherence to consistent updates, maturation of APIs, and expanded integration capabilities.

Exploring Advanced Topics in Flink

Advanced users of Apache Flink can delve into its flourishing toolkit—such as machine learning algorithms harnessed through the FlinkML library, advanced event pattern detection through CEP (Complex Event Processing), and stream graph construction techniques.

As Flink continually evolves, expanded functionalities and optimization strategies keep it aligned with the growing complexities and expectations of cutting-edge real-time process systems.

Apache Flink remains a key enabler for responsive and adaptive analytics, carrying the mantle of data stream processing confidently into an age defined by real-time decision-making and large-scale data acuity.

1.3 Flink Architecture

Understanding the architecture of Apache Flink is imperative for leveraging its full potential as a stream processing framework. Apache Flink boasts an architecture tailored specifically to real-time data processing, which differentiates it from batch processing models and even some other streaming technologies. The architecture of Flink strikes a unique balance by effectively managing stateful stream computation, advanced windowing capabilities, and precise event time semantics while offering strong fault-tolerant mechanisms.

Overview of Flink's Architectural Design

At its core, Flink consists of the following principal components: the JobManager, TaskManager, and the client's API. These components collectively address the complexities of distributed data processing, ensuring high availability, scalability, and robust data handling mechanisms.

- **JobManager**: An integral part of Flink's architecture, the Job-

Manager orchestrates task execution, manages job lifecycle and resources, and handles failure scenarios. It operates as the central coordinator of a Flink application, governing the scheduling and optimization of tasks across the cluster nodes.

- **TaskManager**: Acting as the workhorse, the TaskManager performs the execution of distributed tasks on supplied data. Multiple TaskManagers operate simultaneously within a Flink cluster, each responsible for executing a subset of tasks, known as TaskSlots, to process partitions of the data stream.

- **Client**: The client is used to submit the user-defined Flink job to the cluster. The client translates the user program into an execution plan, encapsulating it into a JobGraph which is then dispatched to the JobManager for execution.

Execution Model and Dataflow

The execution model of Flink is fundamentally based on data streaming, with data processed in continuous streams rather than discrete steps as seen in batch processing. This design ensures low-latency response and high throughput for both bounded and unbounded streams.

- *Plan Construction*: When a user submits a Flink job via the API, it first compiles into an intermediate dataflow representation, known as the StreamGraph. The StreamGraph depicts the logical execution plan of tasks.

- *JobGraph Generation*: The StreamGraph is reduced into a JobGraph, which removes redundant operations and optimizes execution directives. The JobGraph is forwarded to the JobManager, delineating the task dependencies and configurations.

- *Task Deployment*: The JobManager distributes tasks to available TaskManagers. TaskManagers execute tasks as operators, maintaining intermediate states and shuffling data as demanded by the dataflow.

- *Transformation and State Management*: Operators within TaskManagers process data incrementally. They are fundamental in executing transformations such as filter, map, join, and

18

window operations on streaming data. Flink's sophisticated state management mechanisms ensure consistency even in complex operations.

State Management and Consistency

Stateful stream processing is a cornerstone of Flink, distinguishing it as it provides precise control over application state, supporting functionalities such as aggregate computations over extensive datasets.

Flink allows fine-tuned state management through various constructs:

- *Operator State*: Is kept individually for each task operator. It is useful for simple use cases, like maintaining a count or calculating averages.

- *Keyed State*: Provides statefulness across keys, optimizing operations through built-in mechanisms such as keyed functions. It allows developers to preserve and query state tied to specific keys, facilitating advanced operations like windowing.

- *Managed State Backends*: Flink offers multiple backends for state storage, including in-memory and RocksDB configurations. Managed State ensures that checkpoints and failures are mitigated without excessive loss or downtime.

Event Time Processing and Windowing

One of the most compelling features of Flink is its native support for event time semantics, enabling precise timing control for stream processing. This contrasts with processing based on the system (processing) time, offering superior accuracy for real-world datasets.

Flink supports multiple window types to segment streams for individual processing:

- *Time Windows*: Split data by temporal boundaries. These are further classified into fixed, sliding, and session windows to accommodate diverse use cases.

- *Count Windows*: Process data based on the number of events, suitable for scenarios where periodic batch-like patterns are preferred.

- *Custom Windows*: Tailored windows that satisfy special business requirements through user-defined logic.

An example of a Flink application implementing time windowing is as follows:

```
env
    .socketTextStream("localhost", 9999)
    .flatMap(new LineSplitter())
    .keyBy(value -> value.f0)
    .timeWindow(Time.seconds(10))
    .sum(1)
    .print();
```

In this snippet, a source stream is transformed, key-grouped, and processed within ten-second time windows, highlighting Flink's adeptness at handling temporal data segmentation.

Fault Tolerance and Checkpointing

Flink offers robust fault tolerance through clustered architecture built on the design of stateful computations backed by consistent checkpointing. It helps ensure that streaming applications recover cleanly from crashes or unexpected disruptions.

Checkpoints are regularly scheduled to store state snapshots. Flink ensures "exactly-once" semantics for state updates by incorporating synchronous barriers in data streams, inherently supporting eventual state consistency.

Scalability and Resource Management

Flink's distributed nature is ideal for scaling operations across expansive data landscapes. Its architecture supports elastic scaling—through reactive resource adjustments, as driven by Kubernetes or other cluster managers—to optimize resource consumption dynamically.

The streamlined coordination between the JobManager and TaskManagers ensures that resource allocation is balanced based on job requirements, providing a seamless flow of data operations between scaled clusters.

Advanced Features and Integrations

Beyond its core architecture, Flink offers several advanced tools such as:

20

- *Flink SQL and Table API*: Allow for SQL-like querying and tabular data manipulations on streams, extending accessibility for developers familiar with classical data manipulation paradigms.

- *Streaming Connectors*: Enable integration with diverse ecosystems; examples include Kafka, Elasticsearch, Cassandra, and custom sinks, facilitating end-to-end stream data pipelines.

- *CEP (Complex Event Processing)*: Supports pattern detection across multiple event streams using high-level, declarative programming models.

The Flink architecture thus symbolizes a convergence of efficacy and elegance, fostering a fertile ground for the development of next-generation streaming applications. Its meticulously engineered components ensure versatility and resilience, cementing its stance in the realm of real-time data processing.

1.4 Use Cases and Applications

Apache Flink, with its robust architecture and real-time processing capabilities, has become a cornerstone technology across various domains. Its versatility allows it to address a vast array of applications, from real-time analytics to data stream transformations, playing a pivotal role in industries where immediacy and scalability are indispensable. The following section elucidates several prevalent use cases, showcasing Flink's adaptability and effectiveness in solving complex, real-world problems.

Stream Processing in Financial Services

In the financial industry, where transactions are rapid and voluminous, real-time analysis of data streams is crucial for ensuring security, compliance, and efficiency. Apache Flink excels in this niche, providing tools for executing high-speed operations and fostering immediacy in decision-making.

- *Fraud Detection*: Flink's ability to process real-time data streams is instrumental in detecting fraudulent activities instantly. By

21

analyzing transaction patterns and user behaviors in real-time, financial institutions can identify anomalies indicating potential fraud. The system can trigger actions such as alerting analysts or automatically blocking suspect transactions.

- *Algorithmic Trading*: Traders use Flink to ingest massive streams of market data and apply sophisticated algorithms that react to market changes in milliseconds, thereby optimizing trades and offering competitive edges in high-frequency trading environments.

A simple implementation of a real-time classification algorithm for fraud detection might look like this:

```
DataStream<Transaction> transactions = env.fromSource(transactionSource);

transactions
    .keyBy(Transaction::getUserId)
    .process(new FraudDetector())
    .addSink(new AlertSink());
```

Here, FraudDetector represents a custom processing function evaluating incoming transactions for fraudulent indicators.

Telecommunications and Network Optimization

Telecommunications operators manage vast, intricate networks requiring optimized performance. In this landscape, Apache Flink can deploy network monitoring and adjustment solutions:

- *Network Traffic Management*: Flink processes streaming data from network devices and applies analytics for real-time traffic balancing, reducing bottlenecks and preventing outages.

- *Quality of Service (QoS) Monitoring*: By streaming real-time metrics, Flink helps telecoms ensure QoS by dynamically reallocating resources and responding to performance degradations automatically.

In a conceptual Flink application, network data streams might be processed to generate insights used for remediation actions:

```
DataStream<NetworkMetrics> metrics = env.addSource(networkSource);
```

```
metrics
    .keyBy(NetworkMetrics::getDeviceId)
    .window(Time.minutes(1))
    .apply(new QoSAnalyzer())
    .addSink(new ResourceAllocator());
```

E-commerce Personalization and Supply Chain Management

The dynamic nature of e-commerce platforms and their supply chains necessitates real-time data processing capabilities, which Apache Flink caters to effectively:

- *Real-Time Personalization*: By processing user behavior data streams, Flink enables the delivery of personalized user experiences, such as customized product recommendations that adapt to browsing patterns and purchasing history.

- *Inventory Management*: Flink processes transaction data to reflect inventory status in real-time, ensuring stock levels are perpetually up-to-date and item availability is accurately communicated to both procurement systems and end-users.

Example code demonstrating the usage of Flink for real-time recommendations:

```
DataStream<UserActivity> userActivities = env.socketTextStream("ecommerce.com",
    9000);

userActivities
    .keyBy(UserActivity::getUserId)
    .process(new RecommendationEngine())
    .addSink(new RecommendationSink());
```

Smart Cities and IoT Applications

The advent of smart cities and IoT ecosystems has given rise to enormous quantities of streaming data from interconnected devices, necessitating real-time data operations and intelligence at scale which Apache Flink is well-suited for:

- *Traffic Monitoring*: By applying Flink's stream processing against real-time traffic data from various sensors, cities can optimize traffic light cycles, reduce congestion, and improve public transportation.

- *Environmental Monitoring*: Flink can aggregate data from environmental sensors across urban landscapes, providing cities with real-time insights into air quality, temperature variations, or noise pollution for immediate action or long-term planning.

This example illustrates a Flink setup for IoT-driven environmental monitoring:

```
DataStream<SensorData> sensorData = env.addSource(new IoTSource());

sensorData
    .keyBy(SensorData::getType)
    .timeWindow(Time.hours(1))
    .aggregate(new EnvironmentalTrendAggregator())
    .addSink(new AlertingSystem());
```

Media Streaming and Social Media Analytics

Apache Flink supports media platforms by facilitating real-time data operations that enhance user interaction and engagement:

- *Stream Preparation and Encoding*: Real-time stream processing allows media companies to transcode video streams tailored to heterogeneous devices dynamically, improving the delivery and quality of media content.

- *Social Feed Monitoring*: Social media companies leverage Flink for real-time sentiment analysis and the extraction of influential topics, enabling timely user engagement.

The following code illustrates using Flink for sentiment analysis on streaming social feeds:

```
DataStream<Tweet> tweets = env.addSource(new TwitterSource());

tweets
    .flatMap(new Tokenizer())
    .keyBy(value -> value.f0)
    .reduce(new SentimentAggregator())
    .addSink(new SentimentDashboardSink());
```

Complex Event Processing (CEP)

CEP is another noteworthy area where Flink demonstrates substantial prowess. This enables the platform to track sequences of events or specific patterns within real-time data streams. Applications involve anomaly detection in operational systems or complex user interaction sequences to drive automated responses.

Given Flink's capabilities in CEP, an example pattern detection setup might appear as follows:

```
Pattern<Event, ?> pattern = Pattern.<Event>begin("start")
                .where(new SimpleCondition<Event>() {
                    public boolean filter(Event event) {
                        return event.getType() == EventType.START;
                    }
                })
                .next("middle")
                .where(new SimpleCondition<Event>() {
                    public boolean filter(Event event) {
                        return event.getType() == EventType.CONTINUE;
                    }
                })
                .followedBy("end")
                .where(new SimpleCondition<Event>() {
                    public boolean filter(Event event) {
                        return event.getType() == EventType.END;
                    }
                });

PatternStream<Event> patternStream = CEP.pattern(inputEventStream, pattern);

patternStream
    .select(new PatternSelectFunction<Event, String>() {
        public String select(Map<String, List<Event>> pattern) {
            return "Pattern detected!";
        }
    })
    .addSink(new PatternSink());
```

In summary, the versatility of Apache Flink allows it to be deployed effectively in a wide range of sectors demanding real-time, critical data processing. From financial services to media streaming, Flink's ability to process data streams with scalability, fault tolerance, and stateful processing, makes it an invaluable tool in modern data-driven landscapes.

1.5 Comparison with Other Stream Processing Platforms

In big data and real-time processing, several platforms have emerged to address the need for efficient data handling and analytics in streaming contexts. Among these, Apache Flink, Apache Kafka, Apache Storm, and Apache Spark stand out as prominent technologies that offer unique capabilities and features tailored to streamline data processing. Understanding how Apache Flink compares with these platforms is essential for evaluating its suitability for specific applications and environments.

Apache Flink vs. Apache Kafka

Apache Kafka primarily serves as a distributed messaging system rather than a complete stream processing framework. It functions as a storage layer for streaming data via its partitioned log model, facilitating publishing and consuming streams of records in real-time.

- *Design Orientation*: Kafka is designed to ensure durable storage and scalable message coordinates, whereas Flink emphasizes complex event processing with stateful transformations over incoming event data. Kafka provides the transport layer, while Flink executes processing logic on top of data streams.

- *Use Case Focus*: While Kafka inherently focuses on reliable delivery and retention of data streams for consumers, Flink offers advanced data processing, such as windowed analytics, event time processing, and distributed computations.

- *Integrations*: Both projects work well together—Kafka as a robust event bus and Flink performing sophisticated analytical operations on streams originating from Kafka topics.

An example illustrating the interplay between Kafka and Flink for a simple word count might look like this:

```
StreamExecutionEnvironment env = StreamExecutionEnvironment.
    getExecutionEnvironment();

FlinkKafkaConsumer<String> consumer = new FlinkKafkaConsumer<>(
    "my_topic", new SimpleStringSchema(), properties);

DataStream<String> text = env.addSource(consumer);

DataStream<Tuple2<String, Integer>> wordCounts = text
    .flatMap(new Tokenizer())
    .keyBy(value -> value.f0)
    .sum(1);
```

```
wordCounts.addSink(new FlinkKafkaProducer<>(...)); // Output back to a Kafka
    topic
```

Apache Flink vs. Apache Storm

Apache Storm represents an earlier evolution in stream processing platforms, introduced for handling unbounded streams with low latency, designed around a simple spout-bolt topology.

- *Computational Model*: Storm relies on a tuple-based processing architecture focused on real-time computation. However, it lacks Flink's refined state management, precisely-once semantics, and sophisticated event time processing.

- *Performance Optimization*: Flink's DAG-based execution model has advantages over Storm's design by optimizing task execution through operators and chaining, improving resource utilization, latency, and throughput.

- *Complexity and Ease of Use*: Storm's simpler model can expedite smaller, uncomplicated tasks but might be limiting as complexity scales up. Flink offers richer data constructs and support for iterative computations.

A basic Flink pipeline designed similarly to a Storm topology:

```
DataStream<Tuple2<String, Integer>> wordCounts = env
    .socketTextStream("localhost", 9999)
    .flatMap(new Tokenizer())
    .keyBy(value -> value.f0)
    .sum(1);
wordCounts.print();
```

Apache Flink vs. Apache Spark Streaming

As a widely adopted analytics engine, Apache Spark has extended its batch processing capabilities to the streaming world with Spark Streaming, designed for bounded and unbounded data processing via micro-batching.

- *Batch vs. Stream Processing*: Unlike Flink's continuous streaming model, Spark Streaming processes data in blocks, which can introduce higher latency in real-time applications but aids batching-based use cases where latency is less critical.

- *State and Event Time*: Flink provides powerful stateful computations and efficient management of event time. Conversely, Spark has limited evolution in this area with structured streaming enhancing some capabilities, yet Flink remains optimal for time-driven scenarios.

- *Throughput and Latency*: Flink provides lower latency processing due to its native streaming model—ideal for high-frequency, real-time tasks. Spark's batch model inherently can scale, benefiting from advanced ETL and batch analytics tasks.

Below is an example to illustrate real-time windowed processing with Flink:

```
StreamExecutionEnvironment env = StreamExecutionEnvironment.
    getExecutionEnvironment();

DataStream<String> logData = env.socketTextStream("localhost", 9999);

DataStream<Tuple2<String, Integer>> warningCounts = logData
    .filter(new FilterFunction<String>() {
        public boolean filter(String value) {
            return value.startsWith("WARN");
        }
    })
    .map(new MapFunction<String, Tuple2<String, Integer>>() {
        public Tuple2<String, Integer> map(String value) {
            return new Tuple2<>("WARN", 1);
        }
    })
    .keyBy(0)
    .window(TumblingProcessingTimeWindows.of(Time.seconds(5)))
    .sum(1);

warningCounts.print();
```

Key Considerations for Platform Selection

When selecting a stream processing platform, considering the specific use case's demands is crucial. Below are a few key considerations:

- *Data Characteristics*: For real-time stream analytics, Flink offers unmatched capabilities with its stateful processing, event-time support, and exactly-once semantics.

- *Integration and Ecosystem*: The compatibility with existing data pipelines and infrastructure, such as using Kafka for ingesting streams with Flink as the processing component, drives a seamless data architecture.

- *Resource and Scalability Requirements*: Factors like deployment environments, resource management strategies, and job scaling capabilities influence whether Flink's native streaming model or alternatives like Spark's micro-batching model are preferable.

- *Complexity of Operations*: The ability to handle complex transformations, enrichments, and aggregations of data streams may drive choice. Flink excels in these areas, particularly with intricate window operations and stateful computations.

Conclusion of Comparative Strengths

While each platform brings nuanced strengths to the table, the decision ultimately hinges on the specific application requirements and the operational landscape. Apache Flink stands as a compelling choice where low-latency stream processing, advanced state management, and horizontal scalability are essential.

In contexts requiring high-frequency updates, such as dynamic marketplaces or sensor networks, Flink's architecture affords responsiveness and precision that alternative platforms may struggle to match. Nevertheless, hybrid models whereby Flink is coupled with Kafka, and even in conjunction with Spark or Storm for complex workflows, may offer superior solutions harmonizing operational expediency with maximal data insight.

Flink's architecture demonstrates a commitment to embracing both the challenges and opportunities of stream-based processing, making it a robust tool for today's rapidly evolving data ecosystems.

Chapter 2

Setting Up Apache Flink Environment

Setting up the Apache Flink environment is essential for anyone looking to leverage its robust stream and batch processing capabilities. This chapter provides a detailed guide to establishing Flink on both local and cluster environments. It outlines the system requirements, step-by-step installation procedures, and configuration settings needed to optimize Flink's performance. Additionally, it covers verification of the setup by running sample jobs and introduces the use of Docker for streamlined deployment and management. Through these instructions, readers can ensure their Flink environment is correctly configured, paving the way for efficient data processing.

2.1 System Requirements and Prerequisites

Apache Flink is a powerful stream and batch processing framework capable of handling stateful computations over data streams. Before proceeding with the installation and deployment of Apache Flink, it is crucial to ensure that the system meets all necessary hardware and software requirements for optimal performance.

Flink's efficiency and ability to process vast amounts of data rely heavily upon the underlying system's resources. These include CPU, memory, and disk capacity, as well as network connectivity if dealing with distributed setups. It is designed to run on various operating systems, and knowing the compatible environments is an essential first step.

- **Hardware Requirements**

Hardware plays a pivotal role in determining the performance of Apache Flink. The following specifications are generally recommended, although actual requirements will vary based on the size and complexity of the data processing tasks:

- **CPU:** A multi-core processor is recommended to leverage Flink's parallel processing capabilities. Each Flink operator can run on a different core, boosting data handling efficiency.

- **Memory:** At least 8GB of RAM is suggested for development and small-scale testing. Production environments should have significantly more RAM, potentially scaling up to terabytes, to accommodate large stateful operations and cache-intensive computations.

- **Disk:** Adequate disk space is vital, especially when handling large datasets. Flink utilizes the disk for spillover operations from memory. SSDs can substantially increase the speed of disk operations compared to traditional HDDs.

- **Network:** For distributed setups, a high-speed network is essential to support the data exchange between nodes, typically within a cluster.

Cluster environments amplify the need for robust hardware resources, as tasks are distributed across multiple machines, each requiring adequate specifications to handle its share of processing efficiently.

- **Software Requirements**

Apache Flink has several software dependencies. Ensuring these dependencies are installed correctly is integral to Flink's performance and operational reliability.

- **Operating System:** Flink runs on multiple operating systems, including but not limited to Linux, macOS, and Windows. Linux-based distributions such as Ubuntu or CentOS are often recommended for production environments due to their stability and performance in server management.

- **Java:** Apache Flink is a Java-based program. It requires a Java Development Kit (JDK) version 8 or 11. It's paramount to verify the compatibility of Java versions as they introduce features and enhancements which may affect Flink's performance.

- **Hadoop:** For those integrating Flink with Hadoop, the Hadoop version should be compatible with the Flink version being installed. This is particularly relevant for Flink setups that access Hadoop's Distributed File System (HDFS) for distributed storage capabilities.

- **Python (optional):** If you intend to execute PyFlink jobs, Python version 3.5 or higher is necessary. PyFlink enables the execution of Flink programs written in Python, expanding flexibility in job implementations.

- **Prerequisite Software Installation**

Here are some command lines to verify and install the required software:

To check the Java version:

```
java -version
```

The output should resemble:

```
java version "1.8.0_281"
Java(TM) SE Runtime Environment (build 1.8.0_281-b09)
Java HotSpot(TM) 64-Bit Server VM (build 25.281-b09, mixed mode)
```

To install the JDK on a Linux system using apt, the following command can be used:

```
sudo apt-get update
sudo apt-get install openjdk-8-jdk
```

Verifying the Python installation can be done through:

```
python3 --version
```

Should you need to install Python, use:

```
sudo apt-get install python3
```

- **Dependencies**

Flink requires certain additional libraries and configurations, depending on the specific use case:

- **Scala:** If writing Flink jobs in Scala, a compatible version of Scala must be installed. Flink 1.0 and later builds generally recommend Scala 2.11 or 2.12.

- **Apache Kafka:** If you are deploying Flink with real-time data streaming requirements, Apache Kafka can be used as a message broker, necessitating its installation and setup.

- **Development Tools**

While setting up a development environment for Flink, consider the following tools to aid in efficient code management and job execution:

- **Integrated Development Environment (IDE):** IDEs such as IntelliJ IDEA or Eclipse with Maven integration provide a feature-rich environment for writing, debugging, and managing Flink applications. Maven handles the Flink dependencies automatically, simplifying the build process.

- **Command Line Interface (CLI):** The Flink CLI is crucial for submitting and managing Flink jobs. It provides control over the execution of jobs, management of parallelism, and configuration of task managers.

34

To integrate Maven in your project, include the necessary repositories and dependencies in the pom.xml file:

```
<repositories>
    <repository>
        <id>central</id>
        <url>https://repo.maven.apache.org/maven2</url>
    </repository>
</repositories>

<dependencies>
    <dependency>
        <groupId>org.apache.flink</groupId>
        <artifactId>flink-core</artifactId>
        <version>1.15.1</version>
    </dependency>
    <dependency>
        <groupId>org.apache.flink</groupId>
        <artifactId>flink-java</artifactId>
        <version>1.15.1</version>
    </dependency>
</dependencies>
```

- **Networking Considerations**

In distributed Flink environments, particularly when deployed on multiple nodes or using cloud services, robust networking capabilities are essential:

- **IP Addresses:** Machines should be on the same subnet for lower-latency connections. Additionally, having fixed IP addresses ensures that the communication within the cluster is stable and reliable.

- **Ports:** Certain ports need to be open for Flink's runtime environment, job manager, and task managers. By default, port 8081 is used for Flink's web dashboard.

Firewalls should be configured to allow traffic over these necessary ports, aligning with across-cluster communication needs.

- **Scalable Infrastructure**

When planning the infrastructure for intentional scalability, particularly with cloud-based or virtualization scenarios, consider the following:

35

- **Virtual Machines (VMs):** Cloud platforms such as AWS, Google Cloud, and Azure provide flexible options to scale resources up or down based on workload demands.

- **Docker and Containers:** Dockerization of Flink environments allows for modular and portable installations that can be replicated and scaled easily across different environments.

A practical Dockerfile configuration for Apache Flink could look like the following:

```
FROM flink:1.15

RUN apt-get update && \
    apt-get install -y openjdk-8-jdk && \
    apt-get clean;

COPY ./conf /opt/flink/conf

EXPOSE 8081
```

Using containers ensures that each Flink job runs in an isolated environment, preventing dependency conflicts and facilitating easier management and orchestration within clusters.

- **Security Measures**

Implementing security protocols within your Flink environment ensures data integrity and protects against unauthorized access:

- **Encryption:** Implement TLS for securing the communication channels between jobs and data sources.

- **Authentication and Authorization:** Set up user roles and access controls, especially in multi-tenant environments, to ensure only authorized personnel can manipulate Flink operations.

- **Precautions for Scaling**

When planning for high-availability and resource scaling in Flink, the careful consideration of several factors is paramount to maintaining system performance and reliability:

36

- **Replication:** Set up replicas for critical components, such as JobManager and TaskManager, to ensure redundancy and fault tolerance.

- **Resource Management:** Utilize resource management systems like Kubernetes to efficiently allocate and manage resources across the Flink cluster.

Flink's architecture is highly adaptable, allowing for dynamic scaling according to the workloads' requirements. Implementing a well-defined scaling strategy that includes automatic resource adjustments helps in optimizing performance and reducing operational costs.

Configuring JDK, software dependencies, and preparing network infrastructure will aid in seamlessly deploying Flink in suitable environments. With foresight in planning resources, understanding software prerequisites, and embracing modern containerized approaches, Apache Flink setups can be effectively optimized, resulting in high performance and resilient implementations across diverse operational contexts.

2.2 Downloading and Installing Flink Locally

Setting up Apache Flink on a local machine forms the foundational step towards understanding and making full use of this robust stream and batch processing framework. This section provides comprehensive instructions for downloading, installing, and configuring Flink on a local development environment. The focus will be on ensuring that the installation process caters to various development needs and optimizes the setup for testing distributed streaming and batch processing applications.

- **Downloading Apache Flink**

  Apache Flink's binary distributions are freely available from the Apache Flink official website. It is important to download a version compatible with your intended use case and existing infrastructure.

37

To download:

1. Visit the Apache Flink Downloads Page (https://flink.apache.org/downloads.html).
2. Select the binary distribution for the version you wish to install. As a best practice, choose a stable version suitable for your operating environment.
3. Ensure that the chosen download corresponds to your platform needs (such as Hadoop integration if required).

You can download the binary directly using the wget command in the terminal for convenience:

```
wget https://archive.apache.org/dist/flink/flink-1.15.1/flink-1.15.1-bin-
      scala__2.12.tgz
```

- **Verifying Downloads**

Verifying the integrity of the downloaded file ensures that the software has not been tampered with and is safe for installation. Apache provides checksum files and GPG signatures for this purpose.

To verify the checksum, use the sha256sum command:

```
sha256sum flink-1.15.1-bin-scala__2.12.tgz
```

Compare the output with the SHA256 checksum provided on the Flink website.

For GPG signature verification:

1. Import Flink's GPG key:

```
gpg --keyserver keyserver.ubuntu.com --recv-key D1260AE9
```

2. Verify using the downloaded signature file:

```
gpg --verify flink-1.15.1-bin-scala__2.12.tgz.asc flink-1.15.1-bin-
      scala__2.12.tgz
```

- **Installing Apache Flink**

Once the download and verification are successful, proceed with the installation:

38

1. Extract the compressed archive:

```
tar -xzf flink-1.15.1-bin-scala_2.12.tgz
```

   This command will extract the files into a directory named flink-1.15.1.

2. Move the extracted directory to a desired location, such as /opt/flink for standardized access across your system:

```
sudo mv flink-1.15.1 /opt/flink
```

3. Add Flink to your system's path to easily access the Flink CLI tools from any terminal session:

   Edit the .bashrc or .zshrc file to include the flink directory in your PATH:

```
export FLINK_HOME=/opt/flink
export PATH=$PATH:$FLINK_HOME/bin
```

   Complete the change with:

```
source ~/.bashrc
```

- **Environment Configuration**

  Before running any Flink jobs, it's beneficial to configure various environment options to tailor Flink's performance and functionality to your project needs.

  - **Configuration Files**

    Flink configuration is primarily managed via files located in the conf directory of your Flink installation.

    * flink-conf.yaml: This is the main configuration file where you can specify various options such as job manager address, parallelism, and heap memory sizes. A sample configuration adjustment for parallelism:

```
taskmanager.numberOfTaskSlots: 4
parallelism.default: 4
```

    * masters: Used if you run a Flink cluster.

    * workers: Lists the worker nodes if setting up a standalone cluster.

39

Understanding these configurations helps in tuning Flink's environment to optimize job execution and resource management.

- **Memory Allocation**

  Memory allocation in Flink is a key determinant of how efficiently it processes data, particularly in handling stateful transformations. Adjusting the heap sizes of both the Job-Manager and the TaskManager is essential:

  ```
  jobmanager.memory.process.size: 1024m
  taskmanager.memory.process.size: 2048m
  ```

  This example allocates 1GB memory to the JobManager and 2GB to each TaskManager process. Adjust these settings based on the available resources and job requirements.

- **Running Flink Locally**

  Having installed and configured Flink, we can now run it locally. Flink provides an inbuilt job manager and task manager to simulate a cluster on a single machine.

  1. Start the Flink cluster:

     ```
     start-cluster.sh
     ```

     Upon successful execution, you will see messages indicating that the TaskManager and JobManager have been launched.

  2. Open the Flink Web Dashboard to monitor job submission and execution by navigating to http://localhost:8081 in your web browser. This interface provides insights into job operations, task execution, and available resources.

- **Submitting a Sample Job**

  You can verify your Flink setup and familiarize yourself with the execution environment by running a sample job.

  Apache Flink includes a WordCount example in its examples JAR. To submit this job:

  1. Locate the example JAR. It's typically found in the examples directory of your Flink installation, for instance:

40

```
/opt/flink/examples/streaming/WordCount.jar
```

2. Submit the WordCount job using the Flink run command, specifying an input text file and directing the output:

```
flink run /opt/flink/examples/streaming/WordCount.jar --input /
            path/to/input.txt --output /path/to/output.txt
```

3. Inspect the output file to confirm successful job execution. The Web Dashboard will also display the job's completion status and execution metrics.

```
hello 1
flink 2
example 3
```

- **Troubleshooting and Logs**

  Logs serve as a valuable resource in diagnosing issues when running Flink jobs. They are located in the log directory within your Flink installation.

  Viewing console logs in real-time while troubleshooting:

```
tail -f /opt/flink/log/flink-*-taskexecutor-*.out
```

  Monitor both jobmanager and taskmanager logs to diagnose network or resource allocation errors effectively.

- **Accessing Additional Features**

  As you grow familiar with Flink's local setup, explore advanced features and configurations. Possible expansions include:

  - **Batch and Stream APIs:** Beyond the simple WordCount example, dive into Flink's rich API for batch and stream processing, examining examples like DataSet and DataStream operations.

  - **State Management:** For stateful applications, leverage Flink's robust state management. Implement checkpoints that guarantee exactly-once semantics.

  - **Connector Usage:** Explore Flink's connectors which interface with Kafka, HBase, Cassandra, etc. This allows for real-time data processing from diverse sources.

- **Custom Operators and Functions:** Design custom transformations by implementing FlatMap, Map, or Reduce functions that cater specifically to your business logic.

A simple implementation of a custom map function could be:

```
DataStream<String> text = // source such as socketTextStream
DataStream<String> filtered = text.flatMap(new
    FlatMapFunction<String, String>() {
    public void flatMap(String value, Collector<String> out) {
        for (String word : value.split(" ")) {
            if (word.length() > 3) out.collect(word);
        }
    }
});
```

This code snippet demonstrates how a FlatMapFunction is used in processing streamed data, collecting words longer than three characters.

The steps outlined illuminate the process of establishing a local Flink environment, enhancing understanding and supporting the development of sophisticated data processing applications. Harnessing the richness of Flink's tools and configurations in local setups builds a strong foundation beneficial for scaling to larger, production-grade installations.

2.3   Setting Up Flink on a Cluster

Deploying Apache Flink in a clustered environment leverages its distributed processing capabilities, enabling scalable, fault-tolerant stream and batch processing across multiple nodes. This section delves into the intricacies of setting up a Flink cluster, addressing network configurations, resource management, and high availability to ensure efficient and resilient data processing.

Cluster Architecture and Considerations

A Flink cluster consists of multiple components that work together to execute distributed tasks:

- **JobManager:** This is the master node responsible for job scheduling, coordination, and resource allocation. It oversees the execution of programs by coordinating task deployments and fault recovery.

- **TaskManagers:** These are the worker nodes that perform the actual data processing workloads. Each TaskManager manages a subset of the overall tasks, executing and reporting on these to the JobManager.

Understanding the architecture ensures better cluster management, allowing for optimized resource deployment and fault-tolerant execution.

Pre-Requisites for Cluster Setup

Before delving into the setup process, ensure the following:

- **Uniform Environment:** All nodes, including JobManager and TaskManagers, should have a consistent software environment. This includes matching versions of Java, Flink, and other dependencies.

- **Cluster Network Configuration:** Ensure all nodes are interconnected via a high-speed network. Configure hostname resolution (either through DNS or '/etc/hosts') so nodes can communicate seamlessly.

- **SSH Access:** Passwordless SSH access between nodes is recommended for easier cluster management and script automation. Configure SSH keys for secure and seamless connectivity.

43

Installation Steps

Downloading Flink on All Nodes

1. Download and extract Flink on each node within the cluster. This process mirrors the steps highlighted in the local setup section but is mirrored across each participating node.

```
wget https://archive.apache.org/dist/flink/flink-1.15.1/flink-1.15.1-bin-scala_2.12.tgz
tar -xzf flink-1.15.1-bin-scala_2.12.tgz
sudo mv flink-1.15.1 /opt/flink
```

Configuring Cluster Nodes

1. Configure the 'flink-conf.yaml' file:

- Set the 'jobmanager.rpc.address' to the hostname or IP address of the node designated as the JobManager. This tells the TaskManagers where to retrieve their instructions.

```
jobmanager.rpc.address: jobmanager-host
```

2. Define the number of task slots each TaskManager will manage. Task slots represent the parallelism level of tasks managed by each node:

```
taskmanager.numberOfTaskSlots: 4
```

3. Define memory configurations. Adjust these based on the resources available on your nodes:

```
jobmanager.memory.process.size: 2048m
taskmanager.memory.process.size: 4096m
```

Hosts Configuration

Edit the 'masters' and 'workers' configuration files:

- masters: Specify the JobManager host details.

```
jobmanager-host:8081
```

- workers: List all TaskManager nodes with each hostname or IP on a new line.

```
taskmanager-node1
taskmanager-node2
```

These configurations allow Flink to recognize and manage all cluster nodes during operation.

Starting the Flink Cluster

With the configuration complete, the next step is to start the Flink services:

1. On the JobManager node, initiate the cluster:

```
$FLINK_HOME/bin/start-cluster.sh
```

This script will start the JobManager and each TaskManager node listed in the 'workers' configuration file. Validate that all services are running by checking the logs found in 'log' directory on each node.

2. Access Flink's Web Dashboard for monitoring:

```
http://jobmanager-host:8081
```

The Dashboard is a critical interface for monitoring cluster health, viewing running tasks, and managing jobs.

Configuring for Scalability and Reliability

A robust Flink deployment not only considers basic installation but also addresses scalability and reliability. Techniques to enhance these attributes include:

Dynamic Scaling

Leverage resource managers like Kubernetes or YARN to dynamically adjust the number of active TaskManagers based on workload demands.

45

- When using Kubernetes, Flink Kubernetes Operator facilitates scaling by managing Flink jobs as native Kubernetes resources.

Example configuration snippet for Kubernetes resource:

```
apiVersion: flink.apache.org/v1beta1
kind: FlinkDeployment
metadata:
  name: flink-session
spec:
  flinkVersion: v1__15
  flinkConfiguration:
    taskmanager.numberOfTaskSlots: "4"
  infrastructure:
    kubernetes:
      ...
```

High Availability

Flink offers support for high availability configurations which maintain state and ensure job continuity despite failures. This involves persisting checkpoints and integrating with distributed file systems:

1. Configure state checkpoints to ensure that in-flight data and computations can be recovered post-failure:

```
state.checkpoints.dir: hdfs://namenode:9000/flink-checkpoints
```

2. Enable JobManager high availability using ZooKeeper for leader election and persistent state storage:

```
high-availability: zookeeper
high-availability.storageDir: hdfs://namenode:9000/flink-ha
high-availability.zookeeper.quorum: zk1:2181,zk2:2181,zk3:2181
```

These configurations ensure that Flink can recover from failures without restarting from the beginning.

Security Implementations

Security is crucial in cluster environments to prevent data leaks and unauthorized access. Steps to secure a Flink cluster include:

Authentication and Authorization

1. Secure inter-node communication via SSL/TLS:

```
security.ssl.enabled: true
security.ssl.keystore: /path/to/keystore.jks
security.ssl.keystore-password: password
```

2. Manage user roles and ensure access controls. Integrating with authentication systems like Kerberos can help manage authorization effectively.

Data Encryption

Ensure that data at rest and in transit is encrypted using supported libraries and protocols (e.g., AES for data encryption and TLS/SSL for transport security).

Monitoring and Logging

To maintain operational oversight over a Flink cluster:

1. Leverage external monitoring solutions such as Prometheus or Grafana for advanced metrics collection and visualization.

2. Access logs on each node regularly. Flink creates comprehensive logs that detail job submissions, errors, and other operational metrics. Examine:

```
tail -f $FLINK_HOME/log/flink-*-jobmanager-*.log
tail -f $FLINK_HOME/log/flink-*-taskexecutor-*.log
```

Advanced Resource Management and Tuning

Proper resource management and distribution are crucial for an effective Flink cluster:

Resource Profiling

Understand the resource needs of your streams and batch jobs:

47

- Profiling tools can aid in understanding CPU load, memory usage, and I/O performance. Sizing each JobManager and TaskManager appropriately based on this data is crucial.

Optimizing Execution Plans

Execution plans, visible in the Web Dashboard, can inform optimizations. Focus on operations taking excessive time or resources, streamline data flows, and reduce bottlenecked nodes.

Flink's execution plans shed light on task distribution, resource utilization, and network throughput, presenting opportunities for further fine-tuning.

Resource Reservation and Quota Management

For mixed-load environments where multiple teams access the same cluster:

- Implement quota policies to avoid resource contention. - Enforcement through tools like YARN enables controlled resource allocation, avoiding overuse by a single process or user group.

Deploying Flink on a cluster encapsulates configuring and enabling distributed data stream and batch processing across versatile environments. Fine-tuned configurations, robust security measures, and diligent monitoring ensure high performance, enabling Flink to meet enterprise-grade processing needs across broad data-driven applications. Through careful setup, Flink can transform raw data into actionable insights, demonstrating the power and flexibility of modern distributed stream processing architectures.

2.4   Configuring Flink

Configuring Apache Flink is a vital step in optimizing its performance, ensuring it meets the specific needs of your data processing tasks. The ability to fine-tune configurations allows for the customization of resource allocations, task parallelism, and setting operational parameters that optimize both throughput and latency. This section provides an in-depth exploration of Flink's configuration aspects, offering guidance on adjustments that enhance both local and cluster executions.

Understanding Configuration Files

Flink configurations are primarily managed through text files located in the 'conf' directory. Understanding these files is crucial for tailoring the performance settings adequately.

- flink-conf.yaml: The primary configuration file where extensive parameters related to job and task management are set.

- masters and workers: Define master and task nodes in a cluster setup respectively, guiding how jobs are distributed.

- log4j.properties: Sets the logging configuration, crucial for monitoring and troubleshooting.

Detailed knowledge of these files allows administrators to harness Flink's full capabilities.

Key Configuration Parameters

Several parameters in the 'flink-conf.yaml' file affect Flink's behavior significantly, allowing admins to specify memory usage, operational behavior, task scheduling, and more.

Memory and Resource Management

Managing memory effectively is crucial to maintaining Flink's performance, especially as data scales:

- Each Flink process (JobManager and TaskManager) has its memory settings. For example, setting appropriate memory per TaskManager is crucial:

```
taskmanager.memory.process.size: 4096m
```

Memory settings must consider both the heap and off-heap memory needs, especially for intensive stateful processing tasks.

Additionally, the JVM Garbage Collection process is a vital consideration. Configuring JVM options can alleviate performance bottlenecks caused by frequent garbage collections:

env.java.opts: -XX:+UseG1GC -XX:MaxGCPauseMillis=100

Task Slots and Parallelism

The number of task slots determines a TaskManager's processing power, with each slot being capable of hosting one parallel stream or batch task at a time:

```
taskmanager.numberOfTaskSlots: 4
```

Jobs are then parallelized upon execution based on configured slot numbers, influencing both throughput and fault tolerance.

Checkpointing and State Backend

Flink's ability to maintain exactly-once processing semantics is one of its key strengths, supported through checkpointing:

- Configure the checkpointing interval to balance state persistence and the overhead caused by frequent checkpointing:

```
execution.checkpointing.interval: 10000ms
```

This setting facilitates periodic saving of job execution states which are critical for failure recovery.

Selecting the suitable state backend also affects checkpoint storage and retrieval:

```
state.backend: rocksdb
state.checkpoints.dir: file:///opt/flink-checkpoints/
```

RocksDB is often preferred for its ability to handle large state applications effectively. However, the choice between RocksDB and memory-backed states should reflect your performance and reliability trade-offs.

High Availability (HA) Configurations

For robust deployments demanding continuous uptime, setting up high availability is often necessary, enabling Flink's job manager to recover quickly in case of failure:

```
high-availability: zookeeper
high-availability.storageDir: hdfs://namenode:9000/flink-ha/
```

Configuring persistence directories and enabling leader election with tools like ZooKeeper enhances cluster resiliency.

Configuring Execution Modes

Flink supports multiple execution modes, allowing for flexibility in how jobs are deployed and consumed. Understanding and configuring these modes is crucial for optimizing job executions:

Batch vs. Stream Processing

Configure job execution parameters based on whether you are processing batch or stream data:

- For batch processing, it's often beneficial to increase checkpointing intervals or disable it entirely to streamline processing:

```
execution.checkpointing.mode: EXACTLY_ONCE
```

Stream processing, critical in applications demanding immediate response, necessitates configuration to minimize latency. Reducing buffer sizes can lower latency at the cost of potentially increased CPU utilizations.

Interactive and Reactive Mode Configurations

These modes facilitate a more dynamic interaction with Flink jobs, crucial for environments that require rapid changes or agile data model updates:

51

- Set interactive and queryable state settings to enable real-time data querying without disrupting running pipelines:

```
queryable-state.enable: true
```

This setup is invaluable in scenarios like live dashboards or dynamic model inference where current data states are interrogated interactively.

Optimizations for Various Scenarios

Fine-tuning Flink's configuration can significantly improve performance across different scenarios; understanding these scenarios allows for more targeted optimizations:

Resource Bounded Scenarios

In environments where compute resources are limited, configurations must focus on maximizing efficiency without overloading the system:

- Lower the task parallelism to limit resource contention.   - Use memory-efficient serialization libraries like Apache Avro to minimize resource overhead per task.

```
taskmanager.memory.segmentSize: 8mb
```

This configuration optimizes memory segment usage in data swapping, maximizing effective memory management.

High Throughput Environments

In cases where maximum data throughput is targeted, ensure configurations allow sufficient buffer times and capacity to handle extensive data loads seamlessly:

- Increase network buffer timeouts to prevent data loss during spikes:

```
taskmanager.network.memory.fraction: 0.2
```

Aligning network memory fractions allows better queue depths for high-volume data streams, effectively addressing bursty data inflows.

Debugging and Logging Configuration

For robust data processing systems, effective debugging must be supported through configurable and actionable logging settings, crucial for both development and production environments:

Log Levels and Destinations

Adjust the logging configuration in 'log4j.properties' for more granular insight:

```
log4j.rootLogger=INFO, console, file
log4j.logger.org.apache.flink=DEBUG
```

Direct specific processing areas to log at more verbose levels for detailed introspection.

External Monitoring Integration

Integrate Flink with external monitoring and alerting systems such as Prometheus and Grafana:

- Use JMX exporters to bridge Flink's internal metrics with external systems, offering real-time monitoring and alert triggering.

```
metrics.reporter.jmx.class: org.apache.flink.metrics.jmx.JMXReporter
```

By instrumenting metrics into accessible platforms, greater insights into processing efficiency, resource utilization, and operational health can be garnered.

Security Considerations in Configuration

As data sensitivity grows, maintaining a secure Flink processing environment is paramount. This involves configuring operational and data-level security measures:

Transport Layer Security (TLS)

Implement end-to-end encryption through TLS, securing data in transit across Flink nodes and client interactions:

```
security.ssl.internal.enabled: true
security.ssl.internal.truststore: /path/to/truststore.jks
```

Proactively securing data exchanges mitigates risks of interception and unauthorized data exposure across distributed systems.

Access Control and Authentication

Enable secure authentication methods to restrict access to sensitive configurations and user-level modifications:

```
security.authentication: kerberos
security.kerberos.login.contexts: Client,Server
```

By leveraging Kerberos, a common access control protocol, Flink configurations can secure user and component authenticity across respective domains.

Future-Proof Configuration Practices

Adopting forward-thinking configuration practices ensures that Flink deployments remain robust against ever-evolving data demands and processing paradigms.

Version Management and Compatibility

Before any configuration changes, confirm compatibility with current Flink versions and associated modules, ensuring backward compatibility and future-proofing upgrades.

Proactively conducting configuration audits and adhering to semantic versioning principles across dependency upgrades mitigates integration risks and unplanned disruptions.

Automation and Orchestration Enhancements

Harness configuration management tools like Ansible or Kubernetes Operators for defining, automating, and orchestrating complex Flink deployment configurations:

- Utilize Deployment-as-Code approaches to embed version-controlled, repeatable, and scalable configuration scripts, promoting operational efficiency and reducing manual oversight.

By maintaining a disciplined approach to Flink configuration—balancing user-specific adjustments with future scalability and system security requirements—developers and administrators can realize significant gains in system reliability, operational performance, and processing capabilities, vital for comprehensively meeting both current and future data processing demands.

2.5 Verifying Installation and Running a Sample Job

Once Apache Flink is installed, it is crucial to verify that the setup is functioning correctly before starting to deploy complex jobs. This involves executing a sample job to ensure that every component of the Flink environment—from the configuration to resource allocation—is working efficiently. This section provides a step-by-step guide for verifying the installation of Flink and demonstrates how to execute a sample job effectively, with detailed explanations and code examples.

Initial verification steps:

After installing Flink, validate the installation and ensure that all components are working as intended. Begin with these fundamental checks:

Command Line Interface:

Ensure that Flink's command-line tools are accessible. Open a terminal and run:

```
flink --version
```

55

A successful execution should return the version details of both the Flink and Scala environment:

```
Version: 1.15.1, Commit ID: ...
Compiled by user on a date...
```

If the command is not recognized, verify the PATH environment variable settings to ensure the Flink binary is included correctly.

Starting the Cluster Locally:

Flink bundles scripts that allow you to start a standalone cluster on your local machine. Using these scripts ensures that your test environment simulates a full-scale deployment:

Run the start script:

```
$FLINK_HOME/bin/start-cluster.sh
```

Check the output in the terminal to confirm that both the JobManager and TaskManager nodes are running. Furthermore, examine the logs located within the 'log' directory (e.g., 'flink-<username>-jobmanager-<number>.log') for successful startup messages.

To ensure TaskManagers are recognized, verify from the Web Dashboard at 'http://localhost:8081'. This interface is essential for monitoring task execution and overall cluster health.

Executing a Sample Job:

Running a sample job validates the setup with a practical application, providing insights into configuration correctness and operational capacity.

WordCount Sample Job:

The WordCount program is the classic "Hello World" example for stream processing frameworks. It reads a text file, calculates the frequency of each word, and outputs the results.

Preparation:

Ensure the Flink examples JAR is available in the Flink installation directory, typically located in the 'examples' subdirectory:

```
ls $FLINK_HOME/examples/streaming/WordCount.jar
```

Additionally, prepare a sample input text file with content such as:

```
Flink is a stream processing framework
Stream processing is unique to Flink
```

Job Submission:

Execute the sample job using the Flink CLI, specifying the paths for input and output files to verify both reading and writing capabilities:

```
flink run $FLINK_HOME/examples/streaming/WordCount.jar --input /path/to/input.
    txt --output /path/to/output.txt
```

The Flink job will be submitted for processing, with progress and potential errors displayed in the console.

Output Validation:

After the job completes, check the output file for correctness and completion as below:

Examine the contents of the output file:

```
cat /path/to/output.txt
```

The expected result should display the word counts, akin to:

```
Flink 2
is 2
a 1
stream 1
processing 2
framework 1
Stream 1
unique 1
to 1
```

Such results confirm that both the Flink runtime and its processing capabilities are active and correctly configured.

Advanced Verifications and Troubleshooting:

Once the basics are confirmed, delve into more detailed verification to ensure readiness for complex job executions.

Cluster Health Monitoring:

Use the Flink Web Dashboard to check the health of the cluster nodes, particularly focusing on the utilization statistics presented.

- Access network and memory usage graphs to ensure resources are adequately utilized and confirm Task slot allocations. Insights from these graphs can guide further configuration tweaks for performance optimization.

http://localhost:8081/#/overview

Log Analysis and Error Checks:

Logs are instrumental in identifying unidentified issues or configuration mismatches.

- Analyze the JobManager and TaskManager logs for exceptions, warnings, or error messages that could affect Flink's operations:

Tail the logs as follows:

```
tail -f $FLINK_HOME/log/flink-*-jobmanager-*.log
tail -f $FLINK_HOME/log/flink-*-taskexecutor-*.log
```

Common troubleshooting steps based on log outputs may include adjusting heap sizes for JVM, resolving network misconfigurations, or verifying dependency and library paths.

Integrating External Systems for Extended Sample Jobs:

To further test the robustness and integration capacity of Flink, consider executing sample jobs that interact with external systems like Apache Kafka, Hadoop, or custom sources:

Kafka Integration:

For Apache Kafka-based stream ingestion:

- Ensure Kafka is properly configured and running within the environment.

- Utilize Flink's Kafka connector to consume and produce message streams.

Below is a singular example to demonstrate configuration and code structure:

Configure Kafka properties in 'flink-conf.yaml' or an appropriate Kafka properties file:

58

```
bootstrap.servers: localhost:9092
group.id: flink-testing
```

Write or adapt a Flink program utilizing Kafka:

```
env.addSource(new FlinkKafkaConsumer011<>(
        "input_topic", new SimpleStringSchema(), properties))
    .flatMap(new Tokenizer())
    .keyBy(0)
    .sum(1)
    .addSink(new FlinkKafkaProducer011<>("output_topic", new
        SimpleStringSchema(), properties));
```

Submit and execute this pipeline using the CLI tool and validate through Kafka's consumer groups or message queues.

Hadoop Integration:

For Apache Hadoop-based batch or stream operations—integration testing ensures large-scale compatibility:

- Configure Hadoop environment variables and relevant paths similar to:

```
export HADOOP_CONF_DIR=/usr/local/hadoop/etc/hadoop
```

- Adapt Flink Hadoop input state or batch file processing as shown:

```
DataSet<String> text = env.readHadoopFile(new TextInputFormat(), KeyClass.class,
    ValueClass.class, "hdfs://...");
```

Test the integrity of these integrations by submitting appropriate Flink jobs, followed by output validation and log checks.

Extending Verification for Custom Logic:

Beyond pre-packaged examples, validating your environment with custom Flink jobs can illuminate specific operational needs and constraints.

Developing Custom Operators:

Utilize Flink APIs to develop tailored transformations that simulate realistic use-cases of your organization or project.

Example custom flatMap for processing:

```
public class MyDataTransformation extends RichFlatMapFunction<Tuple2<String,
    Integer>, Tuple2<String, Integer>> {
  @Override
  public void flatMap(Tuple2<String, Integer> input, Collector<Tuple2<String,
      Integer>> out) {
    if (input.f1 > 100) {
      out.collect(new Tuple2<>(input.f0, input.f1 * 2));
    }
  }
}
```

Submit, execute, and validate these custom jobs, ensuring they demonstrate successful logic execution across distributed nodes.

Documenting Outcomes and Future Optimizations:

Document outcome observations, such as computational bottlenecks, missed parallelism, or unanticipated resource consumptions during job executions.

Benchmarking and Optimization:

Post-verification, benchmark your tasks as needed:

- Analyze CPU, memory, and network resource utilization for optimization opportunities.

- Evaluate task latencies and throughput to determine parameter adjustments for better performance.

Utilize performance metrics as captured in Web Dashboards, logs, or external monitoring systems integratively tuned with Flink's native metrics.

Verifying Flink installations and running sample jobs serves as both a functional check and a foundational step to iterative learning and optimization. As configuration intricacies become clearer, users can better leverage Flink's capabilities, ensuring precise tuning and robust integrations tailored to specific processing needs. Through detailed verification, the path for scaling and deploying data-intensive applications in production environments is both clearer and more assured.

2.6 Using Docker for Flink Deployment

Deploying Apache Flink with Docker facilitates a streamlined and portable method for creating consistent run-time environments. Docker's containerization capability allows for easy distribution, scaling, and management of Flink applications across diverse platforms. This section provides an extensive guide on employing Docker to deploy Flink, incorporating practical steps, code examples, and considerations for various deployment scenarios.

Understanding Docker Containers and Flink

Docker containers encapsulate Flink applications with all their dependencies, enabling them to run seamlessly across different environments without discrepancies. Docker ensures quick setup times and minimal configuration effort, ensuring that a Flink deployment remains consistent irrespective of deployment location.

Docker Basics:

- **Docker Images:** Immutable templates used to create containers.

- **Docker Containers:** Instances of Docker images running processes in isolated environments.

- **Docker Hub:** A cloud-based repository for sharing Docker images.

Docker provides a conducive environment for developers to manage and deploy applications like Flink within its ecosystem, ensuring that integration tasks are reduced in complexity.

Setting Up Docker for Flink

Before deploying Flink using Docker, ensure your system has Docker installed and functioning correctly.

Installing Docker

Step-by-step instructions to install Docker vary by operating system. For Linux-based systems, follow:

1. Update existing package lists:

```
sudo apt-get update
```

2. Install prerequisite packages:

```
sudo apt-get install apt-transport-https ca-certificates curl software-
    properties-common
```

3. Add Docker's official GPG key:

```
curl -fsSL https://download.docker.com/linux/ubuntu/gpg | sudo apt-key
    add -
```

4. Add the Docker repository to APT sources:

```
sudo add-apt-repository "deb [arch=amd64] https://download.docker.com/
    linux/ubuntu $(lsb_release -cs) stable"
```

5. Install Docker and confirm installation:

```
sudo apt-get update
sudo apt-get install docker-ce
docker --version
```

This sequence installs Docker and confirms its version, preparing the system for container executions.

Obtaining and Using Flink Docker Images

With Docker operational, acquire the official Apache Flink Docker image from Docker Hub, ensuring a uniform and reliable Flink setup.

Pulling the Flink Image

Fetch the Flink image using Docker's pull command:

```
docker pull flink:1.15
```

This downloads the specified version of the Flink image to your local machine, making it ready for deployment. Verify the successful pull by listing available Docker images:

```
docker images
```

Starting Flink as a Docker Container

Once the image is ready, initiate the Flink container. A simple command launches a single-node setup for quick trials:

```
docker run -d -p 8081:8081 flink:1.15
```

This connects the Flink web interface to host port '8081', providing access to the dashboard for job management.

Composing Multi-Node Flink Clusters with Docker Compose

Flink's full potential is realized when deployed as a distributed cluster. Docker Compose simplifies managing multi-container deployments, allowing for coordinated scaling across nodes.

Understanding Docker Compose

Docker Compose organizes multi-container Docker applications through a YAML definition file, streamlining deployment multiple interlinked services.

- Define services: Coordinates multiple Docker containers in a singular file.

- Enable easy scaling: Specify the number of containers per service for scalable infrastructure.

63

Creating a Flink Docker Compose File

Create a docker-compose.yml for deploying a Flink cluster with essential components like JobManager and TaskManagers:

```
version: "3"
services:
  jobmanager:
    image: flink:1.15
    command: jobmanager
    ports:
      - "8081:8081"
    environment:
      - JOB_MANAGER_RPC_ADDRESS=jobmanager
    networks:
      - flink-cluster

  taskmanager:
    image: flink:1.15
    command: taskmanager
    scale: 3
    depends_on:
      - jobmanager
    networks:
      - flink-cluster

networks:
  flink-cluster:
    driver: bridge
```

This configuration provisions a cluster with one JobManager and three TaskManager instances, interconnected through a network bridge.

Deploying the Cluster

Execute 'docker-compose' to bring the cluster to life:

```
docker-compose -f docker-compose.yml up -d
```

This command starts the containers and sets the cluster running in detached mode ('-d'). Access the Flink Dashboard at 'localhost:8081' to interactively monitor and manage cluster-wide tasks.

Managing and Scaling Flink Clusters with Docker

Docker offers inherent simplicity for scaling applications like Flink dynamically and efficiently.

Examine Running Containers

Verify the operation of your Flink helpers with:

```
docker ps
```

This command displays all the containers operating under the Docker Engine.

Scaling Applications

Adjust the number of TaskManagers as workload increases. Using 'docker-compose', scale TaskManagers dynamically:

```
docker-compose scale taskmanager=5
```

By altering the scale factor, Docker effortlessly distributes and adds additional TaskManagers to the network.

Persisting State and Configuration

Handling persistent data in Docker environments involves mounting external volumes to Docker containers. This ensures that configurations and stateful data aren't lost post-container lifecycle:

```
volumes:
  data-volume:
    driver: local
```

Flink configuration files or checkpoint directories point towards these mounted volumes by referencing them directly in the service definitions within 'docker-compose.yml':

```
volumes:
 - data-volume:/opt/flink/checkpoints
```

Such practices promise continuity and reliability across container lifecycles.

65

Networking Configurations and Firewall Settings

Networking for Docker-based Flink deployments requires special attention to ensure seamless communication both within the Docker network and with external clients or systems:

1. Use Docker's bridge network driver to facilitate inter-container communication without public IP exposure.

2. Implement overlay networks for clusters spanning multiple host systems, allowing containers on different hosts to communicate.

```
networks:
  overlay:
    external: true
```

By setting up overlay networks, the containers can engage in efficient communication, vital for distributed Flink operations.

Security Mechanism Implementations

Securing your Dockerized Flink deployment protects against unauthorized access and mitigates risks associated with exposed services:

- Ensure runtime security by configuring container-specific user permissions and capabilities:

```
jobmanager:
  security_opt:
    - no-new-privileges:true
```

- Implement TLS certificates to encrypt communication channels between Flink components and external caller services.

- Build Docker images with minimum permissions and dependencies, to minimize vulnerabilities:

```
FROM flink:1.15
USER flink:flink
```

By incorporating these security measures, you proactively guard against potential intrusions or breaches in data processing pipelines.

66

Advanced Concepts: Orchestration and Deployment

Once Dockerized, Flink deployments can benefit further from container orchestration platforms like Kubernetes, enhancing their scalability and maintenance footprint:

1. **Kubernetes Orchestration**: Kubernetes manages container lifecycles, offering automated deployments, scaling, and management of containerized Flink applications across vast clusters.

   Define Kubernetes resources such as Pods and Services reflecting Docker Compose intentions:

   ```
   apiVersion: apps/v1
   kind: Deployment
   metadata:
     name: flink-jobmanager
   spec:
     replicas: 1
     template:
       ...
   ```

2. **Service Discovery**: Integrate service meshes like Istio for container-level traffic management to optimize cluster communications and secure services with mTLS.

Deploying Apache Flink using Docker simplifies running applications across various environments, offering minimal configuration start-up times and easy scalability. Additionally, Docker Compose and Kubernetes support distributed Flink clusters, enhancing deployment flexibility while maintaining robust performance across data processing tasks. Embracing the Docker ecosystem thus equips developers to leverage Flink's full potential in a coordinated and efficient manner.

Chapter 3

Fundamentals of Flink Data Stream API

This chapter delves into the core principles of the Flink Data Stream API, essential for real-time stream processing applications. It covers the fundamental concepts that distinguish the Data Stream API from other data processing models, providing insight into the handling and manipulation of streaming data. Key topics include the configuration and management of stream data sources and sinks, the diverse range of transformations available, and the use of operators and functions crucial for performing complex computations. Furthermore, it examines the significance of partitioning and parallelism in optimizing data flow, while also addressing event time processing and the role of watermarks in managing late data, thus equipping readers with the foundational knowledge needed to work effectively with streaming data in Flink.

3.1 Understanding the Data Stream API

The Apache Flink Data Stream API forms the backbone of real-time stream processing capabilities, enabling the transformation and management of unbounded data streams. This section comprehensively explores the foundational concepts underpinning the Data Stream API, elucidating the stream data model, the variety of operations available, and the key distinctions from the Dataset API. Understanding these elements is crucial for constructing efficient, high-performance stream applications.

The stream data model in Flink is characterized by continuous data sources producing data instances, referred to as events, which are processed by a dynamic series of operations. Contrary to the traditional DataSet API where the data is static and bounded, the Data Stream API operates over potentially infinite streams, necessitating a distinct approach to computation and state management.

Stream Data Model:

The fundamental unit of data in Flink's Data Stream API is an "event" or a "record," which consists of a set of attributes. These events flow continuously through the system, facilitating real-time analysis and decision-making. Data streams do not require pre-defined sizes, allowing them to adapt to the dynamic nature of real-world data generation.

For instance, consider a use case where data is being transmitted from sensors embedded in an IoT system monitoring environmental conditions:

```
SensorReading {
    String sensorId;
    long timestamp;
    double temperature;
}
```

Each incoming sensor record can be processed as a stream event, enabling immediate response and action based on the data's characteristics.

Operations on Data Streams:

Flink's Data Stream API offers an extensive suite of operations which are crucial for manipulating and analyzing streaming data. These op-

70

erations can be broadly categorized into:

1. *Transformation Operations:* These include map, filter, flatMap, and keyBy, which allow for the modification, filtration, and restructuring of event streams.

```
DataStream<SensorReading> filteredStream =
    sensorStream.filter(r -> r.temperature > 25.0);
```

2. *Windowing Operations:* Since operations on streams need to be bounded in time/space for aggregation, windowing strategies (e.g., tumbling, sliding, session windows) segment streams into finite slices over which computations can be performed.

```
DataStream<AverageTemperature> avgTempStream =
    filteredStream.keyBy("sensorId")
    .timeWindow(Time.minutes(5))
    .reduce(new ReduceFunction<SensorReading>() {...});
```

3. *Stateful Operations:* These allow maintaining state across function calls, indispensable for operations where historical context enhances decision-making. Flink ensures consistency and fault tolerance through state backends.

4. *Join and Co-Group Operations:* These enable the combination of disparate streams, synchronizing data that is logically connected across streams. The join operation can align streams based on keys, integrating related data events.

```
DataStream<Tuple2<SensorReading, Location>> enrichedStream =
    sensorStream.join(locationStream)
    .where(sensor -> sensor.sensorId)
    .equalTo(location -> location.sensorId)
    .window(TumblingEventTimeWindows.of(Time.seconds(10)))
    .apply((sensor, location) -> new Tuple2<>(sensor, location));
```

Distinction from Dataset API:

While there are similarities in the API design for both Data Stream and Data Set, fundamental differences arise due to their target use cases— unbounded versus bounded data. Some noteworthy distinctions include:

- *State and Time Handling:* The Data Stream API emphasizes robust multilevel state management and time semantics, crucial for real-time operations where the order and timing of events are vital.

- *Sync vs. Async Operations:* While the Data Set API executes full dataset transformations synchronously, stream processing often necessitates asynchronous handling to cater to data velocity and volume.

- *Fault Tolerance and Checkpointing:* The dynamic recovery and fault handling mechanisms are particularly sophisticated within the Data Stream API. Flink's abstractions facilitate checkpointing and recovery strategies that ensure minimal processing disruption.

Practical Considerations in Stream Applications:

When developing applications with the Data Stream API, several practical aspects must be considered:

- *Latency vs. Throughput:* Selecting the appropriate windowing strategy and state backend may significantly affect performance, influencing the latency and throughput trade-offs.

- *Partitioned State and Scaling:* Effective use of keyBy partitioning enables scalable state management, allowing for parallel processing across distributed systems.

- *Watermarks and Timestamps:* Managing event-time and processing-time domains are critical, particularly in mitigating the impact of out-of-order events using watermarks.

- *Debugging and Testing:* Comprehensive testing frameworks should be employed to verify the correctness of stream transformations and ensure resilience against data anomalies.

Understanding and effectively utilizing the Data Stream API require familiarity with these concepts and techniques. Through this knowledge, developing robust, scalable, and responsive stream processing applications becomes achievable, supporting diverse real-time data processing requirements.

3.2 Data Sources and Sinks

Data sources and sinks are pivotal components in Apache Flink's architecture, enabling the integration and output of streaming data within the Flink ecosystem. This section delves deeply into configuring and managing data sources and sinks, covering both common and custom implementations to facilitate a robust streaming data pipeline.

In the context of Flink, data sources refer to the origin points from which data streams are ingested into a Flink application. Conversely, data sinks are endpoints where processed data streams are output or stored. These components are critical for connecting Flink applications with external systems, serving as the input-output interface for real-time data processing tasks.

Data Sources:

Data sources in Flink can be broadly categorized as bounded or unbounded. Bounded sources are finite, while unbounded sources represent potentially infinite data streams, such as continuous data from message brokers like Apache Kafka.

Common Data Source Implementations:

- *File and Directory Sources:* Flink supports reading data from static sources such as files and directories across distributed file systems (e.g., HDFS, S3). These are typically used for batch-like processing or as initial input to streaming pipelines.

```
DataStream<String> textStream =
    env.readTextFile("hdfs:///path/to/input/textfile.txt");
```

- *Message Brokers:* Among unbounded sources, message brokers such as Kafka and RabbitMQ are prominently used. Flink provides native connectors to seamlessly ingest streaming data.

```
Properties properties = new Properties();
properties.setProperty("bootstrap.servers", "localhost:9092");
properties.setProperty("group.id", "flink-consumer-group");

FlinkKafkaConsumer<String> kafkaSource =
    new FlinkKafkaConsumer<>("my-topic", new SimpleStringSchema(),
        properties);

DataStream<String> kafkaStream = env.addSource(kafkaSource);
```

73

- *Custom Source Functions:* When working with non-standard data sources, Flink allows for the implementation of custom source functions. Developers can subclass the SourceFunction or use RichParallelSourceFunction for parallel data processing.

```
public class RandomNumberSource implements SourceFunction<Long> {
    private volatile boolean isRunning = true;

    @Override
    public void run(SourceContext<Long> ctx) throws Exception {
        while (isRunning) {
            long number = (long) (Math.random() * 1000);
            ctx.collect(number);
            Thread.sleep(100);
        }
    }

    @Override
    public void cancel() {
        isRunning = false;
    }
}

DataStream<Long> randomNumbers = env.addSource(new
    RandomNumberSource());
```

Data Sinks:

Sinks in Flink are structured to export transformed data streams to various destinations, maximizing utility and accessibility. Similar to sources, sinks encompass a range of implementations, facilitating integration with storage systems and real-time dashboards.

Common Data Sink Implementations:

- *File and Storage Systems:* Sink data to files on distributed systems for durable storage, which is useful for later retrieval or batch processing.

```
stream.writeAsText("hdfs:///path/to/output/")
    .setParallelism(1);
```

- *Database Sinks:* Streaming data can be directed to relational databases or NoSQL databases like Cassandra and HBase, facilitating real-time data warehousing.

- *Message Queues and Topics:* Flink can serve as an intermediary, forwarding processed data to messaging systems like Kafka

74

or RabbitMQ for downstream consumption.

```
FlinkKafkaProducer<String> kafkaProducer =
    new FlinkKafkaProducer<>("output-topic", new SimpleStringSchema(),
        properties);

transformedStream.addSink(kafkaProducer);
```

- *Custom Sink Functions:* For specific requirements not covered by standard connectors, custom sink functions can be implemented, offering flexibility to integrate non-standard destinations.

```
public class ConsoleSink extends RichSinkFunction<String> {
    @Override
    public void invoke(String value, Context context) {
        System.out.println(value);
    }
}

transformedStream.addSink(new ConsoleSink());
```

Connecting Flink to External Systems:

Integration Patterns: The seamless operation of Flink's sources and sinks often requires understanding of integration patterns, such as ensuring consistency between data streams and back-end systems. Techniques like exactly-once or at-least-once delivery semantics enhance reliability.

Performance Considerations: The choice of sources and sinks significantly influences throughput, latency, and resource utilization. For instance, using parallel source functions can increase throughput, whereas synchronous sinks with blocking write operations may impact latency adversely.

State and Fault Tolerance: Integrating state management within sources and sinks requires careful planning, especially for checkpoint intervals and transaction handling. Flink's consistency guarantees allow stateful entities to recover to a consistent state upon failures, but correct configuration is essential to leverage this.

Advanced Customization:

Custom sources and sinks provide higher flexibility, allowing developers to tailor the behavior of the Flink job according to specific appli-

75

cation needs. Detailed attention to serialization, deserialization, and message acknowledgment protocols ensures that the system behaves predictably under load.

Security and Compliance:

Secure data handling is crucial, especially when sources and sinks interact with sensitive data. Implementing secure connectors that use authentication mechanisms like Kerberos for Kafka, or TLS encryption, ensures data privacy and compliance with regulations such as GDPR.

The ability to configure and manage data sources and sinks effectively is fundamental for the successful deployment of stream processing applications. Through deliberate design and careful implementation of these components, Flink can seamlessly integrate with a multitude of data environments, achieving a highly performant and reliable data processing continuum.

3.3 Transformations in Data Streams

Transformations are the essential building blocks for processing and manipulating data streams in Apache Flink. They enable the conversion of input data streams into desired output forms through a variety of operations, each serving distinct analytic and data manipulation purposes. This section delves into the core transformation operations provided by Flink's Data Stream API, explaining their applications, functionalities, and relevant coding examples.

At the heart of data stream processing in Flink lie transformations that allow us to filter, project, aggregate, and join data from one or more streams. By understanding and employing these operations effectively, developers can construct complex workflows that can handle real-time data requirements efficiently and effectively.

Basic Transformations:

- *Map Transformation:* This is a fundamental operation used to apply a specific function to each element of a data stream, transforming each element independently.

```
DataStream<Integer> numbers = env.fromElements(1, 2, 3, 4, 5);
```

```
DataStream<Integer> squaredNumbers = numbers.map(n -> n * n);
```

This operation efficiently transforms input values, making it especially useful for data enrichment and integration tasks.

- *Filter Transformation:* Filter operations allow for the selective passing of elements through a stream based on a predicate logic, creating a resultant stream containing only elements that satisfy the given condition.

```
DataStream<Integer> evenNumbers = numbers.filter(n -> n % 2 == 0);
```

This transformation is crucial in scenarios where data needs to be cleaned or where specific patterns are extracted from a larger data set.

- *FlatMap Transformation:* This extends the capabilities of map by allowing the output of zero, one, or multiple elements per input element. It is particularly beneficial for branching data flows or flattening multi-field inputs.

```
DataStream<String> sentences = env.fromElements("Apache Flink", "Stream
    Processing");
DataStream<String> words = sentences.flatMap((sentence, collector) -> {
    for (String word : sentence.split(" ")) {
        collector.collect(word);
    }
});
```

Such a transformation is pivotal in text processing applications and data normalization tasks.

Keyed Transformations:

Keyed transformations operate on grouped data based on key selection, providing an avenue for parallel processing and stateful computations.

- *KeyBy Transformation:* It partitions a stream into logically connected sub-streams based on a specified key, allowing for localized processing on subsets of data.

```
DataStream<Tuple2<String, Integer>> items = env.fromElements(
    new Tuple2<>("apple", 1),
    new Tuple2<>("banana", 2),
    new Tuple2<>("apple", 3)
);
```

77

```
KeyedStream<Tuple2<String, Integer>, String> keyedItems =
    items.keyBy(item -> item.f0);
```

- *Reduce Transformation:* Often applied post keyBy, this transformation accumulates results over time, outputting updated values as incremental changes occur.

```
DataStream<Tuple2<String, Integer>> sumItems = keyedItems
    .reduce((i1, i2) -> new Tuple2<>(i1.f0, i1.f1 + i2.f1));
```

Reduce transformations are optimal for streaming analytics requiring continuous updates, like running totals or aggregates.

Windowed Transformations:

Windowing applies bounded, temporal constraints to unbounded streams, segmenting data for time-aware processing. Windows can be defined using event time, processing time, or ingestion time semantics.

- *Tumbling Windows:* Non-overlapping, fixed-size time windows for segmenting streams into disjoint sets.

```
DataStream<Integer> summedWindow = numbers
    .keyBy(n -> n % 2)
    .window(TumblingProcessingTimeWindows.of(Time.seconds(5)))
    .sum(0);
```

- *Sliding Windows:* Overlapping windows defined by a window size and a slide interval, capturing every event within the sliding time span.

```
DataStream<Tuple2<String, Integer>> slidingCounts = sentences
    .flatMap(new Tokenizer())
    .keyBy(value -> value.f0)
    .window(SlidingEventTimeWindows.of(Time.seconds(10), Time.seconds(5)))
    .sum(1);
```

- *Session Windows:* Group events separated by inactivity longer than a specified session gap, ideal for analytics based on user activity.

```
DataStream<Tuple2<String, Integer>> sessionedCounts = events
    .keyBy(event -> event.userId)
    .window(ProcessingTimeSessionWindows.withGap(Time.minutes(1)))
    .sum(1);
```

78

Window transformations, by their temporal nature, allow for various time-based analytics and over-rolling calculations, making them highly versatile for real-time stream applications.

Joining and Co-Grouping:

Transformations that involve interactions between multiple streams provide comprehensive insights by combining different data sources.

- *Join Transformation:* Stream join operations align elements from two streams based on key correlation within a shared window, crucial for applications requiring context-enriched data.

```
DataStream<Tuple2<EventA, EventB>> joinedStream =
    streamA.join(streamB)
    .where(event -> event.id)
    .equalTo(event -> event.id)
    .window(TumblingProcessingTimeWindows.of(Time.seconds(10)))
    .apply((a, b) -> new Tuple2<>(a, b));
```

- *CoGroup Transformation:* A more advanced operation, coGroup, allows for independent handling of key-value pairs that do not join as expected.

```
DataStream<String> coGroupedStream = streamA.coGroup(streamB)
    .where(a -> a.id)
    .equalTo(b -> b.id)
    .window(TumblingProcessingTimeWindows.of(Time.seconds(10)))
    .apply((left, right, collector) -> {
        if (!right.isEmpty()) {
            collector.collect("Joined: " + left + " " + right);
        } else {
            collector.collect("Only Left: " + left);
        }
    });
```

Such transformations are indispensable when dealing with heterogeneously sourced data that needs reconciliation or context pairing.

Flink's robust array of transformation functions empowers developers to construct sophisticated, highly customizable stream processing workflows. By mastering these operations, we can harness the power of Flink for real-time big data processing, enabling analytics that cater directly to modern data-centric demands.

3.4   Operators and Functions

Operators and functions are fundamental elements of Apache Flink, providing the computational logic to process data streams. Operators perform data transformations and computations on data elements, while functions encapsulate user-defined logic to be applied over data streams. This section provides an in-depth exploration of the variety of operators and functions available in Flink, elucidating their roles, functionalities, and applications to perform complex computational tasks on streaming data.

Core Operators in Flink:

In Flink, operators serve as the building blocks for transforming data streams, enabling Flink applications to perform efficient distributed computation. These operators can be categorized broadly based on their functionalities:

- *Transform Operators:* These operators include map, flatMap, and filter, which apply user-defined functions to each element in a stream to manipulate or filter data.

```
DataStream<String> lines = env.fromElements("Flink", "Hadoop", "Spark
    ");
DataStream<Integer> lengths = lines.map(String::length);
```

```
DataStream<String> words = lines.flatMap((line, collector) -> {
    for (String word : line.split(" ")) {
        collector.collect(word);
    }
});
```

- *Keyed Operators:* By leveraging keyBy, these operators operate on keyed streams, where elements are grouped according to a specified key, allowing for operations like reduce, aggregate, and sum, which are performed on a per-key basis.

```
DataStream<Tuple2<String, Integer>> countedWords =
    words.map(word -> new Tuple2<>(word, 1))
    .keyBy(t -> t.f0)
    .reduce((a, b) -> new Tuple2<>(a.f0, a.f1 + b.f1));
```

- *Window Operators:* Windowing operators divide streams into finite sets (windows) and perform aggregations such as sum, average, etc., over these windows.

```
DataStream<Integer> summedWindow = numbers
  .keyBy(n -> n % 2)
  .window(SlidingProcessingTimeWindows.of(Time.seconds(10), Time.
      seconds(5)))
  .sum(0);
```

Function Interfaces in Flink:

In Flink, functions encapsulate the user-defined logic applied to operators. These interfaces allow developers to encode transformations, enrichments, and computations via plain Java implementations.

- *MapFunction:* This functional interface is used for transforming elements to another form.

```
public class DoublingMapFunction implements MapFunction<Integer,
    Integer> {
  @Override
  public Integer map(Integer value) throws Exception {
    return value * 2;
  }
}
```

- *FlatMapFunction:* Ideal for mapping each input value to multiple output values, commonly used for splitting and expanding data.

```
public class LineSplitter implements FlatMapFunction<String, String> {
  @Override
  public void flatMap(String line, Collector<String> out) {
    for (String word : line.split(" ")) {
      out.collect(word);
    }
  }
}
```

- *FilterFunction:* For filtering stream elements based on boolean logic.

```
public class EvenNumberFilter implements FilterFunction<Integer> {
  @Override
  public boolean filter(Integer value) throws Exception {
    return value % 2 == 0;
  }
}
```

81

- *ReduceFunction:* This interface handles incremental aggregation, updating the result as each new element in the stream arrives.

```
public class SumReducer implements ReduceFunction<Tuple2<String,
    Integer>> {
    @Override
    public Tuple2<String, Integer> reduce(Tuple2<String, Integer> a,
        Tuple2<String, Integer> b) {
        return new Tuple2<>(a.f0, a.f1 + b.f1);
    }
}
```

Complex Operations with Rich Functions:

Flink provides rich functions that extend basic function interfaces, adding configuration methods, state handling capabilities, and lifecycle management features.

```
public class StatefulMapFunction extends RichMapFunction<Integer, Integer> {
    private transient ValueState<Integer> sumState;

    @Override
    public void open(Configuration config) {
        ValueStateDescriptor<Integer> descriptor =
            new ValueStateDescriptor<>("sum", Types.INT);
        sumState = getRuntimeContext().getState(descriptor);
    }

    @Override
    public Integer map(Integer value) throws Exception {
        Integer currentSum = sumState.value() == null ? 0 : sumState.value();
        currentSum += value;
        sumState.update(currentSum);
        return currentSum;
    }
}
```

Rich functions add significant value by allowing for more complex, contextual transformations through access to both the Flink runtime and internal states.

Advanced Use Cases with Operators:

Operators and functions are not just limited to basic stream processing tasks but also cater to more advanced use cases like pattern detection, anomaly detection, and more.

- *Pattern Detection:* Using Flink's CEP library, complex event patterns can be detected across streams.

```
Pattern<Event, ?> pattern = Pattern.<Event>begin("start").where(e -> e.
    getId() == 1)
    .next("middle").where(e -> e.getId() == 2)
    .followedBy("end").where(e -> e.getId() == 3);

PatternStream<Event> patternStream = CEP.pattern(eventStream,
    pattern);
DataStream<String> alerts = patternStream.select(
    (PatternSelectFunction<Event, String>) patternMap -> "Pattern
        Matched!"
);
```

- *Anomaly Detection:* Leverage reduce and map functions together to flag anomalous patterns indicative of outliers.

```
DataStream<Event> anomalies = eventStream
    .keyBy(event -> event.getType())
    .window(TumblingEventTimeWindows.of(Time.minutes(1)))
    .reduce((event1, event2) -> {
        if (Math.abs(event1.getValue() - event2.getValue()) > threshold) {
            return event1; // indicate anomaly
        }
        return new Event(event1.getType(), event1.getValue() + event2.
            getValue());
    });
```

Understanding the wide array of operators and functions in Apache
Flink is key to leveraging its full potential. These components are powerful tools for building responsive, high-performance data stream applications that can cater to the dynamic needs of modern data processing landscapes. By mastering these operators and functions, developers can tailor solutions that fit precisely within their real-time data processing ecosystems.

3.5 Partitioning and Parallelism

Partitioning and parallelism are integral components of Apache Flink's
design, enabling efficient processing of large-scale data streams by
distributing workloads across multiple nodes. By understanding the
mechanisms of partitioning and parallelism, developers can significantly enhance the performance, scalability, and resilience of stream
processing applications.

Partitioning refers to the distribution of data across different computational units, whereas parallelism represents the concurrent execution of tasks on the data partitions. Together, these concepts facilitate the horizontal scaling of Flink applications, allowing them to handle massive data throughput with reduced processing latency.

Partitioning in Flink:

Partitioning in Flink dictates how data records are routed to parallel operators, playing a critical role in balancing the load and optimizing data locality. There are several partitioning strategies available in Flink:

- *Forward Partitioning:* This simplest form allows data to pass directly from one operator instance to its counterpart downstream without change in partition boundaries. This technique is used when both the upstream and downstream operators have equal parallelism.

- *KeyBy Partitioning:* Often referred to as grouping, this strategy partitions data based on key attributes, directing all records with the same key to the same parallel instance. It is particularly useful for stateful operations, ensuring that consistently keyed data is processed centrally.

```
DataStream<Tuple2<String, Integer>> keyedStream =
    wordCounts.keyBy(word -> word.f0);
```

- *Shuffle Partitioning:* Here, data records are randomly distributed among target partitions without any regard to data ordering or key value. This strategy, effective in equal load distribution, diminishes potential biases from uneven data distributions.

```
DataStream<Integer> shuffledStream = wordCounts.rebalance();
```

- *Rescale Partitioning:* Rescaling allows data to be processed with nearby parallel instances in round-robin fashion, optimizing local data processing by leveraging operational topology, especially in distributed environments.

- *Custom Partitioning:* When application-specific partitions are necessary, custom partitioning through user-defined Partitioner interfaces offers a high level of control over data distribution.

84

```
public class MyPartitioner implements Partitioner<Integer> {
    @Override
    public int partition(Integer key, int numPartitions) {
        return key % numPartitions;
    }
}

dataStream.partitionCustom(new MyPartitioner(), "keyColumn");
```

Parallelism in Flink:

Parallelism is the executor-level concurrency mechanism in Flink, allowing a task to be divided among multiple operators. The degree of parallelism is configurable per operator or as a global job setting, mapped to the number of slots across a Flink cluster.

- *Operator Parallelism:* Each operator in a Flink job can be assigned a parallelism setting that determines the number of concurrent instances that execute its tasks. Adjusting parallelism levels aligns resource allocation with processing demands.

```
DataStream<Tuple2<String, Integer>> keyedCounts =
    wordCounts.keyBy(t -> t.f0).sum(1).setParallelism(4);
```

- *Task Slots and Resource Management:* Flink's runtime environment manages resources through task slots, which encapsulate the concurrent running task subsets. A slot can contain multiple tasks, unified under the same task manager in terms of resource handling.

- *Pipelined Shuffling:* Data exchange between parallel operators achieves high throughput via pipelined shuffling, wherein data flows continuously through buffer pools rather than relying on persistent storage.

Enhancing Performance via Partitioning and Parallelism:

Utilizing effective partitioning and parallelization strategies can dramatically improve data throughput and minimize latency:

- *Stateful Application Optimization:* By using keyBy, it ensures data locality, minimizing the necessity for state shuffles, thereby reducing latency costs associated with network transmission.

85

- *Load Balancing:* Partition strategies such as rebalance and key-based hashing prevent bottlenecks, distributing workloads evenly across computational nodes for optimal performance.

- *Dynamic Adjustments:* Reactive systems may adjust parallelism in response to changing system load, deploying autoscaling techniques to optimize computational costs while maintaining service quality.

Fault Tolerance and Scalability Considerations:

Under the hood, Flink's fault tolerance is achieved via mechanisms like state snapshots and checkpointing, essential for recovering from failures without data loss or inconsistency:

- *Checkpointing:* Ensures that operator states are periodically captured and persisted. Should an operator instance fail, its state can be restored, allowing the system to resume processing transparently.

- *Exact-Once State Consistency:* Controls over state consistency are exercised to meet exactly-once processing guarantees, pivotal for applications requiring strict state integrity.

Advanced Application Patterns:

Partitioning and parallelism are not just about scale but also about enhancing flexibility and dynamic capacity allocation:

- *Stream Joins and Co-Groupings:* Complex interactions between data from multiple streams require conscientious partitioning to keep correlated data together, ensuring timely join operations, reducing lag.

- *Topology-Based Parallelism:* Considering the topology of the task graph influences execution flow and can lead to optimized data paths by aligning stream parallelism with cluster layout.

Developing Efficient Flink Applications:

The effective deployment of Flink applications combines a thoughtful balancing act of partitioning strategy selection and parallelism tuning:

- Investigating workload characteristics can guide setting appropriate parallelism levels.

- Efficient serialization/deserialization prevents bottlenecks in data channels.

- Monitoring tools, such as Flink's Web Dashboard, provide insightful analytics into task execution, with metrics allowing real-time fine-tuning.

The potential of Apache Flink is unlocked through an in-depth understanding of its partitioning and parallelism features, equipping developers with the insights to construct applications capable of handling demanding streaming analytics workloads effectively and reliably.

3.6 Working with Event Time and Watermarks

In stream processing systems, handling time is pivotal for producing accurate and timely results. Apache Flink provides robust support for event time processing, central to applications that require a precise understanding of the temporal aspect of data. To effectively manage out-of-order data and late arrivals, Flink employs the concepts of event time and watermarks, which enable developers to design systems with the required temporal correctness.

Event Time in Flink:

Event time is the time when an event occurred within the data source's context. This contrasts with processing time, which is the time when an event is processed at the stream processor. Event time provides a reliable temporal reference that remains unaffected by network delays or system lags, essential for applications such as real-time analytics, monitoring, and alerting systems where order matters.

1. *Defining Event Time:* Flink allows event time to be defined by extracting timestamps from event data using a timestamp assigner. This timestamp informs Flink when the event originally occurred, setting the basis for all time-dependent operations thereafter.

```
DataStream<Event> eventStream = rawStream
    .assignTimestampsAndWatermarks(
        WatermarkStrategy
            .<Event>forMonotonousTimestamps()
            .withTimestampAssigner((event, timestamp) -> event.getEventTime())
    );
```

2. *Event Time Operations:* When events are processed based on their event time, operations like windowing take into account the timestamps embedded within the event data, accommodating variability in event arrival.

Watermarks in Flink:

Watermarks are essential components that Flink uses to model the progress of event time. A watermark is a marker in the data stream that signifies that no events with earlier timestamps are expected to arrive. By using watermarks, Flink can know when to compute results for window-based operations without waiting indefinitely for out-of-order events.

1. *Watermark Generation:* Watermarks can be generated using predefined strategies depending on the nature of the application and expected data delays. Common strategies include bounded out-of-orderness and periodic watermark increments.

```
DataStream<Event> eventStream = rawStream
    .assignTimestampsAndWatermarks(
        WatermarkStrategy
            .<Event>forBoundedOutOfOrderness(Duration.ofSeconds(5))
            .withTimestampAssigner((event, timestamp) -> event.getEventTime())
    );
```

2. *Late Events Handling:* Events that arrive with timestamps earlier than the current watermark are designated as late. Handling late data is crucial for ensuring the correctness of stream processing results, typically achieved through mechanisms such as allowed lateness and side outputs.

```
windowedStream
    .allowedLateness(Time.seconds(60))
    .sideOutputLateData(lateTag)
    .apply(windowFunction);
```

Windowing with Event Time:

88

Windowing is a primary use case for event time and watermarks, enabling aggregation over finite segments of an unbounded stream. Event-time windows ensure that events are grouped based on their real-world occurrence time, not their arrival order.

1. *Tumbling Windows:* These are fixed-size windows that do not overlap; they segment the stream into mutually exclusive windows of fixed duration.

```
DataStream<AggregateResult> result = eventStream
    .keyBy(event -> event.getKey())
    .window(TumblingEventTimeWindows.of(Time.minutes(10)))
    .aggregate(new AggregateFunction());
```

2. *Sliding Windows:* These overlap, providing a running aggregation over a specified time period.

```
DataStream<AggregateResult> result = eventStream
    .keyBy(event -> event.getKey())
    .window(SlidingEventTimeWindows.of(Time.hours(1), Time.minutes(15)))
    .aggregate(new AggregateFunction());
```

Implementation Strategies and Best Practices:

1. *Choosing the Right Watermark Strategy:* Selecting an appropriate watermark strategy is vital. While bounded out-of-orderness accommodates delays by a fixed time buffer, in some use cases, customizing the watermark generation logic may better suit the data arrival pattern.

2. *Handling Late Data:* Late data strategies should be tailored based on accuracy requirements and latency tolerance. By designating late-arriving data to side outputs, Flink permits corrective processing while maintaining system throughput for on-time data.

3. *Monitoring and Adjusting Watermarks:* Real-world systems should be monitored to understand watermark behavior under various load conditions, facilitating dynamic adjustments to watermark strategies to reflect changing data arrival conditions.

Case Study: Real-Time Analytics with Event Time:

Consider a case where we build a real-time analytics system for transaction data. The transactions are associated with timestamps indicating their occurrence. To ensure accurate analytics, the system relies on event time to group transactions occurring within prescribed periods.

- Using watermark strategies, we mitigate delays due to network congestion.

- Event time windows assure analytics results correspond to transaction timings, offering insights unaffected by when data is processed.

- By monitoring watermark delays and late data collection, corrective measures refine analytics outcomes, enhancing prediction precision and consistency.

Event time and watermarks enable Apache Flink to precisely handle the challenges of real-time stream processing across various domains where temporal accuracy is paramount. By offering mechanisms to create time-aware applications, they provide the ability to manage the complexities of data delays, ensuring that applications can process streams reliably despite the challenges posed by the order and timing of data arrival. By mastering these elements, developers can build stream processing systems that meet the demands of time-sensitive data applications with robust accuracy and efficacy.

Chapter 4

Batch Processing with Flink Dataset API

This chapter provides a comprehensive overview of batch processing using the Flink Dataset API, which is integral for handling static datasets efficiently. It discusses the differences between stream and batch processing, emphasizing scenarios where batch processing is most beneficial. The chapter covers the structure and operation of the Dataset API, including how to set up and manage data sources and outputs for batch jobs. Key attention is given to various transformations applicable to batch data and techniques for data partitioning and grouping to optimize computational tasks. Additionally, the chapter explores the use of iterative processing and delta iterations, enabling the execution of complex batch workflows with precision and efficiency.

4.1 Distinction Between Stream and Batch Processing

In data processing, stream and batch processing represent two fundamental paradigms, each with distinctive characteristics and suitable operation scopes. Traditional batch processing systems, with their robust ability to handle large volumes of data, are critical for scenarios that demand comprehensive analysis on static datasets. Conversely, stream processing models shine in environments where real-time analytics and rapid response to data events are paramount. Understanding the differences between these two approaches is pivotal in selecting the appropriate processing mechanism to meet specific computational and business requirements.

Batch processing involves the execution of operations on a complete dataset. This method accumulates raw data over a period, which is then sequentially processed as a single unit or batch. Such systems encapsulate advantages including but not limited to efficient data processing by leveraging full dataset availability and the application of comprehensive and complex analytical models. The operations in batch processing tend to be predictably scheduled, as data is not processed until a triggering event, such as a scheduled time, prompts execution.

One core feature of batch processing is its ability to perform repetitive, scheduled tasks that are computationally demanding, without being restrained by latency concerns inherent in waiting for new data. This makes batch processing ideal for financial end-of-day reports, large-scale scientific simulations, and comprehensive business analytics workflows.

In contrast, stream processing enables real-time data analysis. Data streams are continuous and arrive in real-time, necessitating that operations be applied instantaneously or at very low latencies. Stream processing systems handle infinite datasets with updating incoming data events, making them optimal for applications such as live traffic monitoring, fraud detection in financial transactions, and IoT sensor data analysis.

Key features distinguishing stream processing include adaptability

92

to real-time data dynamics, low-latency computation, and often, reduced data storage requirements due to the ephemeral nature of processed streams. Stream systems emphasize time-sensitive computations, where the immediacy of insights is essential.

The following code snippets illustrate the conceptual differences between batch and stream processing in a simplified pseudocode format:

```
# Batch Processing Example
def process_batch_data(dataset):
    retrieved_data = read_data_from_storage()
    processed_data = perform_batch_operations(retrieved_data)
    save_processed_data(processed_data)
    generate_report_from_data(processed_data)

execute_on_schedule(trigger_time="end-of-day", function=process_batch_data)
```

```
# Stream Processing Example
def process_stream_data():
    while True:
        data_event = read_real_time_data()
        processed_event = perform_real_time_operations(data_event)
        store_or_forward_data(processed_event)

initialize_stream_processor(process_stream_data)
```

In the batch processing pseudocode, data is processed in one go after being loaded from storage, illustrating how processing is delayed until a batch of data is available, whereas stream processing operates continuously, applying operations as data arrives.

One significant advantage of batch processing is its ability to perform complex transformations and aggregations on stored data. Batch executions can utilize entire dataset access to fine-tune analytical models, whereas stream processing often approximates or utilizes windowing operations to handle real-time constraints.

Batch processing can afford to simulate predictive analysis and forecast scenarios by using complete datasets, while stream processing must rely on the latest data trends and rely on stateful operations across windows to maintain relevance.

Consider a scenario for calculating daily sales reports in a retail environment. Batch processing effectively processes accumulated daily sales records overnight, allowing time-intensive analytics to report comprehensive insights. A batch processing framework efficiently handles these operations, optimizing resources to execute scheduled tasks in optimal data windows.

Stream processing, inversely, is beneficial for monitoring checkout terminals for real-time discounts and promotional reactions. Here, immediate feedback is vital, necessitating a stream processing system that continually ingests sales data and dynamically adjusts strategies based on the emerging trends.

In summary, the decision to employ batch or stream processing hinges on the latency tolerance, data volume, and real-time requirements of the application in question. Selecting the optimal processing paradigm involves balancing the need for quick insights against extensive, detailed post-processing. Acknowledging these factors ensures efficient resource utilization, accuracy of output, and alignment with operational goals. The choice between these models is not mutually exclusive, and hybrid approaches often leverage the strengths of both systems, deploying batch processing for robust backlog operations and stream processing for immediate analytics.

4.2 Exploring the Dataset API

The Dataset API is a pivotal element within Apache Flink's framework for executing batch processing tasks. This API is designed to facilitate the manipulation and processing of bounded data, enabling users to perform complex transformations, aggregations, and analytics on large datasets residing in static storage. Unraveling the key components and functions of the Dataset API is essential for exploiting its capabilities to efficiently manage and execute batch operations.

At its core, the Dataset API provides a programming abstraction for distributed data collections. These collections, or datasets, are immutable and transformations applied to them result in new datasets. Within the Dataset API, users can access a wide range of operations tailored to process and analyze data, such as map, filter, reduce, join, and aggregate. Understanding these operations is fundamental for constructing precise and effective data processing jobs.

Creating Datasets: Datasets are typically created from data sources, which can be varied, including local file systems, distributed storage systems like HDFS, or databases. The API provides methods for read-

94

ing data into dataset objects. Consider the following example, which illustrates loading data from a CSV file:

```
DataSet<Tuple2<String, Integer>> csvInput = env.readCsvFile("path/to/file.csv")
    .fieldDelimiter(",")
    .types(String.class, Integer.class);
```

In this example, a dataset is created from a CSV file with fields of type String and Integer. The ability to specify data types ensures that data is correctly interpreted and processed.

Transformations: Once datasets are instantiated, the Dataset API allows a plethora of transformations to be performed. Key transformation operations include:

- Map: Applies a specified function to each data element.

- Filter: Selects elements from the dataset based on a conditional evaluation.

- Reduce: Combines elements using an associative binary function.

Transformation examples:

```
DataSet<String> lines = env.readTextFile("path/to/textfile");
DataSet<Integer> lineCounts = lines
    .map(new MapFunction<String, Integer>() {
        public Integer map(String s) {
            return s.length();
        }
    })
    .filter(new FilterFunction<Integer>() {
        public boolean filter(Integer i) {
            return i > 5;
        }
    });
```

In this example, a map function computes the length of each line, and a filter function retains lines longer than five characters. Mapping and filtering enable efficient data preparation and cleaning, essential for accurate analysis.

Keyed Operations and Aggregations: The Dataset API supports operations on keyed datasets, which partition data into subsets in order to perform aggregations or grouping. Keyed datasets facilitate operations such as grouped reduce, and use of combiners for optimization:

95

```
DataSet<Tuple2<String, Integer>> wordCounts = lines
    .flatMap(new Tokenizer())
    .groupBy(0)
    .sum(1);
```

In this scenario, a dataset is generated that tokenizes lines into words and utilizes grouping on words to count occurrences. The sum operation aggregates counts across identical keys.

Iterative Data Processing: The Dataset API provides capabilities for iterative processing which are often necessary for advanced machine learning or numerical computations where repeated refinements of results over multiple iterations are needed. The API's Iterative-DataSet interface governs iterative tasks and controls execution flow:

```
IterativeDataSet<Double> initial = dataset.iterate(10);
DataSet<Double> iterationResult = initial
    .map(new IterationStep())
    .reduce(new SumReducer());
DataSet<Double> output = initial.closeWith(iterationResult);
```

Iterations are controlled by specifying the number of iterations or convergence criteria. The iterative step refines the dataset until completion criteria are satisfied, emphasizing its utility in complex algorithmic solutions such as optimization problems.

Joining Datasets: Datasets can be joined based on common fields, empowering us to perform relational operations equivalent to SQL joins:

```
DataSet<Tuple2<String, Integer>> userRatings = userDataset.join(ratingDataset)
    .where(0)
    .equalTo(0)
    .with(new JoinFunction<Tuple2<Integer, String>, Tuple2<Integer, Double>,
            Tuple2<Integer, String, Double>>() {
        public Tuple3<Integer, String, Double> join(Tuple2<Integer, String> user,
                Tuple2<Integer, Double> rating) {
            return new Tuple3<Integer, String, Double>(user.f0, user.f1, rating.f1);
        }
    });
```

In the join operation above, two datasets are combined based on a user ID key, creating a dataset pairing user information with their corresponding ratings, exemplifying how the Dataset API supports complex relational data manipulations.

Optimizations and Execution Planning: Underneath the opera-

96

tions, the Flink runtime rigorously optimizes execution plans, striving for parallel execution and resource-efficient computations through optimally scheduled task graphs. Users of the Dataset API can thus trust the system to handle the intricacies of distributed computations while they focus on logical data transformation specifications.

The interplay of these operations and the underlying system optimizations empowers the Dataset API to handle large-scale computations beyond conventional capacities. Mastery of the API ensures users can transition data into insights, leveraging transformations, keyed operations, joins, and iterations effectively to align computing tasks with specific analytical objectives. Understanding these facets positions Apache Flink's Dataset API as an invaluable tool for executing robust batch processing pipelines.

4.3 Data Sources and Outputs for Batch Jobs

In the context of batch processing, selecting and configuring data sources and outputs is a critical step in constructing efficient data pipelines. Apache Flink provides the Dataset API, which offers a versatile and comprehensive suite of options for both data input and output. This adaptability is essential, as it allows seamless integration with a variety of storage systems, including distributed file systems, databases, and cloud-based data platforms.

Data Sources: The Dataset API supports a wide range of data sources, enabling the ingestion of data from local files, distributed storage, and various database systems. This flexibility ensures that batch jobs can access the data required for processing, regardless of the original storage format or location.

Local and Distributed File Systems: One of the most common data sources for batch jobs is files stored locally or on distributed file systems. Apache Flink offers native support for reading from Hadoop Distributed File System (HDFS), the Amazon Simple Storage Service (S3), and network file systems. Users can easily read structured and unstructured data files in different formats, such as CSV, JSON, Avro, and Parquet.

97

```
DataSet<Tuple3<String, Integer, Double>> data = env.readCsvFile("hdfs://path/to/
    data.csv")
  .fieldDelimiter(",")
  .ignoreInvalidLines()
  .types(String.class, Integer.class, Double.class);
```

In the example above, a CSV file stored on HDFS is read into a dataset, where each row consists of a string, integer, and double type, facilitating structured data processing.

Database Systems: The Dataset API allows batch jobs to read data from relational databases using JDBC. This capability is crucial for batch operations on structured datasets stored within traditional database architectures, ensuring that comprehensive analytics can be performed on data extracted from operational systems.

```
DataSource<Tuple3<String, String, Double>> dbSource = jdbcEnvironment
  .createInput(Schema.inputSchema({
    { "id", java.sql.Types.VARCHAR },
    { "name", java.sql.Types.VARCHAR },
    { "balance", java.sql.Types.DOUBLE }
  }))
  .read("SELECT id, name, balance FROM accounts");
```

Using JDBC connectivity, datasets can pull records from database tables, allowing batch tasks to transform and analyze data held in enterprise systems.

NoSQL Databases and External Sources: Flink's support for NoSQL databases, such as Apache Cassandra and Elasticsearch, further extends its capability. By interfacing with these systems, users can process large volumes of semi-structured or unstructured data typical of modern big data applications.

Data Outputs: The Dataset API provides mechanisms for writing the results of batch processing operations to various output sinks, such as files, databases, and message queues. This versatility ensures that processed datasets can be stored and further analyzed in downstream applications or systems.

File System Outputs: Like inputs, outputs can be directed to local or distributed file systems, where results are stored in a variety of formats. Supported export formats include delimited text files, JSON, Avro, and Parquet, among others.

```
resultDataSet.writeAsCsv("s3://path/to/output.csv", "\n", ",", WriteMode.
    OVERWRITE);
```

This example demonstrates writing a dataset to an S3 location as a CSV file, mirroring the flexibility of using distributed storage for batch processing outputs.

Database and Cloud Storage Outputs: Using connectors like JDBC, datasets can be written back to relational databases, facilitating synchronization with transactional systems post-processing. Furthermore, integration with cloud storage solutions such as AWS S3 and Google Cloud Storage enables flexible positioning of output data.

```
results.output(new JDBCOutputFormat()
    .setDrivername("org.postgresql.Driver")
    .setDBUrl("jdbc:postgresql://dbserver/db")
    .setQuery("insert into results (id, value) values (?, ?)")
    .setSqlTypes(new int[]{Types.VARCHAR, Types.DOUBLE}));
```

Here, processed data is inserted into a PostgreSQL database, showcasing scenarios where analytic results need to be integrated into business systems.

Message Queues and Streaming Systems: Beyond static storage, the Dataset API can also output data to streaming platforms such as Apache Kafka. By doing so, batch-processed data can be published to real-time consumers, blending the boundary between batch and stream processing environments.

```
resultDataSet.output(new FlinkKafkaProducer<String>(
    "kafka-broker:9092",
    "output-topic",
    new SimpleStringSchema()));
```

This example illustrates how to publish processed data to a Kafka topic, supporting real-time processing scenarios that require batch results.

Configuration and Tuning: Optimal interaction between the Dataset API and storage systems necessitates proper configuration and resource management. Tuning parameters such as parallelism, buffer sizes, and read/write consistency settings play a fundamental role in achieving resource-efficient operations, thereby balancing performance and reliability.

The API's adaptive nature allows alignment with various infrastructural needs, promoting a balance between computational cost and processing speed. Advanced users may deploy data partitions to parallelize read/write operations and utilize data locality features to minimize resource-intensive I/O operations.

Interplay with Data Ecosystems: The seamless integration of data sources and outputs stands as a testament to Flink's robustness in orchestrating batch workflows across intricate data ecosystems. The Dataset API positions Apache Flink as a central unit in data engineering pipelines, fostering robust connections between raw data reservoirs and analytical insights.

Understanding and leveraging the wide array of supported data inputs and outputs within the Dataset API empowers organizations to capture the full analytical potential of their data assets. By establishing flexible, efficient, and resilient data pipelines, Flink enhances the value delivered through comprehensive batch processing, promoting actionable intelligence from diverse data substrates.

4.4 Transformations in Batch Processing

Transformations are the cornerstone of the data manipulation capabilities in batch processing using the Apache Flink Dataset API. These operations enable the systematic conversion, restructuring, and aggregation of datasets, allowing users to derive insights and execute data-driven analytics. By understanding and applying a variety of transformations, practitioners can efficiently process large datasets while preserving the integrity and meaning of the underlying data.

Map Transformation: The map operation is a fundamental transformation that applies a specified function to each element of a dataset, generating a new dataset of equal size. This operation is used to perform element-wise transformations, such as converting data types, scaling values, or extracting specific fields.

```
DataSet<String> input = env.readTextFile("input.txt");
DataSet<Integer> lengths = input.map(new MapFunction<String, Integer>() {
    public Integer map(String value) {
        return value.length();
    }
```

```
});
```

This example demonstrates mapping a string dataset to its corresponding lengths, where the map function computes the length of each string.

Filter Transformation: With the filter operation, elements are evaluated against a predicate function, ensuring that only those satisfying the condition are retained in the resulting dataset. Filter transformations are pivotal in data cleaning and preprocessing tasks, helping remove irrelevant or erroneous data entries.

```
DataSet<String> longLines = input.filter(new FilterFunction<String>() {
    public boolean filter(String value) {
        return value.length() > 10;
    }
});
```

Through this filter example, only lines exceeding ten characters are included in the output dataset, aiding in refining input data for specific analyses.

FlatMap Transformation: The flatMap operation extends the capabilities of map by allowing one input element to produce zero or more output elements. This is especially useful for operations that require data expansion, such as tokenization of text documents, where each document may yield multiple words.

```
DataSet<String> words = input.flatMap(new FlatMapFunction<String, String>() {
    public void flatMap(String sentence, Collector<String> out) {
        for (String word : sentence.split(" ")) {
            out.collect(word);
        }
    }
});
```

In this word tokenization example, each line is split into words, resulting in a dataset representing all words across the input text.

Reduce Transformation: The reduce transformation applies a binary associative operator to combine elements of a dataset into a smaller result set, where each key group is reduced to a single value. This transformation is crucial for aggregating values, such as summing numeric fields or concatenating strings within groups.

```
DataSet<Integer> numbers = env.fromElements(1, 2, 3, 4, 5);
DataSet<Integer> sum = numbers.reduce(new ReduceFunction<Integer>() {
    public Integer reduce(Integer val1, Integer val2) {
```

```
        return val1 + val2;
    }
});
```

Here, each pair of numbers is successively summed until a single over-all total remains, exemplifying a classic reduce operation for summing integers.

GroupBy and Aggregate Transformations: The combination of groupBy and aggregate operations allows sophisticated group-wise computations, facilitating the calculation of statistics within segmented datasets. By partitioning data into groups and applying aggregate functions, such as sum, average, min, and max, specific analytics insights can be drawn from specific dimensions.

```
DataSet<Tuple2<String, Integer>> wordCounts = words
    .map(new MapFunction<String, Tuple2<String, Integer>>() {
        public Tuple2<String, Integer> map(String word) {
            return new Tuple2<>(word, 1);
        }
    })
    .groupBy(0)
    .sum(1);
```

This example counts word occurrences by mapping each word to a (word, 1) tuple, grouping by the word field, and aggregating the count, thus producing a frequency distribution of words.

Join Transformation: Join transformations merge elements from two datasets based on shared keys, analogous to SQL joins. This oper-ation enables relational data processing, where records from different datasets are combined to form enriched datasets.

```
DataSet<Tuple2<Integer, String>> dataset1 = // Dataset with id and name
DataSet<Tuple2<Integer, Double>> dataset2 = // Dataset with id and value

DataSet<Tuple3<Integer, String, Double>> joinedDataset = dataset1.join(dataset2)
    .where(0) // Key for dataset1
    .equalTo(0) // Key for dataset2
    .with(new JoinFunction<Tuple2<Integer, String>, Tuple2<Integer, Double>,
            Tuple3<Integer, String, Double>>() {
        public Tuple3<Integer, String, Double> join(Tuple2<Integer, String> first,
                Tuple2<Integer, Double> second) {
            return new Tuple3<>(first.f0, first.f1, second.f1);
        }
    });
```

This join operation merges two datasets based on a shared identifier, producing a dataset that combines information from both sources.

Cross and CoGroup Transformations: The cross transformation computes the Cartesian product of two datasets, generating all possible pairs. Though computationally intensive, this operation is useful for specific classes of problems, such as similarity measurements and combinatorial analyses.

Conversely, the coGroup transformation allows parallel processing of grouped elements from two datasets, bridging the divide between groupBy and join, offering more refined control over paired dataset operations.

Practical Implications and Considerations: By mastering these transformations, practitioners can enforce robust data manipulations that cater to diverse analytical needs. Understanding when and how to employ each transformation makes batch pipelines more efficient and adaptive to complexity.

Flink's transformation offerings are further enhanced by optimization features such as lazy evaluation, where actual execution plans are dynamically optimized at runtime. This optimization ensures that resources are used judiciously, and performance is maximally exploited by minimizing data shuffling and unnecessary computations.

Custom User-Defined Functions (UDFs): Users are not restricted to predefined transformations; Flink empowers users to design their own custom transformations via user-defined functions (UDFs). By implementing MapFunction, ReduceFunction, or comparable interfaces, users introduce custom logic tailored to their unique processing requirements, which can then be seamlessly integrated within the execution environment.

Deciphering the vast ensemble of transformations available in the Dataset API is tantamount to wielding a versatile toolkit capable of addressing a spectrum of batch processing problems. As users assimilate these concepts, they achieve greater dexterity in constructing pipelines tailored for diverse data contexts, converting raw datasets into actionable insights with precision and efficacy. The harmony of transformations within batch workflows embodies the essence of the Dataset API's prowess in processing static datasets comprehensively, heralding a domain where data governs intelligent decision-making.

4.5 Managing Data Partitioning and Grouping

Data partitioning and grouping are fundamental techniques in batch processing that significantly enhance performance, scalability, and efficiency in data processing workflows. Understanding how to manage and apply these techniques effectively with the Apache Flink Dataset API enables developers to optimize resource utilization and improve the throughput of batch processing jobs.

Data Partitioning: Partitioning involves dividing a dataset into distinct segments, which allows for parallel processing across distributed computing resources. This is crucial in large-scale data processing where the volume of data cannot be efficiently handled by a single computational node. Partitioning ensures that each partition can be processed independently, maximizing parallel execution potential.

Flink provides several strategies for partitioning datasets. Key methods include:

- *Hash Partitioning*: Distributes data based on the hash value of partitioning keys, ensuring even distribution across partitions.

- *Range Partitioning*: Segments data into contiguous ranges, ideal for numeric or ordinal data when ordering needs to be preserved within partitions.

- *Custom Partitioning*: Allows customized partitioning logic based on specific criteria or functions.

```
DataSet<Tuple2<String,Integer>> dataset = // Dataset initialization
DataSet<Tuple2<String,Integer>> partitionedData = dataset.partitionByHash(0);
```

This code snippet illustrates hash partitioning of data based on the first field of the tuple, aiding in balanced partition distribution for efficient parallel processing.

Data Grouping: Grouping involves clustering dataset records based on shared keys, which simplifies operations like aggregation and joins that are performed on subsets of data. Effective grouping is pivotal

104

for operations that require cumulative calculations, such as sums, averages, or identifying minimum/maximum values within groups.

```
DataSet<Tuple2<String, Double>> salesData = // Dataset initialization
DataSet<Tuple2<String, Double>> totalSales = salesData
    .groupBy(0)
    .sum(1);
```

Here, sales data is grouped by the first field (e.g., product category) and then aggregated to calculate total sales per category.

Advanced Partitioning Strategies: While traditional partitioning methods suffice in many scenarios, domain-specific needs may necessitate advanced strategies. Flink allows the definition of custom partitioning logic, enhancing flexibility in data distribution.

```
dataset.partitionCustom(new Partitioner<String>() {
    public int partition(String key, int numPartitions) {
        // Custom logic to determine partition index
        return Math.abs(key.hashCode() % numPartitions);
    }
}, 0);
```

A custom partitioner implemented here uses a modular hash function to allocate data, ensuring specific distribution patterns, potentially reducing data skewness and balancing load among nodes.

Combining Partitioning and Grouping: Commonly, data processing applications require both partitioning for parallel execution and grouping for logical operations. Managing composite strategies can reduce data shuffling—a costly operation in distributed processing—and enhance performance.

Consider the task of computing average sales per region, where an initial partitioning by region balances the load, while subsequent grouping within partitions enables efficient local aggregation.

```
DataSet<Tuple2<String, Double>> partitionedByRegion = salesData.
    partitionByHash(0);
DataSet<Tuple3<String, Double, Integer>> regionSalesWithCount =
    partitionedByRegion
    .map(new MapFunction<Tuple2<String, Double>, Tuple3<String, Double, Integer
        >>() {
        public Tuple3<String, Double, Integer> map(Tuple2<String, Double> s) {
            return new Tuple3<>(s.f0, s.f1, 1);
        }
    });

DataSet<Tuple2<String, Double>> averageSalesPerRegion = regionSalesWithCount
```

```
.groupBy(0)
.reduceGroup(new GroupReduceFunction<Tuple3<String, Double, Integer>,
      Tuple2<String, Double>>() {
   public void reduce(Iterable<Tuple3<String, Double, Integer>> values,
         Collector<Tuple2<String, Double>> out) {
      double sum = 0.0;
      int count = 0;
      for (Tuple3<String, Double, Integer> v : values) {
         sum += v.f1;
         count += v.f2;
      }
      out.collect(new Tuple2<>(values.iterator().next().f0, sum / count));
   }
});
```

This example initiates partitioning by region for parallel task execution, followed by grouping to compute per-region statistics, illustrating the synergy between partitioning and grouping operations.

Optimizing Grouping and Partitioning for Performance: Effective partitioning and grouping are critical to minimizing network communication and I/O costs, which are major factors in the performance of batch processing jobs. Careful attention to these operations ensures that:

- *Data Locality*: Operations maintain data locality, avoiding unnecessary data transfer.

- *Data Skew*: Balanced partitioning mitigates data skew, preventing certain partitions from becoming bottlenecks.

- *Resource Utilization*: System resources are optimally utilized by evenly distributing load.

Analyzing Grouped Data: Once data is partitioned and grouped, Flink allows comprehensive and complex data analyses using advanced operators, such as custom grouping functions and windowed aggregations.

```
dataset.groupBy(0).reduceGroup(new GroupReduceFunction<>() {
   @Override
   public void reduce(Iterable<Tuple2<String, Double>> values, Collector<Tuple2<
         String, Double>> out) {
      double total = 0.0;
      for (Tuple2<String, Double> val : values) {
         total += val.f1;
      }
      // Emit grouped analysis result
```

106

```
        out.collect(new Tuple2<>(values.iterator().next().f0, total));
    }
});
```

This custom reduction procedure calculates total values per group, accommodating specialized aggregation logic and supporting domain-specific analyses.

Considerations and Challenges: Implementing a robust partitioning and grouping strategy requires diligent planning to address potential challenges such as data imbalance, processing latency, and resource contention. Practitioners must carefully determine partitioning keys and grouping strategies based on data characteristics, estimated workloads, and system architecture. Iterative testing and tuning permit adaptation to real-world data distributions, ultimately driving efficiency in batch processing environments.

The ability to manage data partitioning and grouping effectively with Apache Flink's Dataset API facilitates high-performance, scalable batch processing solutions. By leveraging these techniques meticulously, data engineers and analysts can ensure their systems are equipped to handle vast datasets swiftly and accurately, transforming raw data into actionable insights with minimal resource expenditure.

4.6 Iterative Processing and Delta Iterations

Iterative processing is a technique often employed in data analytics to refine solutions through repeated computation cycles, particularly in tasks like machine learning, optimization, and graph processing. Delta iterations, a refinement of standard iterations, address the inefficiencies of recomputing results for unchanged data by focusing only on the differences (deltas) between successive iterations. Apache Flink's Dataset API offers robust support for both types of iterative processing, enhancing its utility in complex batch processing workflows.

Iterative Processing: Traditional iterative processing involves repeatedly applying a computation over a dataset until a condition is met, such as reaching a specified number of iterations or achieving convergence. This process is crucial for algorithms that require refinement over multiple passes, such as k-means clustering, logistic regression, and PageRank.

In Flink, iterative processing is handled through the IterativeDataSet abstraction. An iteration begins with an initial dataset, and iterative transformations are applied until the iteration is closed either by reaching a maximum iteration count or by meeting a convergence condition.

```
DataSet<Double> initialData = // Initialize dataset
IterativeDataSet<Double> iterativeDataSet = initialData.iterate(10);

DataSet<Double> iterativeStep = iterativeDataSet.map(new MapFunction<Double,
    Double>() {
  public Double map(Double value) {
    return value * 0.85 + 0.15;
  }
});

DataSet<Double> terminationCriteria = // Define convergence criteria

DataSet<Double> finalData = iterativeDataSet.closeWith(iterativeStep,
    terminationCriteria);
```

This example illustrates an iterative map operation where each dataset element undergoes a transformation for a set number of iterations, exemplifying basic PageRank logic.

Delta Iterations: Delta iterations are an enhancement designed to optimize iterative processes by processing only the modified subset of data that changes between iterations. This approach reduces computational overhead, particularly in scenarios where only a small portion of the dataset changes iteratively, such as updating connected components in a graph or refining neighborhood-centric calculations.

Flink's support for delta iterations is articulated through the DeltaIteration abstraction, which differentiates between the *solution set* (complete data) and the *workset* (delta data). The workset adjusts during each iteration to reflect updates, expanding efficiency by reducing redundant computations.

```
DataSet<Vertex> vertices = // Initialize vertex dataset
DataSet<Edge> edges = // Initialize edge dataset

DeltaIteration<Vertex, Vertex> deltaIteration = vertices.iterateDelta(vertices, 100, 0);

DataSet<Vertex> deltaWorkset = deltaIteration.getWorkset()
   .join(edges).where("id").equalTo("source")
   .with(new JoinFunction<Vertex, Edge, Vertex>() {
```

```
        public Vertex join(Vertex vertex, Edge edge) {
            // Perform directed update
            return new Vertex(edge.target, vertex.value);
        }
    });

DataSet<Vertex> result = deltaIteration.closeWith(deltaWorkset, deltaWorkset);
```

Here, a delta iteration tackles an example from graph processing, where only altered vertex values are propagated, conserving computations associated with static vertices.

Applications of Iterative Processing: The applicability of iterative and delta iterations extends across a broad spectrum of domains:

- *Machine Learning*: Iterative algorithms are at the core of training models, where data passes through multiple iterations for convergence to optimal parameters.

  Example: Gradient descent in neural network training.

- *Graph Processing*: Iterative graph algorithms, particularly those analyzing connectivity or influence, leverage delta iterations for efficient computation on evolving graph structures.

  Example: Connected components, shortest path computation.

- *Optimization Problems*: Mathematical optimization often demands iterative approaches to iterate towards optimal solutions using techniques like simulated annealing or genetic algorithms.

  Example: Routing and network optimization problems employing iterative refinement.

Optimizing Iterative Operations: While iterations enable sophisticated computations, their inherent repetitiveness demands strategic optimization:

- *State Management*: Iteration efficiency relies on effectively managing state, ensuring that memory use remains within bounds, especially with stateful operations in delta iterations.

- *Lazy Evaluation*: Benefit from Flink's optimization strategies through lazy evaluation, deferring computation until execution, allowing a cost-effective synthesis of execution plans over iterative cycles.

- *Efficient Data Model*: Choosing an appropriate data model that minimizes state transfer and maximizes data locality aids in improving iterative execution performance.

Challenges in Iterative Processing: Practitioners face challenges in designing optimal iterative solutions due to:

- High Data Volume: Large state requirements and data volume may necessitate architectural solutions to distribute load and manage resources effectively.

- Convergence Criteria: Choosing appropriate convergence criteria is critical to avoid premature termination or endless iteration scenarios.

- Debugging and Tuning: Iterative processes add layers of complexity in debugging and require tuning for tailored performance, calling for profiling solutions to analyze iteration behavior and resource utilization.

Ultimately, effective use of iterative and delta iterations enhances the capability of batch processing systems to handle extensive and complex computational tasks. The ability to strategically apply these iterative techniques within Flink allows practitioners to build scalable and adaptive data pipelines, empowering high-performance data engineering platforms that exploit the potential of iterative refinement methods. With careful management of iteration parameters and judicious application of delta iterations, Flink's iterative processing capabilities unlock powerful avenues for in-depth analysis and robust predictive modeling.

Chapter 5

State Management and Fault Tolerance

This chapter delves into the crucial aspects of state management and fault tolerance in Apache Flink, which are pivotal for maintaining consistency and reliability in streaming applications. It examines the function and significance of state in stream processing, including stateful operators and managed state features. Flink's sophisticated checkpointing mechanism is detailed, highlighting how it preserves state and enables recovery during failures. The chapter also discusses different state backends, such as RocksDB, exploring their roles in performance and storage optimization. Strategies for handling failures and ensuring seamless recovery underscore Flink's capabilities in providing resilient and high-availability data processing solutions.

5.1 Key Concepts of State in Stream Processing

Stream processing is integral to many applications that demand real-time data analysis. One of the pivotal components in stream processing is the concept of **state**. Understanding and effectively managing state is crucial for integrating stream transformations and aggregations. State in stream processing refers to data that workers (or nodes) in a distributed system accrue over time, which persists throughout the computation's lifecycle beyond the processing of individual streams. This concept empowers systems to perform a variety of operations such as windowed calculations, session data handling, and complex event processing.

1. The Nature of State in Stream Processing

The state in stream processing can manifest in multiple dimensions, such as *local versus global state* and *persistent versus transient state*. Local state is confined to a single processing node or operator, while global state spans multiple nodes or the entire processing topology. These states can be persistent, meaning they are stored in a durable medium such as a database or file system, or transient, existing only in memory.

Stream processing engines such as Apache Flink consider the state as first-class citizens and provide mechanisms to manage them robustly. The state is tightly integrated with stream processing logic, executed within the constraints of limited processing time and space. A common conceptual distinction in stream processing uses the terms *stateless* and *stateful*. Statelessness implies computations whose output depends only on the current input, with no preserved historical information. Conversely, stateful computations utilize historical state data to produce current output, which allows for more sophisticated functions like aggregation, joins, and pattern detection.

2. Types of State in Stream Processing

The types of state include, but are not limited to, the following:

- **Keyed State**: This state is associated with each key within a dataset. It enables aggregates, counters, or any type of accumulators tied specifically to keys, facilitating operations such as *reduce* and *aggregate*.

- **Operator State**: This pertains to state scoped to an operator rather than an individual keyed element. Operator state can be seen in scenarios where data across keys might have some collective association or when performing partitioned state operations.

With the rapid velocity of data, effective state management demands both optimal performance and low-latency accesses. The key here is to choose the appropriate types of state storage that fit the application's requirements seamlessly.

3. State as a Core Component in Flink

Apache Flink exemplifies a stream processing engine that employs an advanced state management system. It provides a fault-tolerant mechanism to manage state both reliably and efficiently. Flink handles state serialization, persistence, and recovery, catering to both local and remote state accessibility based on user requirements.

```
public class StateExample extends KeyedProcessFunction<Long, Tuple2<Long, Long
    >, Tuple2<Long, Long>> {

    // ValueState to hold the characteristic of each key
    private transient ValueState<Long> sumState;

    @Override
    public void open(Configuration parameters) {
        ValueStateDescriptor<Long> descriptor =
            new ValueStateDescriptor<>("sum", TypeInformation.of(new TypeHint<
                Long>() {}));
        sumState = getRuntimeContext().getState(descriptor);
    }

    @Override
    public void processElement(
            Tuple2<Long, Long> value, Context ctx, Collector<Tuple2<Long, Long>>
                out) throws Exception {

        Long currentSum = sumState.value();

        if (currentSum == null) {
            currentSum = 0L;
        }
```

```
        currentSum += value.f1;
        sumState.update(currentSum);

        out.collect(Tuple2.of(value.f0, currentSum));
    }
}
```

This Flink code snippet demonstrates a simple scenario where a running sum is maintained as state for each key extracted from the stream. The state example shows the Flink API's ability to offer lightweight resolution of state interactions through Flink's state descriptor API.

4. Significance of State in Transformations and Aggregations

State makes possible the sophisticated transformations often necessary in real-time stream processing applications. For instance, whether implementing a simple count of items grouped by a key or maintaining session data across user interactions, state is indispensable.

Flink's architecture allows users to write such stateful applications without manually addressing state checkpointing, failover, or recovery. This is primarily due to Flink's state abstraction, which abstracts complexities and provides automatic crash recovery through checkpointing mechanisms, offering robustness in stream computation processing.

Consider a scenario wherein a stream processing application must account for an order's lifecycle, continually updating the total for orders processed. Using keyed state, every unique order ID would be associated with its aggregate total, maintained and updated as records stream in.

```
public class OrderProcessor extends KeyedProcessFunction<Long, Order, TotalOrder>
    {

    private transient ValueState<Double> totalAmount;

    @Override
    public void open(Configuration parameters) {
        ValueStateDescriptor<Double> descriptor =
            new ValueStateDescriptor<>("totalAmount", Double.class);
        totalAmount = getRuntimeContext().getState(descriptor);
    }
```

```
@Override
public void processElement(
        Order value, Context ctx, Collector<TotalOrder> out) throws Exception {

    Double currentTotal = totalAmount.value();

    if (currentTotal == null) {
        currentTotal = 0.0;
    }

    currentTotal += value.getAmount();
    totalAmount.update(currentTotal);

    out.collect(new TotalOrder(value.getOrderId(), currentTotal));
    }
}
```

In this illustrative example, the order processing application uses Flink's stateful processing facilities to retain the totalAmount state. It continuously sums up the amounts from Order records keyed by order ID.

5. Challenges in State Management

While state management is essential for meaningful stream processing applications, it also introduces challenges in consistency, latency, and scalability. The distributed nature requires state to be managed concurrently across nodes, raising issues around access synchronization, consistency models, and the performance impact of large state sizes.

To optimize state access and persist state effectively, practitioners must often choose between in-memory and disk-based state backends. In-memory storage offers rapid access times suitable for applications requiring high-throughput and low-latency, while disk-based backends provide scalability and durability at the cost of increased access time delay.

6. Streams and Event Time Processing

The handling of state is intricately tied to event time processing, where event timestamps—rather than system processing time—govern the progression of logical time. This allows for event ordering based on their occurrence rather than arrival times, offering more accurate results in diverse time-sensitive applications.

115

Flink, for example, uses watermarking, which indicates current event time progress, ensuring state operations are synchronized with the temporal context of processing tasks.

```
public class TimestampAndWatermarkAssigner implements
    AssignerWithPeriodicWatermarks<MyEvent> {
    private final long maxOutOfOrderness = 3500; // 3.5 seconds

    private long currentMaxTimestamp;

    @Override
    public long extractTimestamp(MyEvent element, long previousElementTimestamp)
        {
        long timestamp = element.getTimestamp();
        currentMaxTimestamp = Math.max(timestamp, currentMaxTimestamp);
        return timestamp;
    }

    @Override
    public Watermark getCurrentWatermark() {
        return new Watermark(currentMaxTimestamp - maxOutOfOrderness);
    }
}
```

Through well-configured watermarking and state synchronization based on event time, applications can ensure precision in scenarios involving late arrivals or out-of-order data.

The complexities introduced by event time necessitate that state is handled with consideration to both the demands of temporal accuracy and the limitations inherent in distributed processing environments. Factors like window size, state expiration, and event order handling are tightly interwoven into state management practices.

Successful stream processing architects balance these considerations by employing stateful components with a comprehensive understanding of their utility, limitations, and performance characteristics. As systems grow in complexity and data volumes increase, robust state management becomes a cornerstone in sustaining operational efficiency and accuracy.

5.2 Stateful Operators and Managed State

Stream processing systems, such as Apache Flink, leverage **stateful operators** to manage complex transformations and aggregations, thus enabling sophisticated analytics on streaming data. Stateful operators are at the heart of Flink's architecture, facilitating an efficient mechanism to maintain and manipulate state directly within the data flow. This concept of operators, combined with Flink's managed state capabilities, ensures fault-tolerant processing by consistently maintaining the state in the face of system failures or disruptions.

1. Understanding Stateful Operators

Stateful operators in Apache Flink are defined as those operators which maintain some form of state. This is in contrast to stateless operators, where outputs are strictly a function of the current input, independent of past input. Stateful operators use stored state to produce output, maintaining continuity across streams and ensuring data integrity.

Flink's dataflow programming model is centered around the abstraction of operators that transform data. When these operators store data between invocations—such as counting events, maintaining user session state, or tracking aggregation windows—they are considered stateful. This capability enables Flink to mitigate the challenges posed by the dynamic nature of streams, such as variability in volume and velocity, while providing mechanisms to cope with the eventual consistency of stream data.

Flink provides various operators like *FlatMap*, *ProcessFunction*, and *RichFunction*, which can all be utilized as stateful operators. The state can be keyed, meaning each partition of the operator has separate states based on data keys, which is pivotal for isolating state handling to minimize contention.

```
public class WordCountWithState extends KeyedProcessFunction<String, String,
    Tuple2<String, Integer>> {

    private transient ValueState<Integer> countState;

    @Override
```

```
public void open(Configuration parameters) {
    ValueStateDescriptor<Integer> descriptor =
        new ValueStateDescriptor<>("wordCount", Integer.class, 0);
    countState = getRuntimeContext().getState(descriptor);
}

@Override
public void processElement(String value, Context ctx, Collector<Tuple2<String,
    Integer>> out) throws Exception {
    Integer currentCount = countState.value();
    currentCount += 1;
    countState.update(currentCount);
    out.collect(new Tuple2<>(value, currentCount));
}
}
```

In this example, each word is processed through a stateful operator maintaining a count state, demonstrating how Flink retains state independently for each key (i.e., each word in this context).

2. Managed State in Flink

Managed State refers to the mechanism by which Flink manages the state for operators. This transcends simple storage; it entails Flink handling serialization, deserialization, partitioning, and agreeing on the state's physical representation. Managed state offers durability and reliability, which are core competencies of Flink's design, delivering compliance with consistency models while facilitating fault tolerance.

Flink allows for two key forms of state: *Keyed State* and *Operator State*. These variants integrate seamlessly with the process through folding and reducing aggregations. Flink's architecture standardizes interaction with these state abstractions, even across complex distributed systems.

Keyed state is accessible when an operator can be assigned a key that ensures state partitioning, such as during a keyed stream. This produces data-local state scoped by the key, allowing for optimizations at the data shard level.

Operator state is pertinent when operations require non-keyed associations, distributing state beyond single elements. Use-cases include storing state for dynamic workflows or maintaining as yet unmatched event data in pattern recognition scenarios.

118

```
public class NonKeyedOperatorState extends RichFlatMapFunction<String, Integer> {

    private ListState<String> checkpointedState;

    @Override
    public void open(Configuration parameters) throws Exception {
        ListStateDescriptor<String> descriptor =
            new ListStateDescriptor<>("buffered-", String.class);
        checkpointedState = getRuntimeContext().getListState(descriptor);
    }

    @Override
    public void flatMap(String value, Collector<Integer> out) throws Exception {
        checkpointedState.add(value);
    }
}
```

This example illustrates the use of operator state to maintain an un-keyed list of strings, encapsulating state across a computation that requires holistic data assertions beyond simple keying.

3. Consistency and State Management in Flink

Consistency in distributed systems is a major theme within Flink's state management strategies. Flink is designed to comply with strong consistency paradigms via exactly-once state management. Despite the processing semantics that may be configured to enable additional laxness and performance efficiency (at-most-once), the default exactly-once semantics provide robust fault tolerance.

Flink's **checkpointing** mechanism captures the engaged state periodically, ensuring a synchronized point of recovery. During data processing, these checkpoints safeguard the state, enabling Flink to resume operations from the most recent checkpoint should a failure occur. The integration of this with Flink's Watermark Handling allows it to be consistent even with event times aligning, leveraging state with time constraint functionalities.

Managed state also informs compaction and cleanup strategies. The ability to define state Time-To-Live (TTL) policies allows for better resource management in applications where bounded state is preferable.

```
ValueStateDescriptor<Integer> stateDescriptor =
  new ValueStateDescriptor<>("ttlState", Integer.class);
// Set the state TTL to 1 hour
StateTtlConfig ttlConfig = StateTtlConfig
```

```
.newBuilder(Time.hours(1))
.setUpdateType(StateTtlConfig.UpdateType.OnCreateAndWrite)
.build();

stateDescriptor.enableTimeToLive(ttlConfig);
```

By configuring TTL for state, state updates trigger TTL resets and en-sure idle state purging. This alleviates resource demands on the pro-cessing system, maintaining fiscal state storage allocation.

4. Analytical Advantages of State Management

Stateful operators play a crucial role in optimizing streaming analytics, allowing for the following:

1. **Event-Time Processing Optimization**: Flink's state allows processed streams to factor order latency, guaranteeing timely execution and consistency in outputs.

2. **Pattern Recognition and Complex Event Processing**: Managed state facilitates maintaining the context of broad data patterns for real-time, complex event processing (CEP).

3. **Windowed Aggregation and Counting**: Leveraging state enables efficient aggregation, where windows accumulate data rather than simple transitional output production.

The state relates directly to Flink's performance as it scales with the ap-plication. Distributed data sharding, combined with optimized check-points, ensures that the system bears minimal overhead while reaching scalable capacities in executing complex transactional workflows.

In conjunction with stream processing ability, managed state inte-grates transactional boundaries that ensure no loss or repetition of data across processing nodes, even during a failover expected in dis-tributed environments. This negates possible ambiguities associated with non-deterministic data flows and guarantees system consistency in near-real-time applications.

Ultimately, stateful operators and managed state are foundational elements that define Flink's capacity to uphold comprehensive analytic solutions with low messaging latency, high throughput, and robust availability. Through automated yet user-definable state configuration, Flink deploys a robust underpinning facilitating real-time data processing capable of adhering to the demands of modern, scalable data systems.

5.3 Checkpointing and Saving State

In the landscape of stream processing, checkpointing represents a critical mechanism by which systems maintain state consistency and facilitate robust fault tolerance. Apache Flink's efficient and reliable checkpointing system is pivotal in ensuring resilience, providing the foundation necessary to recover state after failure without data loss or duplication. Understanding the inner workings of Flink's checkpointing mechanism, its configuration, and its role in state management enables developers to implement resilient stream processing applications.

1. The Checkpointing Process

Checkpointing in Flink involves creating consistent images of the distributed state of a program at specific points in time. This enables recovery while ensuring that the state is synchronized with all data sources and transformations. During this process, Flink captures snapshots of the entire state of a program's data operators and persists them to durable storage such as HDFS, S3, or any other supported storage backends.

This model creates so-called "consistent points" in the application's state timeline, to which Flink can revert during a failover scenario. The Chandy-Lamport algorithm, a classic consistency model, forms the theoretical backbone of Flink's checkpoint creation, achieving distributed snapshots without blocking stream processing.

The checkpointing process adheres to the following steps:

1. A checkpoint coordinator initiates the process at regular inter-

vals by broadcasting checkpoint barrier messages throughout the stream topology.

2. As these barriers propagate through each task's input channels, they trigger the state backend to snapshot its current state.

3. The snapshots, executed in a non-blocking fashion, divide the stream of data into pre-barrier and post-barrier segments, ensuring that state captured remains consistent and isolated.

4. Upon capturing all barrier messages, operators flush any buffered state changes and emit them as part of the consistent checkpoint state to durable storage.

Achieving low latency and high throughput in applications necessitates mastering these checkpointing flows, configuring them for optimal balance between system resiliency and processing velocity.

2. Configuring Checkpointing

Flink offers flexible checkpointing configuration options, ensuring that it caters well to the distinct needs of various use cases. Aspects such as checkpoint frequency, timeout settings, and storage strategies typically concern themselves with developers seeking to harness state durability effectively.

Basic checkpointing configuration is as follows:

```
StreamExecutionEnvironment env = StreamExecutionEnvironment.
    getExecutionEnvironment();
env.enableCheckpointing(60000); // checkpoint every minute

env.getCheckpointConfig().setCheckpointTimeout(10000); // 10 seconds timeout
env.getCheckpointConfig().setMinPauseBetweenCheckpoints(500); // 500ms delay
    between checkpoints
env.getCheckpointConfig().setMaxConcurrentCheckpoints(1); // Only one checkpoint
    at a time
```

This essential configuration initiates checkpointing every minute, setting a timeout limitation preventing excessively prolonged intervals that might degrade performance or induce unnecessary latency.

Advanced configurations might additionally involve:

122

- **Externalized Checkpoints**: Flink allows checkpoint data to be retained after job cancellation (i.e., externalized), facilitating easier fault recovery and state examination post-job termination.

- **Incremental Checkpoints**: For state backends such as RocksDB, Flink supports incremental checkpoints wherein only state deltas are saved since the last checkpoint, enhancing performance in state-heavy applications.

- **State Backends Selection**: Configuring a suitable backend influences that state check activities. For example, MemoryState-Backend is suitable for lightweight state contexts, while RocksDBStateBackend suits larger datasets demanding durable persistence.

```
RocksDBStateBackend rocksBackend = new RocksDBStateBackend("hdfs://namenode
    :8020/flink/checkpoints", true);
env.setStateBackend(rocksBackend);
```

Such configurations significantly enhance scalability and recovery times, optimizing backend interactions for efficient reading and writing activities.

3. Consistency and Mode Selection

Flink supports different spectral modes—the trade-offs between processing guarantees and performance:

- **Exactly-Once**: The default and strongest processing guarantee, ensuring that each event affects the state exactly once.

- **At-Least-Once**: Processing may produce duplicate events in case of a failure but generally offers less overhead than exactly-once semantics.

Understanding the need for these modes largely depends on anticipated business scenarios. For financial transactions, exactly-once is crucial. For analytics querying near real-time service insights, at-least-once might suffice with enhanced throughput. Deploying suitable consistency policies within checkpointing extends beyond mere processing; it becomes imperative to facilitate application demands in both performance and consistency.

4. Long-Term State Management and Retention

State retention refers to maintaining state consistency concerning timeouts and size limits, ensuring older, unused states are systematically purged without affecting integrity. Flink's retention policies are directly linkable to checkpointing strategies. Practitioners consider deployment configurations such as Time-to-Live (TTL) states which define bounds for state retention efficiently.

```
StateTtlConfig ttlConfig = StateTtlConfig
    .newBuilder(Time.hours(1))
    .setUpdateType(StateTtlConfig.UpdateType.OnReadAndWrite)
    .setStateVisibility(StateTtlConfig.StateVisibility.ReturnExpiredIfNotCleanedUp)
    .build();

ValueStateDescriptor<Integer> descriptor =
    new ValueStateDescriptor<>("valueState", Integer.class);
descriptor.enableTimeToLive(ttlConfig);
```

Leveraging these configurations requires implementing the elasticity which balances state cleanup with continuous procession demands and ensuring that operational states do not stale or invalidate due to endurance compensations.

Properly regulated state persistence helps maintain a streamlined, performance-aligned pipeline capable of adjusting to both increased data loads and future scaling.

5. Fault Recovery Mechanisms

Flink's checkpointing integrates seamlessly with its failover strategies. Upon detecting a fault, whether a node failure or hardware disruption, Flink is able to restore state from its most recent consistent checkpoint. This recovery strategy ensures that downstream data consumers can resume operations without any loss of data fidelity or duplication of state manipulation.

The critical element in recovery relies on both the frequency and integrity of the checkpoints. Too frequent snapshots can result in processing overhead, but too sparse saves can lead to sizable data loss risks. Thus, properly understanding load characteristics and network stability provides insights into suitable checkpoint configuration.

Upon recovery, the Flink runtime re-deploys task managers using the preserved state. Utilizing historical checkpoint data, Flink sequentially applies the recoverable state back into the data flow network, re-initializing any operators and data paths as configured. This even applies to parallel streams and multi-branched topologies, ensuring systemic coherence.

The integration of large-scale distributed environments is also backed with "savepoint" mechanisms, which allow user-initiated snapshots independent of the automatic checkpoint cadence, enabling seamless state migration across cluster updates or topology changes.

Adopting a comprehensive strategy involves aligning pipeline design, business analytics throughput, and computational resource availability with Flink's checkpoint capacities. This determines not just crash safety but system optimizations—achieving a balance between resilience, scalability, and performance target thresholds.

Visualizing checkpointing as part of a broader data governance strategy accentuates its functionality; it's integral not only in data alignment during operations but equally in durable state preservation for compliance and operational pleasure. Flink's robust checkpoint framework offers a reusable model, where deploying iterative learning and real-time analytics necessitates continuous improvement and integration, leveraging dynamic elasticity that scales towards operational excellence.

5.4   Fault Tolerance Mechanisms in Flink

Apache Flink offers comprehensive fault tolerance mechanisms, ensuring resiliency and continuity in data processing even in the face of failures. These mechanisms are integral to Flink's ability to provide strong consistency guarantees and ensure minimal downtime across distributed streaming applications. By maintaining data integrity and robustness, Flink supports real-time analytics applications that demand high availability and reliability. Understanding these fault tolerance features provides insight into how Flink implements failure detection, state recovery, and assures message processing guarantees.

1. Execution Model and Failure Handling

Flink's execution model is based on distributed stream dataflow, where programs are modeled as graphs of stateful operators. The execution pipeline operates continuously to process incoming data streams. Fault tolerance within this model requires identifying points of failure — nodes, tasks, or entire operators — and ensuring that operations can continue seamlessly upon failure resolution.

When a failure occurs within Flink, several strategies are deployed to ensure continuous processing, including:

- **Task Level Failures**: These account for failures in a single task or operator. Flink leverages checkpoints to restore the state of a failed task and rerun it to achieve state consistency.

- **Node Failures**: Affecting an entire processing node, Flink uses the same checkpoint strategy, re-deploying affected tasks on different nodes if necessary.

- **Job Manager Failures**: Addressed through HA configurations, Flink allows standby Job Managers to take over active duties seamlessly, ensuring that processing does not halt.

In each case, Flink ensures that upon detecting a failure, it halts ongoing computations, retrieves the latest successful checkpointed state, and recomputes the affected portions of the application graph to reestablish consistency.

2. Checkpoint and State Recovery

The cornerstone of Flink's fault tolerance is its checkpoint-based state management strategy. Flink periodically captures the state of streams and their operators during runtime, achieving distributed, consistent snapshots by using checkpoint barriers.

```
StreamExecutionEnvironment env = StreamExecutionEnvironment.
    getExecutionEnvironment();
env.enableCheckpointing(10000); // every 10 seconds

env.getCheckpointConfig().setCheckpointingMode(CheckpointingMode.
    EXACTLY_ONCE);
env.getCheckpointConfig().enableExternalizedCheckpoints(
    CheckpointConfig.ExternalizedCheckpointCleanup.
        RETAIN_ON_CANCELLATION);
```

The above code snippet highlights the configuration set up to employ exactly-once processing semantics, ensuring that state and results remain consistent with each processing cycle. Retention strategies handle post-cancellation scenarios, offering durability for longer-term fault recovery.

Upon encountering a failure, Flink proceeds as follows:

1. Detecting a failure results in suspending ongoing task processing.

2. Through the Job Manager, Flink responds by organizing checkpoints.

3. It restores state from the last successful checkpoint, ensuring the aligned event sequences and state applications are consistent.

4. Tasks are redistributed, resuming execution with seamless continuity aided by durable state backends.

The focus on minimizing downtime and performance overhead during state recovery makes Flink well-suited for high-demand analytics workloads that operate nearer to real-time constraints.

3. Savepoints for Flexible Recovery

In addition to checkpoints, Flink supports **savepoints** as a mechanism to manually trigger state snapshots. Savepoints are particularly useful for controlled shut-downs, version updates, or migrations across cluster configurations.

```
# Triggering a Savepoint
$ bin/flink savepoint <jobId> s3://my-bucket/savepoints/

# Resuming a job from Savepoint
$ bin/flink run -s s3://my-bucket/savepoints/savepoint-<id> path/to/myJob.jar
```

By using savepoints, operators can pause processing, make configuration changes, and resume operations without loss of intermediate state, catering to strategic operational requirements beyond conventional failure recovery.

4. High Availability Configurations

To bolster operational reliability, particularly in mission-critical environments, Flink facilitates high availability (HA) setups. These configurations often involve redundant Job Managers, the primary controller for orchestrating tasks within Flink.

Flink's HA arrangement typically involves running several Job Managers with leader election capabilities powered through systems like ZooKeeper. The leader Job Manager manages active jobs and coordinates tasks, while standby Job Managers stay synchronized and assume control if the lead Job Manager fails.

```
high-availability: zookeeper

high-availability.storageDir: "hdfs:///flink/recovery/"
high-availability.zookeeper.quorum: "localhost:2181"
high-availability.cluster-id: "my-flink-cluster-id"
```

These configurations ensure a seamless leadership transition, minimizing downtime if a Job Manager fails, while preserving configuration continuity and checkpoint integrity.

5. Exactly-Once vs. At-Least-Once Processing Guarantees

Flink's fault tolerance mechanisms are characterized primarily by their adherence to either **exactly-once** or **at-least-once** semantics:

- **Exactly-Once**: Guarantees that each record updates the state exactly one time, essential for transactional applications where data integrity mandates strict adherence to data accuracy.

- **At-Least-Once**: Guarantees that each record is processed one or more times, offering improved performance but possibly introducing duplicates during failure recovery.

Choosing between these models involves assessing trade-offs between performance demands and the level of consistency needed by applications. For instance, financial applications typically necessitate exactly-once for precise transactions, while streaming pipelines for log analytics may prioritize throughput efficiency typical of at-least-once.

```
env.getCheckpointConfig().setCheckpointingMode(CheckpointingMode.
    AT_LEAST_ONCE);
```

Tailored checkpointing modes that align with specific business logic allows for flexible application design, adapting processing guarantees pragmatically.

6. Network and Resource Reliability Considerations

Flink's architecture further accentuates its fault tolerance through network-layer resilience and allocation strategies:

- **TaskManager Resilience**: Flink's reliance on TaskManager resilience avoids single points of failure, redistributing loads through healthy TaskManagers should one fail.

- **Network Partitioning**: Ensures data consistency, employing resilient network protocol configurations for maintaining data streams through failover, typically handling task recovery independently of network disruptions.

Elastic scalability further complements this model, allowing for dynamic adjustments in computational resource deployment reacting to changing workloads, underpinning seamless real-time processing.

7. Conclusion and Strategic Implementation

Successfully implementing Flink's fault-tolerance strategies requires comprehending both the technical constructs and strategic business intimation. Integrating a resilient architecture deciphered into transparent operational configurations splits effort across both high-availability and rapid state turnover mechanics.

Continued accrual of empirical insights informs the procedural refinements necessary to uphold operational excellence while tuning Flink's numerous configuration layers, each piece yielding redundancy, scalability, and assurance inherent to modern real-time stream processing mandates.

Expanding upon theoretical paradigms with practical insights facilitates intelligent enhancing of cluster models, yielding functional systems capable of tolerating failure without user-facing repercussions. Consequently, by building on sophistication in execution and insight through configuration understanding, Flink persists as a key asset achieving widespread reliable stream processing.

5.5 State Backends and Snapshots

Apache Flink's performance and efficiency in stream processing are underpinned by its ability to manage state seamlessly through the implementation of **state backends** and **snapshots**. These components are fundamental in ensuring that stateful tasks are performed with high availability and resiliency across distributed systems. Understanding and efficiently managing these pointers bolster the processing framework's ability to handle large-scale data with finesse and reliability.

1. Understanding State Backends

Flink separates the process-level state and the physical representation (or storage) of the state using state backends. A state backend in Flink is a configurable component where state is stored and checkpoint data is persisted. Each state backend has distinct characteristics impacting application performance, storage needs, and throughput.

Commonly used state backends in Flink include:

- **MemoryStateBackend**: Stores state within JVM memory with serialized bytes in the execution graph representing checkpoints. It is light, fast, and beneficial for testing or development environments where state size is minimal.

- **FsStateBackend**: Writes checkpoint data as files to an accessible filesystem such as HDFS, ceasing usage of JVM storage. The FsStateBackend facilitates larger fault-tolerant state sizes beyond MemoryStateBackend's capacity.

- **RocksDBStateBackend**: Integrates with RocksDB, a key-value store, offering disk-based state storage enabling very large state management whilst maintaining high throughput even under intensive I/O.

Choosing an appropriate state backend involves evaluating application-specific needs, including state size, durability, and processing performance considerations. An understanding of operational dynamics—order of data processing, type of processing guarantees—guides backend configuration.

```
RocksDBStateBackend rocksBackend = new RocksDBStateBackend("hdfs://namenode
    :8020/flink/checkpoints", true);
env.setStateBackend(rocksBackend);
```

This illustrates setting up a RocksDB state backend, persisting state data to HDFS, ideal for high-scale operations with durable storage demands.

2. MemoryStateBackend vs. FsStateBackend vs. RocksDB-StateBackend

Each state backend has unique attributes making them suitable for disparate use cases:

- **MemoryStateBackend** is optimized for scenarios where state size is relatively small (typically less than a few hundred MB) as it resides in JVM heap space, providing rapid access times at the cost of volatility and size constraints.

- **FsStateBackend** stores checkpoints in file systems, bridging the gap between memory limitations and massive-scale resilience needed by larger states. While it sacrifices access speed due to I/O operations, it supports larger state size persistence with network or distributed filesystem durability.

- **RocksDBStateBackend** allows persistence directly on disk, independently from heap size limitations. Built for vast state-heavy applications, it handles key-value pairs efficiently and supports incremental snapshots, facilitating fast recoveries of modified states without hashing unnecessary duplication.

The choice of state backend impacts application processing characteristics, determining scalability, access performance, and failure recovery dynamics. Developers therefore often switch among backends in response to state growth or underlying storage infrastructure.

3. Snapshots in Flink

A vital tool in maintaining service reliability, snapshots ensure resilience and state integrity in stream processing. Flink incorporates

131

snapshots as part of its fault-tolerant architecture, capturing the state of streams alongside operator states at consistent checkpoints.

Snapshots effectively function as stateful "pictures" capturing operator state at given instants, thus aiding recovery pathways during failures. The snapshot process encompasses the following:

1. **Barrier Alignment**: Flink's checkpointing utilizes barrier messages injected into the network stream to initiate a global, asynchronous snapshot.

2. **Operator Participation**: Each processing task uses defined state backends to capture their local state during barriers. These tasks, through internal mechanisms, serialize, store, and transmit snapshots to pre-defined checkpoint storage.

3. **State Consistency**: Post operation, the stream's captured points form concurrent images of active operators, bearing enough information to recover tasks upon tasks of failure.

This snapshot capability powered through orchestration ensures low-error tolerance for state-dependent tasks, facilitating data flow resumption with minimal data losses during operational failures.

4. Incremental Snapshots with RocksDB

One advanced feature of the RocksDB backend is its support for incremental snapshots, allowing only state differences to be recorded since the previous snapshot rather than duplicating the entire data set. This functionality significantly reduces the storage space necessary for checkpoints and accelerates recovery times, particularly advantageous for applications perpetually modifying extensive state builds.

```
RocksDBStateBackend rocksBackend = new RocksDBStateBackend("hdfs://namenode
    :8020/flink/checkpoints", true);
rocksBackend.setIncrementalCheckpoints(true);
env.setStateBackend(rocksBackend);
```

Implementing incremental snapshots involves enabling this feature within the RocksDB backend configuration, allowing efficient state change recordings while maintaining operational fluency.

5. Performance Considerations and Tuning

Optimizing performance with state backends includes acknowledging limitations and setting configurations that support the workload structure. Key elements to consider involve:

- **Checkpoint Interval and Timeout**: Align timeout settings to circumvent blocking in state-heavy sequences whilst maintaining agility in save operations.

- **Backend Configuration and State Size**: Evaluate state memory consumption limitations and disk access times, especially around node replication and network speed concerns.

- **Scaling and Parallelism**: Incorporating scaling provisions entails augmenting parallelization where state backends afford flexibility in distributed state sharps throughout tasked deployments.

```
env.enableCheckpointing(30000); // Set 30 seconds interval
env.getCheckpointConfig().setCheckpointTimeout(15000); // 15 seconds timeout
```

This configuration establishes practical checkpoint frequencies appropriate for operations that demand more extended processing time versus failure correction precision.

6. Strategic Backend Selection for Different Workloads

Flink's ability to toggle state backends permits leveraging feathered backend attributes, aligning operational goals with backend capabilities:

- For rapid development, testing, or constrained-memory applications, deploying MemoryStateBackend is conducive, entailing minimal set-up for trial simulations.

- Deploying FsStateBackend suits when continuity and retention of comprehensive historic states are necessary, bridging gap with connection pipelines serving consumption repositories like HDFS.

- For high-throughput operations characterized by expansive state accumulation, selecting RocksDBStateBackend enables intensive state size management, efficiently cycling through state changes translating processing equivalence against needs for persistent continuity.

Selecting a state backend effectively involves a diagnostic analysis of application throughput requirements, journeying through state evolutions, and balancing application drawbacks relating to resource taxation. These choices manifest substantially in the operationalized trade-offs inherent to streamline analytics or continuous transactional commitments.

In summary, understanding the nuances of different state backends and snapshot mechanisms unlocks advanced operational agility, enabling Flink to sustain robust streaming applications scalable under complex requirements. Through iterative observation, enhancements in the way state backends reside substantiate organizational objectives, yielding sustainable paths to articulate smart analytics capable of transformation across multiple streams and vistas.

5.6 Handling Failures and Recovery Strategies

Apache Flink's formidable standing in stream processing is largely attributed to its robust failure handling and recovery mechanisms. These features are designed to ensure continuous operation and data flow consistency in distributed applications, minimizing downtime and data loss. Understanding how Flink effectively manages faults and the strategies employed to recover from disruptions underscores the platform's reliability and efficiency.

1. Types of Failures in Flink

In large-scale distributed environments, failures are multifaceted and can occur at various levels:

- **Task Failures**: These occur when a processing operator or task fails due to exceptions such as arithmetic errors, null pointer access, or code bugs. Task failures necessitate immediate attention to prevent data loss.

- **Task Manager Failures**: This relates to the crashes or failures of worker nodes (Task Managers) responsible for executing and managing tasks. Common causes include node crashes, resource exhaustion, or network issues.

- **Job Manager Failures**: The Job Manager orchestrates the execution of jobs, hence its failure can disrupt task scheduling and state checkpointing, demanding a robust failover mechanism.

- **Network Partitioning and Connectivity Issues**: Such failures result from network outages, leading to difficulties in communication between distributed nodes, affecting data stream continuity.

Addressing these failures requires coordinated strategies that ensure Flink's runtime environment can quickly recover, maintaining both data accuracy and processing guarantees.

2. Checkpointing as a Recovery Pillar

Flink utilizes checkpointing, capturing consistent snapshots of the stream processing state at regular intervals as a core strategy to handle task and node-level failures. The use of checkpoint barriers enables Flink to achieve these consistent snapshots while the application continues processing incoming data.

In the event of a failure, Flink can fall back to the last successful checkpoint and resume processing without data duplication or loss, adhering to exactly-once processing semantics unless configured otherwise for at-least-once semantics.

```
StreamExecutionEnvironment env = StreamExecutionEnvironment.
    getExecutionEnvironment();

env.enableCheckpointing(5000); // Checkpoint every 5 seconds
env.getCheckpointConfig().setCheckpointingMode(CheckpointingMode.
    EXACTLY_ONCE);
env.getCheckpointConfig().setMinPauseBetweenCheckpoints(3000);
env.getCheckpointConfig().setCheckpointTimeout(60000); // 1 minute timeout
```

Configurations such as checkpoint intervals and timeouts are integral to defining the balance between processing overhead and the likelihood of precise recovery.

3. Savepoints for Enhanced Recovery Control

Beyond automated checkpointing, Flink supports the use of developer-triggered **savepoints**, allowing users to manually store the state of the application consistently. Savepoints are useful for operational control, enabling safe updates, migrations, or shutdowns with state preservation.

```
# Triggering a Savepoint
$ bin/flink savepoint <jobId> s3://my-bucket/savepoints/

# Resuming a job from Savepoint
$ bin/flink run -s s3://my-bucket/savepoints/savepoint-<id> path/to/myJob.jar
```

Savepoints offer flexibility, particularly in scenarios where state-savvy adjustments are necessary beyond mere failure recovery, such as version upgrades or system scaling.

4. Handling Task and Task Manager Failures

Task Failures typically stem from software errors within user-defined functions. Flink's runtime environment automatically detects task failure, aborts the fail-prone operator, and restarts it from the last checkpoint. Any transient state, therefore, remerses progressively without user intervention, securing continuity in downstream processing.

Task Manager Failures involve the reallocation and redistribution of tasks to other available Task Managers. Flink dynamically reschedules these jobs across remaining nodes to uphold pre-configured parallelism levels. This failover process capitalizes on idle computational capacities and leverages checkpoint states to instantiate tasks resiliently.

```
env.setRestartStrategy(RestartStrategies.fixedDelayRestart(
   4, // Number of restart attempts
   Time.seconds(10) // Delay between attempts
));
```

The configuration above exemplifies a fixed-delay restart strategy where a task can retry processing, establishing redundancies against transient errors or temporary task misalignments.

5. Job Manager Failover via High Availability

The **Job Manager Failures** are addressed using Flink's high availability (HA) setups, often employing solutions like ZooKeeper for leader election and state management. Under an HA configuration, a failed Job Manager is replaced by a standby, ensuring that orchestration responsibilities are transferred seamlessly with minimal interruption.

Such configurations necessitate persistence of metadata and checkpoints within distributed file systems conducive to re-election protocols.

```
high-availability: zookeeper

high-availability.storageDir: "hdfs:///flink/recovery/"
high-availability.zookeeper.quorum: "localhost:2181"
high-availability.cluster-id: "my-flink-cluster-id"
```

Through this setup, Flink guarantees job metadata and state persistence, ensuring leaders resume operations with reduced latency, rebounding effectively from disruptions in high-scale environments.

6. Coping with Network Partitioning

Ensuring robustness against network disruptions requires a combination of strategies ranging from buffer management to retrying messaging protocols. Flink's architecture supports opaque, non-blocking processing paths, enabling progress through barriers designed for eventual synchronization despite the occurrences of connection dropouts.

The role of maximum concurrent checkpoints, buffer timeout strategies, and heartbeat intervals collaborates to maintain network reliability.

```
env.getCheckpointConfig().setMaxConcurrentCheckpoints(1); // Allow max one
    checkpoint
env.setBufferTimeout(20); // 20ms buffer timeout
```

By tuning net-bound configurations, applications can adequately antic-

137

ipate fluctuating network conditions, managing stream timeliness and alignment during progressive streaming.

7. Strategy Considerations for Real-Time Scaling

Agile adjustment to topical data influxes is fundamental to resilience in stream processing. Flink leverages scaling techniques – horizontal and vertical – maneuvering varied workloads without compromising failure management strategies.

- **Horizontal Scaling**: Involves adding more nodes or containers to accommodate growing state and task distribution requirements, amplified processing reached non-intrusively.

- **Vertical Scaling**: Entails enhancing resource categories such as CPU, memory, or disk space of existing nodes, counterbalancing complex computation against refined resources.

Kubernetes and Docker environments ease these covariate modeling techniques, whereby state is safely negotiated with State Backends during escalating deployments.

8. Integrated Monitoring and Logging

Continuous oversight over task execution, state transitions, and data flows is vital for early fault detection and flawless recovery planning. Flink offers metrics and logging frameworks — tools that integrate effortlessly with monitoring solutions like Prometheus, Grafana, and ELK stack — enabling developers to conduct health checks and analysis pre-emptive to faults.

```
Configuration conf = new Configuration();
conf.setString("metrics.reporter.prom.class", "org.apache.flink.metrics.prometheus.
    PrometheusReporter");
conf.setString("metrics.reporter.prom.port", "9249");
```

By maintaining 360-degree, real-time visibility over streams, organizations harness actionable insights that refine efficiency ensuring Repair with the added flair of empirical data shaping comprehensive operational methodologies.

138

Deployments tuned to administer cognitive recovery will judiciously marry legacy fault-tolerance, state-of-the-art backend orchestration, and empirical stakeholder settings, establishing Flink as an indispensable framework in catering to global-scale, high-reliability processing commitments. Each configured thread, task, and boundary consideration interlaces nuanced architecture and recovery skillsets towards resilient, uninterrupted execution in stream processing at-scale.

Chapter 6

Flink's Windowing and Time-Based Operations

This chapter explores Flink's windowing and time-based operations, essential for segmenting continuous data streams into manageable sets for analysis. It examines the various window types available in Flink, such as tumbling, sliding, session, and global windows, each suited for different processing needs. The importance of time characteristics—processing time, event time, and ingestion time—is discussed, along with their impact on windowing behavior. Additionally, the configuration of window assigners and triggers is explained, offering precision in control over data processing timelines. The chapter also addresses implementing custom windows for specific use cases and strategies to manage late events, ensuring accuracy and completeness in stream processing.

6.1 Understanding Windowing in Stream Processing

Windowing is a fundamental concept in stream processing that allows operations to be executed over finite subsets of data within a continuous stream. This technique is critical for transforming seemingly endless data flows into manageable and analyzable units. Stream processing frameworks like Apache Flink leverage windowing to enable users to perform computations over real-time data streams effectively.

In stream processing, data flows continuously and indefinitely. Unlike batch processing systems, where data is static and bounded, stream processing emphasizes the immediacy and perpetuity of data streams. The task of deriving meaningful insights from such streams requires partitioning the infinite data into finite, analyzable chunks—windows.

Windows are essentially subsets of a stream that accumulate data for a specified timeframe or data condition before triggering computation. They define the boundaries over which computations are performed. Carefully designed windowing strategies yield efficient processing while delivering accurate results. A comprehensive understanding of windowing entails not only comprehension of what windows achieve but also how they are formulated, managed, and utilized in practical applications.

In Flink, windows are used to segment the continuous data streams, thus enabling operations such as aggregations, joins, or transformations on bounded data. The implementation involves both the selection of an appropriate windowing strategy and the configuration of the window parameters. The following sections further elucidate the intricacies of windowing in the context of Flink, supplemented with relevant examples and detailed explanations.

One fundamental aspect of windowing is the choice of how the end of a window is triggered. This is functionally referred to as the windowing logic, which determines when accumulated data within a window is processed. Windows can be triggered based on time, data counts, or more complex conditions. The kinds of operations performed over these windows depend heavily on the window type and the conditions under which they operate.

```
DataStream<String> stream = // Initialize your streaming source

// Applying a time window of 5 seconds
DataStream<Aggregate> aggregateStream = stream
    .keyBy(value -> value.getKey())
    .timeWindow(Time.seconds(5))
    .reduce((value1, value2) -> new Aggregate(value1, value2));
```

In the example above, windowing is performed with a simple time window of five seconds. The operations specified after the window are applied to each key's collected data within these five-second intervals.

A critical concept in windowing is the notion of a consistent state throughout the execution of operations. Each window maintains state information over its desired scope of data, ensuring that operations such as aggregations or transformations produce consistent and expected results. The preservation and management of this state are crucial for maintaining the integrity of the outcome.

Understanding the purpose of windowing leads us into exploring the 'how' and 'why' of their implementation. Here's a breakdown of key considerations in windowing:

- **1. Granularity and Scope**

  The size of the window, whether based on time intervals or counts of events, dictates the granularity of analysis possible. Smaller windows allow more frequent updates but result in greater computational overhead and state management requirements. Conversely, larger windows reduce the computational load but may delay the derived insights.

  ```
  DataStream<Event> eventStream = // Initialize your streaming source

  // Applying a count window of 100 events
  DataStream<Aggregate> countWindowStream = eventStream
      .keyBy(event -> event.getCategory())
      .countWindow(100)
      .sum("value");
  ```

  In this example, a count window captures 100 events before executing the sum operation. The choice of window type and size should align with the performance and accuracy objectives of the application.

- **2. Considerations of Latency and Throughput**

143

By determining the appropriate windowing strategy, a balance between low latency and high throughput can be achieved. Event time windows help maintain accurate temporal sequencing necessary in many data-driven applications, where the timing of incoming data is critical.

```
DataStream<Event> eventStream = // Initialize your event source

// Set up to utilize event time
eventStream
    .assignTimestampsAndWatermarks(new EventTimeExtractor())
    .keyBy(event -> event.getId())
    .timeWindow(Time.seconds(10))
    .reduce((value1, value2) -> // Reduction logic);
```

Here, event time with watermarks is utilized to manage latency effectively while maintaining the sequence of data based on the event occurrence time. The watermarks indicate the progress of event time in the stream, allowing the system to process late events correctly.

- **3. Composition and Overlapping of Windows**

An advanced consideration is the use of overlapping windows such as sliding windows, which provide a balance of detailed and holistic views of the data over time. Sliding windows process overlapping segments of data, meaning events can contribute to multiple windows.

```
DataStream<String> stream = // Initialize your streaming source

// Applying a sliding window of 10 seconds with a slide of 5 seconds
DataStream<Aggregate> slidingWindowStream = stream
    .keyBy(value -> value.getKey())
    .timeWindow(Time.seconds(10), Time.seconds(5))
    .reduce((value1, value2) -> new Aggregate(value1, value2));
```

Sliding windows facilitate higher operational thoroughness by re-evaluating overlapping sets of data, which can be especially useful for trend analysis or anomaly detection.

Each windowing pattern offers distinct advantages and serves specific purposes in stream processing. Tumbling windows are non-overlapping, fixed-size blueprints ideal for batch-like processing of streams. Sliding windows provide ongoing, repetitive analyses over dynamic datasets. Session windows are particularly suitable for data streams that exhibit variable patterns, such as user activity sessions.

Implementing an effective windowing strategy also involves accounting for late data, an inevitable characteristic of real-world streams. The framework has built-in mechanisms to handle such scenarios gracefully, ensuring that delayed elements are incorporated into ongoing computations, preserving the sequence and correctness of the results.

Beyond these rudimentary strategies for windowing, adaptive windowing strategies can dynamically adjust window sizes in response to changing data patterns. Incorporating machine learning models or predictive analyses can inform modifications to the windowing approach, granting additional layers of customization and precision to stream processing workflows.

Compiler optimization, resource allocation, and computational scheduling are enhanced through the efficient design of window processes. Understanding these mechanisms is paramount for effective resource management, particularly in environments with mixed workloads or heterogeneous data sources requiring specialized handling. Coupling windowed operations with stateful processing and backpressure management strategies can uphold performance efficiency.

Incorporating the various windowing features, each tailored to specific stream attributes and operational goals, empowers developers to craft robust and adaptable stream processing solutions. As we continue to explore the interplay between various time characteristics, windowing turns into a versatile tool critical for unlocking the full potential of real-time data analysis frameworks. The evolution and expertise in windowing initializes a pathway to developing high-throughput, low-latency, and resilient streaming services tailored to diverse domains. Therefore, the practical application and theoretical understanding of windowing remain pivotal to advancing stream processing technology.

6.2 Types of Windows in Flink

Apache Flink provides a rich set of windowing mechanisms, each tailored to address specific needs and challenges in stream processing.

Understanding the various types of windows available in Flink is crucial for implementing effective data processing strategies that align with specific business and application requirements. This section explores the core types of windows offered by Flink, including tumbling, sliding, session, and global windows, providing detailed explanations and examples for each.

Tumbling Windows

Tumbling windows are fixed-size, non-overlapping windows that partition the data stream into contiguous chunks. Each window contains events that occur within a specific interval, processing them as a complete unit. This approach is similar to batch processing in that data is aggregated at fixed intervals, ensuring consistent segmenting of data regardless of the time or data count.

```
DataStream<Event> eventStream = // Initialize your event source

// Defining a tumbling window of 30 seconds
DataStream<AggregationResult> tumblingWindowStream = eventStream
    .keyBy(event -> event.getKey())
    .timeWindow(Time.seconds(30))
    .aggregate(new MyTumblingWindowFunction());
```

In this example, the tumbling window spans a period of 30 seconds. Events are grouped by a key, and all events within each window period are subjected to an aggregation function MyTumblingWindowFunction. The window closes at fixed boundaries, ensuring a neat division of time-series data.

Tumbling windows are particularly effective for applications needing consistent time-bound metrics, such as monitoring system health over fixed intervals or aggregating user actions in gaming applications at regular time spans.

Sliding Windows

Unlike tumbling windows, sliding windows can overlap, enabling events to be part of multiple windows. This characteristic allows users to perform a more granular analysis of data over successive time frames. Each window is of fixed size, but the windows progress over time with a sliding offset, providing overlapping frames of data for repeat observations.

```
DataStream<Event> eventStream = // Initialize streaming data source
```

```
// Implementing a sliding window with a 30 seconds size and 10 seconds slide
DataStream<AggregationResult> slidingWindowStream = eventStream
    .keyBy(event -> event.getKey())
    .timeWindow(Time.seconds(30), Time.seconds(10))
    .aggregate(new MySlidingWindowFunction());
```

The sliding window in this snippet operates over 30 seconds, with a slide of 10 seconds. This setup results in each new window opening every 10 seconds, capturing events from the current 30-second span. Sliding windows are invaluable in scenarios requiring dynamic analysis and insights, including trending data, noise reduction, or forecasting, as each window can incorporate slightly different datasets for comprehensive time-based evaluations.

Session Windows

Session windows are unique as they do not rely on fixed interval sizes. Instead, session windows are determined by user activity, commencing with the first event and grouping all subsequent events until a defined inactivity gap or session timeout is encountered. As such, session windows capture user sessions bounded by periods of inactivity, which can vary in real-world data streams depending on the use case context.

```
DataStream<UserEvent> userEventStream = // Load your user events

// Defining a session window of 1-minute inactivity
DataStream<SessionSummary> sessionWindowStream = userEventStream
    .keyBy(event -> event.getUserId())
    .window(ProcessingTimeSessionWindows.withGap(Time.minutes(1)))
    .process(new MySessionWindowFunction());
```

In this example, a session window with a 1-minute inactivity gap is set for a stream of user events. The session window is suitable for tracking user interactions over time until no actions occur within the inactivity window. Session windows are especially useful in application scenarios like tracking user session behavior in web analytics, online gaming, or customer interaction logging.

Global Windows

Global windows are not constrained by time or event counts and remain open indefinitely. Instead, their closure is managed explicitly via triggers, compelling customization of when computations should execute over the aggregated data. This flexibility allows for complex, condition-driven data processing tasks.

```
DataStream<EventType> eventTypeStream = // Load streaming source

// Applying a global window with a custom trigger
DataStream<GlobalSummary> globalWindowStream = eventTypeStream
    .keyBy(event -> event.getCategory())
    .window(GlobalWindows.create())
    .trigger(new MyCustomTrigger())
    .aggregate(new GlobalAggregationFunction());
```

The global window in this code block is designed for a stream categorized by event type. A customized trigger MyCustomTrigger manages when the computation will proceed. Global windows are critical in scenarios necessitating non-time-based triggers, such as accumulating data until a specific recognition pattern is met, making them ideal for advanced data science applications.

Each type of window bears unique properties, impacting how data is gathered, processed, and interpreted within bounded contexts. The choice of window type needs to consider factors like data arrival patterns, processing requirements, latency sensitivity, and computational resource allocation.

Windows are integral to data-driven applications because they facilitate aggregation, computation, and the summarization of streamed datasets while enabling the system to handle data in bite-sized portions suitable for memory constraints. The correct windowing strategy ensures insights are gleaned efficiently, meeting both analytics demands and operational matters. Flink's flexibility in window configuration enables users to tailor their applications for myriad use cases through these distinct window types.

Further evolving the power of windowing, Flink allows for the creation of custom windows leveraging user-defined logic. Developers can tailor window behavior to adhere to specific business logic or performance objectives, expanding the application potential of stream processing beyond predefined constructs.

Windowing concepts, alongside Flink's robust processing capabilities, empower developers with fine-grained control, enabling the conversion of continuous streams into valuable, actionable intelligence consistently and efficiently. This examination of Flink's windowing mechanisms reinforces its versatility and adaptability in meeting diverse processing needs, bridging the gap between raw data and meaningful insights.

6.3 Working with Time Characteristics

In stream processing, time is an essential dimension that dictates how data streams are interpreted and processed. Apache Flink provides sophisticated mechanisms for handling different time semantics, which are crucial for ensuring accurate and reliable stream processing. The primary time characteristics that Flink handles are processing time, event time, and ingestion time, each serving distinct use cases based on the temporal nature of data streams.

Processing Time

Processing time refers to the local system time at the machine that performs the stream processing operation. It is the simplest time characteristic since it relies solely on the system clock of the machine executing the Flink job. However, using processing time can lead to inaccuracies, especially in distributed and networked environments where delays and variations are possible.

```
DataStream<Event> stream = // Initialize your streaming data source

// Configuring a processing time window of 15 seconds
DataStream<Stats> processedStream = stream
    .keyBy(event -> event.getType())
    .timeWindow(Time.seconds(15))
    .reduce(new StatsReductionFunction());
```

In the example, a processing time window is applied to a data stream. While this is a straightforward method to compute statistics for incoming events, it assumes that the system's clock reflects the data's temporal reality, which may not be accurate in a real-time streaming setup with potential latencies or clock drifts.

Processing time is suitable for applications where latency is minimal, and precise temporal alignment is not crucial, or where system time provides sufficient accuracy, such as monitoring local device metrics or processing synthetic data streams.

Event Time

Event time reflects the time when data events were originally generated

149

on the producing device, as represented by a timestamp included in the data. It is the most accurate time characteristic since it corresponds to the actual occurrence of each event, making it paramount for use cases requiring precise temporal analysis, such as financial transactions or sensor data analytics.

Event time processing in Flink involves assigning timestamps and generating watermarks, which denote the progress of event time in the stream. Watermarks indicate that no events with a timestamp older than the watermark timestamp are expected, enabling Flink to manage out-of-order events gracefully.

```
DataStream<Event> eventStream = // Initialize event source

SingleOutputStreamOperator<Event> timestampedStream = eventStream
    .assignTimestampsAndWatermarks(WatermarkStrategy
        .<Event>forBoundedOutOfOrderness(Duration.ofSeconds(30))
        .withTimestampAssigner((event, timestamp) -> event.getTimestamp()));
```

Here, a timestamp is set from an event's attribute, and a watermark strategy accommodates an expected out-of-orderness of 30 seconds, allowing Flink to handle any disruptions in the event sequence due to delays.

With event time, stream processing logic can align with the actual event chronology, thereby providing accuracy in analytics, especially in domains where backdated or late-arriving data must be processed accurately.

```
DataStream<Event> userActivityStream = timestampedStream
    .keyBy(event -> event.getUserId())
    .window(TumblingEventTimeWindows.of(Time.hours(1)))
    .reduce(new ActivityAggregator());
```

In this example, event time windows categorize user activity over hourly intervals. Each window aggregates activities, providing reliable snapshots at each hourly mark, in sync with the timestamps of the events rather than the machine's processing time, preventing discrepancies due to event arrival inconsistencies.

Ingestion Time

Ingestion time is an intermediate approach between processing time and event time. It captures the time when events are incorporated into the Flink system, offering a balance by providing time analysis without the complexity of handling event time and watermarking.

Flink assigns the ingestion timestamp automatically when data enters the system, which can be advantageous when dealing with systems where event timestamps are unavailable or where causal ordering and low latency are more significant than pinpoint precision.

```
DataStream<Event> ingestedStream = env.addSource(new CustomSourceFunction())
    .assignTimestampsAndWatermarks(WatermarkStrategy.forIngestionTime());
```

Here, a stream is initialized with ingestion time as the timestamp strategy, allowing standard analytics without needing explicit timestamp assignments.

Ingestion time is practical for systems working with semi-realtime scenarios or where external systems interfacing with Flink do not expose event timestamps. It provides a lightweight yet effective approach to aligning events chronologically based on the time of entry into the Flink pipeline.

Comparative Analysis

Choosing the appropriate time characteristic involves considering several factors, such as the data source's inherent characteristics, latency requirements, and the need for temporal accuracy.

- **Accuracy**: Event time offers the highest accuracy as it aligns events based on real-world occurrences. Processing time is less accurate since it depends on processing system clocks.

- **Latency Handling**: Event time, with watermarking, can robustly handle late data. Processing time has minimal handling for late events due to its dependency on system time of processing.

- **Simplicity**: Processing time configurations are straightforward with minimal setup. Event time requires timestamp assignment and watermarking, thereby increasing configuration complexity.

- **Use Cases**: Event time is crucial for time-critical applications like network monitoring, event logging, and fraud detection, where order precision is necessary. Processing time is applicable in simpler, latency-friendly contexts like monitor localization or internal batch processes.

Flink's provision for time characteristics empowers developers to tailor stream processing operations to the temporal dynamics of their data, enabling them to maintain accuracy, streamline processing, and optimize results based on time-critical considerations.

Given the significance of temporal alignment, developers often opt for event time wherever feasible, notwithstanding the complexity it introduces. This approach ensures that data processing aligns with actual business dynamics and external factors affecting the data's chronological flow. Flink's capabilities embrace robustness, precision, and flexibility, offering unparalleled operational control over streamed data.

However, making effective use of these time semantics requires understanding the specific application context, expected data patterns, and readiness to deal with late or out-of-order data. Investment in mastering these components guarantees enhanced processing, reduced anomalies, and accurate data-driven insights, aligning computational outputs with strategic enterprise objectives.

The profound utility of time characteristics lies in their dual role of improving the computational integrity and efficacy of streaming systems while tailoring the deployment to specific performance needs. Flink's adaptability in these respects ensures its relevance as a tool for high-performance, real-time data operations.

6.4 Configuring Window Assigners and Triggers

In the context of Flink's stream processing capabilities, window assigners and triggers play crucial roles in defining how data is segmented and when processing occurs. Configuring these components effectively is essential for achieving efficient and precise streaming analytics. This section elaborates on the mechanisms and strategies for configuring window assigners and triggers, offering detailed insights and examples to enrich understanding and application.

Window Assigners

Window assigners are responsible for segmenting a continuous stream of data into discrete windows. They determine the shape, size, and overlap of windows, thereby setting the boundary conditions for subsequent data processing operations. Flink provides various pre-defined window assigners, including TumblingEventTimeWindows, SlidingEventTimeWindows, ProcessingTimeSessionWindows, and GlobalWindows. Each assigner has distinct characteristics that cater to specific data processing needs.

```
DataStream<String> sourceStream = // your input data stream;

// Configuring a tumbling window via a window assigner
DataStream<AggregateResult> tumbledStream = sourceStream
    .keyBy(value -> value.getCategory())
    .window(TumblingEventTimeWindows.of(Time.minutes(5)))
    .reduce(new AggregateReducer());
```

In the above example, TumblingEventTimeWindows is used to create non-overlapping windows of five minutes each, assigned based on event time. The AggregateReducer function processes events within each distinct window.

Sliding Window Assigner

Sliding windows allow overlap by progressing the window frame at specified intervals, defined as the slide. This configuration enables data points to be part of multiple windows, offering a denser analytical perspective on the data stream.

```
DataStream<String> stream = // your input data stream;

// Configuring sliding event time windows
DataStream<Aggregation> slidingWindowStream = stream
    .keyBy(event -> event.getKey())
    .window(SlidingEventTimeWindows.of(Time.minutes(10), Time.minutes(5)))
    .aggregate(new SlidingAggregateFunction());
```

In this configuration, windows are 10 minutes long, with a 5-minute sliding interval, enabling comprehensive data inspections at frequent intervals to highlight trends or detect changes effectively.

Session Window Assigner

Session windows are derived from the concept of dynamic window lengths based on activity scope, marked by inactivity gaps (timeouts). Session windows segment data associated with user or process sessions across fluid timeframes defined by interim inactivity.

```
DataStream<Event> eventStream = // your input event stream;
```

```
// Session window with an inactivity gap
DataStream<SessionSummary> sessionWindows = eventStream
   .keyBy(event -> event.getSessionId())
   .window(ClientSessionWindows.withGap(Time.seconds(30)))
   .process(new SessionWindowFunction());
```

Here, Flink segments sessions within a 30-second inactivity gap, acknowledging the fluid nature of sessions, capturing user actions, and analyzing them as logically related activity clusters.

Global Window Assigner

Global windows span the whole data stream and are executed based on custom triggers instead of window boundaries. They support applications needing complex, custom, or long-term data views.

```
DataStream<SensorData> sensorStream = // your sensor data stream;

// Assign global window
DataStream<GlobalAggregate> globalWindow = sensorStream
   .keyBy(sensor -> sensor.getType())
   .window(GlobalWindows.create())
   .trigger(new ThresholdTrigger())
   .aggregate(new GlobalAggregateFunction());
```

Here, the global window does not have a preset boundary but waits for the ThresholdTrigger to execute processing, making it suitable for specific conditions like a statistical threshold breach.

Triggers

Triggers determine when a window's computation should be emitted or executed. Once a window is assigned, a trigger assesses data or temporal conditions to execute the associated logic. Flink offers pre-defined triggers such as EventTimeTrigger, ProcessingTimeTrigger, CountTrigger, and PurgingTrigger. Moreover, developers can create custom triggers for specialized processing needs.

```
DataStream<ClickEvent> clickStream = // your user clickstream;

// Using an event-time trigger on a tumbling window
DataStream<UserSummary> userSummaryStream = clickStream
   .keyBy(click -> click.getUserId())
   .window(TumblingEventTimeWindows.of(Time.minutes(10)))
   .trigger(EventTimeTrigger.create())
   .process(new ClickAggregateProcessFunction());
```

In this case, an EventTimeTrigger ensures that the window computation considers the watermark-driven event time to handle late data and

154

out-of-order events appropriately.

Custom Triggers

For specialized conditions or multi-dimensional criteria, custom triggers offer a flexible approach for executing windowed computations beyond pre-defined triggers.

```
public class CustomTrigger extends Trigger<Event, TimeWindow> {

    @Override
    public TriggerResult onElement(Event element, long timestamp, TimeWindow
        window, TriggerContext ctx) {
        if (element.getValue() > THRESHOLD) {
            return TriggerResult.FIRE;
        }
        return TriggerResult.CONTINUE;
    }

    @Override
    public TriggerResult onEventTime(long time, TimeWindow window,
        TriggerContext ctx) {
        return TriggerResult.CONTINUE;
    }

    @Override
    public TriggerResult onProcessingTime(long time, TimeWindow window,
        TriggerContext ctx) {
        return TriggerResult.CONTINUE;
    }

    @Override
    public void clear(TimeWindow window, TriggerContext ctx) {
        // Implement functionality to clear any state
    }
}
```

In this example, a custom trigger fires computation when an event value exceeds a predefined threshold, illustrating how trigger logic can be tailored to specific event conditions beyond simple time-based activation.

Understanding the Interplay Between Assigners and Triggers

The synergy between window assigners and triggers defines the dynamism of streaming operations in Flink. Assigners shape the data input subsets at varying granularities, while triggers dictate the timing and conditions for processing those subsets.

Selecting a window assigner should align with the nature of tasks— whether examining non-overlapping batches, tracking ongoing trends, session-based analysis, or custom conditions. Triggers further refine these analyses by honing the execution to necessary, opportune moments ensuring computational resources focus on momentous data points, preserving system throughput and reducing redundant calculations.

Impact on System Performance

Configuring window assigners and triggers profoundly impacts processing speed, resource utilization, and result accuracy. Proper settings optimize computation, ensuring timely analytics without overwhelming system capacity. Misconfigurations can inadvertently increase latency, induce state overflow, or compromise result accuracy, particularly where real-time data swift changes demand.

Flink provides mechanisms to balance performance, precision, and complexity, ensuring that developers harness potent stream processing solutions tailored to real-world requirements through proficient assigner and trigger configurations. This flexibility enables handling diverse and dynamically evolving stream processing challenges efficiently.

In summary, the architecture around window assigners and triggers manifests Flink's richness in adaptability and precision in streaming analytics. Proper application of these configurations translates into operational agility, enhancing real-time data processing and actionable insights. Each defined strategy around assigners and triggers sharpens the analytical framework, driving meticulous and responsive stream processing workflows.

6.5 Implementing Custom Windows

Implementing custom windows in stream processing with Apache Flink provides the capability to tailor window behavior to meet specific operational needs, enabling more nuanced handling of data streams compared to standard window types. The ability to define custom windows is particularly beneficial when specific patterns or conditions in data processing cannot be addressed by conventional window configurations. This section delves into the intricacies of implementing custom windows within Flink, illustrating how developers can extend the framework's capabilities to handle unique data processing scenarios.

Conceptualizing Custom Windows

The fundamental premise behind custom windows is to move beyond the limitations imposed by predefined window structures such as tumbling, sliding, session, and global windows. Custom windows offer users the flexibility to specify how data segments are accumulated based on bespoke criteria, whether driven by event attributes, external signals, or complex temporal relations.

Leveraging WindowAssigner

The key to implementing custom windows lies in creating a unique 'WindowAssigner'. This is a central component that determines the precise boundaries over which data is aggregated, playing a similar role to predefined assigners but with customized logic.

```
public class CustomWindowAssigner extends WindowAssigner<Object, TimeWindow>
    {

    @Override
    public Collection<TimeWindow> assignWindows(Object element, long timestamp,
        WindowAssignerContext context) {
      long windowStart = calculateWindowStart(timestamp);
      return Collections.singletonList(new TimeWindow(windowStart, windowStart +
          WINDOW_SIZE));
    }

    private long calculateWindowStart(long timestamp) {
      // Custom logic to calculate the beginning of the window
      return timestamp - (timestamp % WINDOW_SIZE);
    }

    // Required override methods omitted for brevity...
}
```

In this example, the custom window assigner calculates the window start based on a specified logic that can account for unique data characteristics or external conditions, thereby allowing window boundaries to extend beyond simple fixed intervals.

Utilizing Custom Trigger

With custom windows, exclusive triggers might be necessary to manage window emissions. Custom triggers can be devised to fire based on complex business logic or external inputs, providing control over when results should be computed and exposed.

157

```
public class ThresholdBasedTrigger extends Trigger<Object, TimeWindow> {

    @Override
    public TriggerResult onElement(Object element, long timestamp, TimeWindow
        window, TriggerContext ctx) {
        if (checkThresholdCondition(element)) {
            return TriggerResult.FIRE;
        }
        return TriggerResult.CONTINUE;
    }

    private boolean checkThresholdCondition(Object element) {
        // Logic to determine if the threshold condition is met
        return ((CustomEvent) element).getValue() > THRESHOLD;
    }

    // Other required overrides...
}
```

The 'ThresholdBasedTrigger' functions by firing when a specific event attribute exceeds a defined threshold, illustrating how custom triggers allow for dynamic processing aligned with real-time data variations.

Custom Window Functionality

Implementing custom window logic within Flink also involves defining how data should be processed once windows are assigned and triggers are activated, using specialized window functions—such as ProcessWindowFunction or ReduceFunction—depending on the exact requirements.

```
public class CustomProcessWindowFunction
    extends ProcessWindowFunction<Event, Output, String, TimeWindow> {

    @Override
    public void process(String key, Context context, Iterable<Event> elements,
        Collector<Output> out) {
        // Implement custom aggregation logic
        int sum = 0;
        for (Event event : elements) {
            sum += event.getValue();
        }
        Output result = new Output(key, sum, context.window().getEnd());
        out.collect(result);
    }
}
```

Here, the 'CustomProcessWindowFunction' demonstrates how aggregated results can be derived using bespoke calculations or transformations tailored to specific analytics or business needs.

Combined Custom Windowing

Flink permits combining custom window assigners with refined triggers and processing functions, delivering sophisticated windowing mechanisms adept at tackling complex data requirements unique to industry-specific applications such as predictive maintenance, personalized recommendations, or adaptive analytics.

Alongside customization, dimensions such as window state management, checkpointing efficiencies, and resource optimization are uniquely influenced by custom window configurations, driving gains in processing resilience and system throughput.

The practical applications for custom windows extend across various domains:

- **Telecommunications**: Monitoring and alerting systems with dynamic thresholds based on network performance metrics.

- **Healthcare**: Patient data analytics, leveraging irregular sampling rates, to determine critical health events or trends.

- **Financial Services**: Banking transaction analysis constrained by unpredictable market factors or intraday anomalies.

Emphasizing state and fault-tolerance, custom window implementations must consider stateful operations, accommodating efficient recovery processes. Flink's robust state management ecosystem ensures data stateful operations such as these are synchronic with both speed and data accuracy, fulfilling stringent requirements prevalent in high-demand environments.

Effective application design for custom windows requires in-depth exploration of both the data semantics and intended operational outcomes, ensuring custom window frameworks are seamlessly phased into existing processing paradigms while augmenting their effectiveness. The adaptability Flink offers through custom window functionality epitomizes its stature as a versatile, applicable tool for dynamic and evolving data streams, capable of adapting to the challenges inherent in modern digital ecosystems.

Custom windows allow developers to harness Flink's extensive processing capabilities, bridging gaps unapproachable with standard configurations. Migration towards bespoke windowing logic within Flink serves as a pivotal step forward, granting scalability and precision in high-fidelity stream processing workflows. Consequently, investing time in holistically understanding and leveraging custom window functionalities results in transformative, data-driven insights tailored to contemporary business landscapes.

6.6 Late Events and Allowed Lateness Strategies

In stream processing environments where 'event time' semantics are used, managing late events is a critical concern. Late events are those that arrive after a window has already fired, based on watermarks or system timings. These events, if not handled appropriately, can create inaccuracies in the computed results. Flink provides a robust framework for dealing with late data through mechanisms such as watermarks and allowed lateness strategies. This section delves into handling late arrivals and implementing allowed lateness strategies, exploring both theoretical and practical implications to ensure data accuracy and integrity.

Understanding Late Events

Late events occur when message propagation delays or processing latencies cause data to arrive after the designated event time windows have been processed. This latency might be due to network delays, slow producers, or clock inaccuracies in the distributed system. Ignoring late events can lead to incorrect aggregations or insights, particularly in scenarios where temporal precision is crucial, such as financial markets or sensor data applications.

For instance, consider a scenario where sensor readings are collected for environmental monitoring. If some readings arrive late due to network congestion, ignoring these late events could lead to incomplete or misleading reports on conditions such as temperature changes or pollution levels.

Role of Watermarks

Watermarks are a Flink construct used to keep track of time progress within a stream, allowing the framework to manage event time operations effectively. Watermarks help signal when a window's operations should be triggered, giving the system a virtual timeline for processing order.

```
DataStream<SensorData> sensorStream = // obtain the sensor data stream;

sensorStream.assignTimestampsAndWatermarks(
    WatermarkStrategy.<SensorData>forBoundedOutOfOrderness(Duration.ofSeconds
        (5))
    .withTimestampAssigner((event, timestamp) -> event.getTimestamp()));
```

In this example, a 'WatermarkStrategy' is implemented, permitting data reordering with a maximum allowable latency of 5 seconds. Watermarks help determine when windows should emit results but also designate when no older timestamps should appear.

Determining Allowed Lateness

Allowed lateness is a strategy in Flink that defines the additional time a system waits before discarding late events that could potentially update previously triggered window results. By setting a boundary of allowed lateness, users provide a buffer within which late data can still be accurately processed and incorporated.

```
DataStream<Event> stream = // data stream of events;

// Defining an allowed lateness interval of 2 minutes
DataStream<Summary> latenessHandledStream = stream
    .keyBy(event -> event.getKey())
    .window(TumblingEventTimeWindows.of(Time.minutes(10)))
    .allowedLateness(Time.minutes(2))
    .sideOutputLateData(lateOutputTag)
    .aggregate(new MyAggregateFunction());
```

Here, 'allowedLateness(Time.minutes(2))' sets a 2-minute tolerance for late arrivals during a 10-minute event time window. This method allows incoming late events to update previously computed windowed aggregates within the allowance period, ensuring more complete analysis.

Side Outputs for Late Events

Flink supports side output streams where late events can be redirected for additional processing or storage, ensuring no data is omitted inadvertently. This feature is particularly useful for subsequent review or delayed inclusion.

```
final OutputTag<Event> lateOutputTag = new OutputTag<Event>("late-data"){};
```

```
DataStream<Event> processedStream = sensorStream
  .keyBy(event -> event.getId())
  .window(SlidingEventTimeWindows.of(Time.minutes(15), Time.minutes(5)))
  .allowedLateness(Time.minutes(3))
  .sideOutputLateData(lateOutputTag)
  .process(new EventProcessingWindowFunction());

DataStream<Event> lateEvents = processedStream.getSideOutput(lateOutputTag);
```

In this configuration, late events are rerouted via 'sideOutputLateData'
into an auxiliary stream 'lateEvents' for further handling or storage.
This dual-path approach ensures all data, regardless of timeliness, is
accounted for and processed effectively.

Practical Considerations and Trade-offs

While configuring allowed lateness and handling late data, several
trade-offs require consideration:

- **Complexity vs. Completeness**: Increasing the allowed lateness interval improves result completeness; however, it adds
  complexity in managing state and potential backlogs in computations.

- **Resource Utilization**: Longer lateness periods may force additional resource usage, specifically in-memory states or checkpoint sizes, impacting scalability.

- **Result Timeliness and Accuracy**: Balancing the lag introduced by waiting for late data against the necessity for immediate results is vital, especially in applications driven by real-time
  decision-making.

- **Data Patterns and Arrival Variability**: Knowledge of typical data patterns or event timing attributes aids optimal lateness
  configurations, reducing over or under-adjustments in window
  period allowances.

Advanced Strategies

Advanced strategies can involve dynamic lateness adjustments based
on real-time system metrics or adopting predictive models to estimate
lateness probability. These methods can shift lateness handling from

static configurations to more responsive strategies that customize resource use and processing efficiency.

Also, comparative systems might adopt rolling buffer methodologies or hybrid streaming modes to finesse data timeliness challenges. Flink's extensibility supports diverse approaches towards integrating newer methodologies, refining late event management effectiveness further.

Conclusions and Implications

Effective late event and allowed lateness strategies are paramount for achieving correct and comprehensive results in time-sensitive applications. By setting appropriate lateness policies with Flink, real-time systems gain resilience against temporal discrepancies inherent in dynamic streaming environments. Given the adaptability of Flink, continual explorations for optimizing lateness strategies promise enhanced decision-making insights and data processing robustness.

In essence, these strategies enhance the stream processor's reliability and credibility, particularly in domains demanding high frequency or precision, such as IoT networks, trading platforms, or mission-critical alert systems. Hence, mastering late event management is pivotal for developers intending to employ Flink extensively in realizing time-aware, data-intensive distributed applications.

Chapter 7

Flink's Connectors and Integrations

This chapter focuses on Flink's connectors and integration capabilities, which are vital for connecting with diverse data sources and sinks. It provides insights into the range of built-in connectors Flink offers, such as those for Apache Kafka, JDBC, and file systems, facilitating seamless data flow in and out of Flink applications. The integration with cloud storage solutions, including AWS S3 and Google Cloud Storage, is also covered, highlighting Flink's adaptability in cloud environments. Additionally, it discusses the development of custom connectors to meet specific data handling requirements and presents best practices for managing connectors, ensuring performance and reliability in complex data processing systems.

7.1 Overview of Flink Connectors

Connectors in Apache Flink are pivotal components that enable the integration of Flink applications with external data systems. They serve as interfaces for data interchange between Flink and various external systems, such as databases, message queues, file systems, and cloud storage services. The potency of connectors lies in their ability to provide seamless data flow, which is crucial for both stream processing and batch processing. This capacity for integration extends Flink's capabilities significantly, transforming it into a comprehensive real-time data processing framework.

Flink connectors can be broadly classified into sources and sinks. A source is responsible for reading data from external systems into Flink applications, while a sink writes processed data from Flink applications to external systems. This bidirectional capability enables Flink applications to act as intermediaries, performing necessary data transformations on the fly or aggregating data as required by downstream applications.

The available connectors are designed with optimality and efficiency in mind, allowing for rapid data ingestion and dissemination. These connectors are built upon well-established protocols and libraries to ensure compatibility and robustness across different types of external data systems. An understanding of how to utilize these connectors effectively is imperative for any Flink-based solution architecture.

Consider the Kafka connector, which exemplifies the seamless integration between Flink and a predominantly popular messaging system. Kafka is renowned for its ability to handle massive volumes of real-time data. The connector abstracts the complexities of setting up reliable data communication channels. Developers only need to specify configurations such as broker lists, topic names, and consumer group IDs. Here's a simple example demonstrating how to configure a source to read from a Kafka topic using the Flink Kafka connector:

```
Properties kafkaProperties = new Properties();
kafkaProperties.setProperty("bootstrap.servers", "localhost:9092");
kafkaProperties.setProperty("group.id", "flink-consumer-group");

FlinkKafkaConsumer<String> kafkaSource = new FlinkKafkaConsumer<>(
    "input_topic",
    new SimpleStringSchema(),
    kafkaProperties
);

DataStream<String> messageStream = env.addSource(kafkaSource);
```

This snippet illustrates an efficient and straightforward setup. Flink's integration with Kafka ensures fault tolerance by leveraging Kafka's inherent fault recovery mechanisms, thus guaranteeing at-least-once processing semantics.

Data streaming scenarios often involve interactions with relational databases. Here, JDBC connectors serve as essential tools for accessing and updating transactional data, providing a bridge between Flink's in-memory computations and persistent data storage. This is particularly crucial for applications that require transformation and analysis of structured datasets originating from online transaction processing (OLTP) systems. JDBC connectors come with flexibility, allowing developers to define SQL queries for data ingestion or updates. A typical configuration might appear as follows:

```
JdbcConnectionOptions.JdbcConnectionOptionsBuilder builder = new
    JdbcConnectionOptions.JdbcConnectionOptionsBuilder();
builder.withUrl("jdbc:mysql://localhost:3306/flinkdb")
    .withDriverName("com.mysql.jdbc.Driver")
    .withUsername("flinkuser")
    .withPassword("password");

JdbcSink.sink(
    "INSERT INTO events (id, event_type, event_time) VALUES (?, ?, ?)",
    (statement, event) -> {
        statement.setInt(1, event.getId());
        statement.setString(2, event.getType());
        statement.setTimestamp(3, new Timestamp(event.getTimestamp()));
    },
    builder.build()
);
```

In this example, data is consumed and transformed within Flink and then sent to a MySQL database. The ability to interface directly with relational databases ensures that Flink can participate in workflows extending beyond mere stream processing, enabling effective integration in enterprise data ecosystems.

File systems form another category of external systems interfaced by Flink connectors. File-based connectors support reading from and writing to various file systems such as Hadoop HDFS, local file systems, or cloud-based storage like AWS S3. These connectors are indispensable when dealing with large-scale, batch-oriented data processing tasks. Using file-based systems with Flink ensures data durability and offers an abstraction layer for interacting with actual file systems, thereby simplifying the management of read and write operations.

The RealizationContext component aids developers in executing fault-tolerant and state-consistent file operations. Consider a common setup where a file sink writes processed data to HDFS:

```
StreamingFileSink<String> hdfsSink = StreamingFileSink
    .forRowFormat(new Path("hdfs://localhost:8020/flink/output"),
        new SimpleStringEncoder<String>("UTF-8"))
    .build();

messageStream.addSink(hdfsSink);
```

This file sink ensures data is consistently written into HDFS, allowing subsequent batch processing or archival tasks to be performed easily. It also supports rolling policies, which control how files are split and managed on the file system.

Integrating Flink with cloud storage services like AWS S3 elevates its credentials as a tool for cloud-native applications. The AWS S3 connector ensures that Flink applications can scale elastically while tapping into virtually unlimited storage potential. This feature is particularly advantageous in scenarios requiring rapid deployment of data pipelines in cloud environments devoid of traditional on-premises hardware constraints.

Flink's connector ecosystem, characterized by its extensibility and adaptability, allows the development of custom connectors tailored to specific needs. Situations that existing connectors cannot cover effectively require custom connector development. Custom connectors expand Flink's architectural plasticity, supporting specialized data formats or proprietary systems. To implement a custom connector, developers create source and sink interfaces, defining how data should be retrieved or written, followed by setting up configuration parameters and fault-tolerance mechanisms. Such extensibility allows Flink to adapt to an expanding array of operational environments.

Using and managing Flink connectors effectively requires attention to several best practices. These involve tuning performance by balancing parallelism and buffer sizes, employing checkpoints judiciously to guarantee consistency without compromising latency, and ensuring proper exception handling to maintain system resilience. Proper deployment architecture that considers failure points, load balancing, and resource allocation further enhances connector performance.

As Flink continues to evolve, its connectors benefit from continuous improvements, both in terms of performance optimization and broadening of supported external systems. Developers utilizing Flink must stay informed on these developments to leverage the full potential of connectors in their streaming and batch processing workflows.

Thus, connectors within the Flink ecosystem are indispensable for real-world applications that demand high throughput, low-latency processing, and robust integration with a myriad of data systems. Mastery of these connectors and their configurations is key to achieving scalable and maintainable Flink applications that meet contemporary data processing challenges.

7.2   Integrating with Apache Kafka

Integrating Apache Flink with Apache Kafka brings together two of the most powerful technologies in the realm of large-scale data processing. Apache Kafka, a distributed streaming platform, is designed to handle high-throughput, fault-tolerant, and real-time data feeds. Apache Flink, renowned for its high-performance stream processing capabilities, leverages Kafka's robust queueing and publish-subscribe model to achieve distributed, fault-tolerant data streaming. The union of these technologies allows for the construction of sophisticated data pipelines that handle large volumes of data efficiently.

In a typical Flink-Kafka integration, Flink reads data from Kafka topics through a Kafka connector, processes the data applying transformations and computations, and then writes the results back to Kafka or to other external systems. Understanding the intricacies of this integration enables developers to build responsive, resilient, and scalable data-driven applications.

Understanding Kafka's Role:

Kafka's architecture revolves around the concept of producers, consumers, topics, and brokers. A producer publishes messages to topics, partitions spread across different brokers ensuring data is distributed and parallelized. Consumers, such as Flink applications, subscribe to topics to retrieve data. The consumer group feature allows for load balancing, where multiple consumers divide the workload by automatically coordinating which consumer reads specific partitions.

The integration of Flink with Kafka involves the usage of Flink's Kafka connector, which abstracts the mechanics of subscribing, partitioning, and offset management for Kafka topics. The connector supports Flink's continuous processing model, enabling exactly-once or at-least-once semantics. When setting up this integration, consider both the source and the sink connectors. Let us delve into configuring and using these connectors effectively.

Kafka as a Source in Flink:

Flink's Kafka source connector is adept at consuming data from Kafka topics. It handles Kafka's partitioning and offset management transparently, thus allowing developers to focus on their application logic without delving into Kafka's operational complexities. The source can be configured to handle different modes of fault tolerance - at least once or exactly once, each with implications on processing guarantees and performance.

Configuring a Kafka source is straightforward. You need to specify the Kafka broker details, consumer group ID, the desired processing guarantees, and optionally the Kafka deserialization schema. Here's a typical configuration:

```
Properties kafkaProperties = new Properties();
kafkaProperties.setProperty("bootstrap.servers", "broker1:9092,broker2:9092");
kafkaProperties.setProperty("group.id", "flink-app-consumer-group");
kafkaProperties.setProperty("auto.offset.reset", "earliest");

FlinkKafkaConsumer<String> kafkaSource = new FlinkKafkaConsumer<>(
    "input_topic",
    new SimpleStringSchema(),
    kafkaProperties
);

kafkaSource.setStartFromEarliest();

DataStream<String> stream = env.addSource(kafkaSource);
```

In this setup, the consumer group ensures that only one instance of this consumer will read a partition at a time, thus providing parallelism and load balancing capabilities across different Flink tasks.

Kafka as a Sink in Flink:

Using Kafka as a sink in Flink allows processed results to be published back to Kafka topics for consumption by downstream systems. This might involve feeding results into machine learning pipelines, alerting

170

systems, or dashboards. Setting up a Kafka sink is akin to configuring producers in a Kafka system. You define the Kafka brokers, topics, and serialization schemas:

```
Properties kafkaProducerProperties = new Properties();
kafkaProducerProperties.setProperty("bootstrap.servers", "broker1:9092,broker2:9092")
    ;

FlinkKafkaProducer<String> kafkaSink = new FlinkKafkaProducer<>(
    "output_topic",
    new SimpleStringSchema(),
    kafkaProducerProperties
);

stream.addSink(kafkaSink);
```

The Kafka producer in Flink is responsible for managing data serialization and ensuring message delivery guarantees, thus integrating seamlessly with Kafka's underlying message delivery mechanisms.

Delivering Exactly-Once Semantics:

When integrating Flink with Kafka, maintaining data consistency and correctness is paramount, especially in applications where accumulated errors from duplicate events can lead to costly outcomes. Flink's support for exactly-once semantics in Kafka ensures that each record is processed once, despite failures or retries that might occur during processing.

Exactly-once semantics require enabling Flink's checkpointing mechanism alongside Kafka's transaction API, which together coordinate to synchronize the offsets in Kafka with the state in Flink. Here, the enablement of exactly-once semantics through checkpoints is illustrated:

```
env.enableCheckpointing(10000, CheckpointingMode.EXACTLY_ONCE);
FlinkKafkaConsumer<String> kafkaSource = new FlinkKafkaConsumer<>(
    "input_topic",
    new SimpleStringSchema(),
    kafkaProperties
).setStartFromGroupOffsets();

FlinkKafkaProducer<String> kafkaSink = new FlinkKafkaProducer<>(
    "output_topic",
    new SimpleStringSchema(),
    kafkaProducerProperties,
    FlinkKafkaProducer.Semantic.EXACTLY_ONCE
);

stream.keyBy(value -> value.getFieldToKey())
    .process(new CustomProcessFunction())
    .addSink(kafkaSink);
```

Performance Tuning:

The efficiency of data pipelines utilizing Flink and Kafka can depend significantly on the parameter tuning of both systems. Careful consideration of Kafka partition counts, Flink parallelism, and Kafka producer configurations can help maximize throughput while minimizing latency.

Kafka partitions should be chosen in alignment with the desired degree of parallelism in Flink and underlying infrastructure capabilities. Additionally, producer configurations such as linger.ms and batch.size should be optimized to balance the trade-off between latency and throughput. Kafka's retention policies should align with the data lifecycle requirements of the application to ensure storage infrastructure is not overloaded.

Security and Monitoring:

Incorporating best practices for security and monitoring when integrating Kafka with Flink is indispensable for resilient operations. Enabling SSL/TLS and SASL authentication fortifies the data pipeline against unauthorized data access and eavesdropping. Moreover, setting up JMX monitoring on Kafka and utilizing Flink's metrics API aides in proactively monitoring system health and identifying performance bottlenecks.

Capture error metrics, consumer lag, and throughput for Kafka while observing Flink's task manager metrics to gain insights into pipeline performance and resource utilization. Operational alerts can be configured to detect anomalies based on these metrics, enabling immediate action to rectify adverse conditions.

Handling Schema Evolution:

When data flows through Kafka, schema evolution is a recurring challenge in dynamic data environments. Leveraging Confluent Schema Registry alongside Kafka can ease this challenge, ensuring schema compatibility across producers and consumers. Flink types can integrate with Avro schemas, maintaining full control over serialization and deserialization alongside seamless inclusion of schema evolution policies.

172

By using the Schema Registry, you define schemas for all Kafka topics. Flink reads these schemas, which facilitates forward or backward-compatible data transformations even in the face of evolving data structures.

In summary, integrating Kafka as a source and sink in Flink applications presents robust opportunities for scalable data processing. By tuning configurations, ensuring secure practices, and managing schemas carefully, developers can leverage Kafka's distributed messaging prowess alongside Flink's efficient processing engine to create powerful data-driven applications.

7.3 Using JDBC and File System Connectors

Apache Flink connectors for JDBC and file systems fulfill vital roles in making Flink a versatile tool for both stream and batch data processing. JDBC connectors bridge the gap between Flink applications and relational databases, thus allowing seamless data reading and writing in a structured format. Conversely, file system connectors facilitate data exchange between Flink and various storage structures, enabling integration with different file-based data sources. Together, these connectors enhance Flink's capability to operate within diverse data ecosystems, making it suitable for enterprise applications and analytics involved in data warehousing and big data processing.

JDBC Connectors: Bridging to Relational Databases

The JDBC (Java Database Connectivity) API is a well-established tool that facilitates interaction with a wide array of relational databases. Flink's JDBC connectors exploit this API, enabling real-time data ingestion and persistence with databases such as MySQL, PostgreSQL, Oracle, and others. These connectors serve as conduits for data that require integrity and transactionally consistent updates.

Using JDBC connectors involves defining operations to either read data from a database (as a source) or to write data into a database (as a sink). When operating as a source, SQL queries drive the data extraction process, while as a sink, data updates are achieved through parameterized SQL statements or prepared statements.

```
// Configuring a JDBC source connector
JdbcInputFormat jdbcSource = JdbcInputFormat.buildJdbcInputFormat()
    .setDrivername("com.mysql.jdbc.Driver")
    .setDBUrl("jdbc:mysql://localhost:3306/eventdb")
    .setQuery("SELECT id, event_type, event_time FROM events")
    .setRowTypeInfo(new RowTypeInfo(Types.INT, Types.STRING, Types.
        SQL_TIMESTAMP))
    .finish();

DataSet<Row> dbData = env.createInput(jdbcSource);
```

This example establishes a source connector reading data from a MySQL database table. The 'RowTypeInfo' indicates expected column types, while the SQL query defines what data to extract. This operation often requires proper database permissions and connection configurations to ensure secure and efficient data retrieval.

JDBC as a Sink:

Employing JDBC as a sink involves constructing SQL insert statements or updating existing rows within a database. This requires defining how Flink's processed outputs translate into database writes. Here, transaction management becomes critical, particularly in distributed systems where correct semantics ensure data integrity.

```
// Configuring a JDBC sink connector
JdbcConnectionOptions.JdbcConnectionOptionsBuilder optionsBuilder =
    new JdbcConnectionOptions.JdbcConnectionOptionsBuilder()
    .withUrl("jdbc:mysql://localhost:3306/eventdb")
    .withDriverName("com.mysql.jdbc.Driver")
    .withUsername("user")
    .withPassword("password");

JdbcSink.sink(
    "INSERT INTO processed_events (id, processed_event_type,
        processed_event_time) VALUES (?, ?, ?)",
    (statement, event) -> {
        statement.setInt(1, event.getId());
        statement.setString(2, event.getProcessedType());
        statement.setTimestamp(3, new Timestamp(event.getProcessedTime()));
    },
    optionsBuilder.build()
);
```

In this code fragment, the JDBC Sink API is utilized for inserting processed results into a database. The 'JdbcSink.sink' method requires a statement mapping function to bind data stream elements to SQL parameters. Transactional updates are essential here for maintaining

174

data consistency.

Handling Transactions and Fault Tolerance:

Flink's approach to managing fault tolerance with JDBC sinks hinges on the checkpointing mechanism. By tightly coupling checkpointing with transactional sinks, Flink ensures that data is written exactly once, even in the presence of failures. This consistency is typically achieved using two-phased commit protocols where a pre-commit transaction phase confirms that all data can be committed, followed by a commit phase that ensures all data changes are durable in the event of a success.

File System Connectors: Interfacing with Storage Systems

File system connectors in Flink facilitate batch processing and data archival through seamless interaction with various file stores. These connectors allow data extraction from, and insertion to, systems like the Hadoop Distributed File System (HDFS), local file systems, and cloud storage architectures such as AWS S3 or Google Cloud Storage.

Reading from File Systems:

A file system source typically requires specifying a file format and defining how data should be parsed into Flink's processing model. Flink supports several file formats, including Text, CSV, and Parquet, each suitable for different use cases.

```
// Reading from a CSV format file
DataSource<Tuple3<Integer, String, Timestamp>> fileSource = env.readCsvFile("
    hdfs://namenode:8020/data/events.csv")
    .fieldDelimiter(",")
    .ignoreFirstLine()
    .pojoType(Tuple3.class, "id", "eventType", "eventTime");
```

This operation reads a CSV file from HDFS, parsing lines into tuples where the delimiter is a comma, and the first line is treated as header metadata.

Writing to File Systems:

File system sinks manage data serialization and involve specifying a target directory, format, and write control strategies. A common output scenario involves writing data to Parquet or CSV formats for analytics processing.

```
// Writing to an output file in Parquet format
```

175

```
StreamingFileSink<Tuple3<Integer, String, Timestamp>> fileSink =
    StreamingFileSink.forBulkFormat(new Path("hdfs://namenode:8020/results/output.
        parquet"),
    ParquetAvroWriters.forReflectRecord(MyEvent.class))
    .withBucketAssigner(new DateTimeBucketAssigner<>())
    .build();

processedData.addSink(fileSink);
```

Bucket assignment strategies play an important role by allowing control over how files are split and organized within the file system, usually based on time or other criteria, which assists in efficient data retrieval and aggregation.

Interfacing with Cloud Storage:

For cloud-native applications, Flink's file system connectors extend their functionality to AWS S3 or Google Cloud Storage. These cloud storage systems provide scalable, cost-effective means for large data storage and easy setup without traditional hardware constraints. Configuring connectors involves setting up access credentials and specifying bucket names, paths, or object keys for data storage.

Implementing cloud storage as a file sink generally follows patterns similar to that of HDFS or local file architectures, enhanced by cloud-specific configurations such as IAM roles (for AWS) and OAuth authentication tokens (for GCP).

Considerations and Best Practices:

Using JDBC and file system connectors in Flink applications introduces several design considerations aimed at optimizing performance and maintaining the resilience of processing pipelines:

- Serialization and Deserialization: Custom serialization/deserialization logic should be implemented carefully to avoid performance bottlenecks and ensure correct data type mappings with schemas.

- Concurrency Management: For JDBC, it's crucial to configure proper concurrency settings in the underlying database to handle simultaneous updates from parallel Flink tasks without locking contention.

- Data Partitioning and Sharding: For file system operations, en-

176

sure data is partitioned and sharded appropriately to balance workload across distributed storage nodes, ensuring both read and write throughput is optimized.

- Fault Handling and Recovery: Implement robust fault handling mechanisms to cope with network failures, transient errors, or node downtimes without data loss.

- Security: Employ secure connections using TLS for database connections and configure encryption for data both at rest and in transit, especially when interacting with cloud storage systems.

- Efficient Schema Management: Regular evolution of data schemas should be managed with version control strategies and schema registries to avoid disruptions in processing pipelines.

By adhering to these strategies, the integration of JDBC and file system connectors into Flink pipelines can significantly enhance the capability of enterprises to derive value from large-scale, real-time data processing systems, extending analytic capabilities from structured relational models to unstructured or semi-structured big data environments.

7.4 Interfacing with AWS S3 and Google Cloud Storage

In the modern era of cloud computing, integrating big data processing systems like Apache Flink with cloud storage services such as AWS S3 (Amazon Web Services Simple Storage Service) and Google Cloud Storage (GCS) is essential for leveraging the scalability, durability, and flexibility provided by cloud infrastructures. These integrations enable Apache Flink applications to efficiently ingest, process, and persist large volumes of data in and from the cloud, supporting analytics, machine learning, and data archiving tasks without the need for costly and complex on-premises infrastructure.

Overview of Cloud Storage in Data Processing:

Cloud storage solutions like AWS S3 and Google Cloud Storage are object-based storage systems designed for 99.999999999% durability and high availability, making them well-suited for data-processing workloads. They allow organizations to store and retrieve any amount of data, at any time, from anywhere over the Internet, providing a cost-effective solution to manage data lakes or process unstructured and semi-structured data at scale.

Configuring and Using AWS S3 with Flink:

AWS S3 is one of the most widely used cloud storage services. Flink's integration with S3 leverages the Hadoop FileSystem API, allowing seamless interaction with S3 buckets as if they were local or HDFS (Hadoop Distributed File System) storage, thus abstracting the complexity of underlying communication protocols.

When integrating Flink with S3, a fundamental requirement is the establishment of credentials and the configuration of S3 as a target storage layer. This involves setting up the AWS access credentials, region specifications, and bucket names, typically through the 'flink-conf.yaml' or programmatically using environment properties.

```
// Sample setup for connecting Flink to AWS S3
Configuration hadoopConfig = new Configuration();
hadoopConfig.setString("fs.s3a.access.key", "YOUR_AWS_ACCESS_KEY");
hadoopConfig.setString("fs.s3a.secret.key", "YOUR_AWS_SECRET_KEY");
hadoopConfig.setString("fs.s3a.endpoint", "s3.amazonaws.com");

env.setConfiguration(hadoopConfig);

StreamingFileSink<String> s3Sink = StreamingFileSink
    .forBulkFormat(new Path("s3a://my-bucket/my-directory"), ParquetAvroWriters.
        forReflectRecord(MyRecord.class))
    .build();

myDataStream.addSink(s3Sink);
```

The code configuration example demonstrates connecting to S3, using the S3A scheme for Hadoop FileSystem compatibility. It initializes configuration properties required for authentication and specifies data storage in Parquet format, a common choice for its efficient columnar storage mechanism.

Benefits of S3 Integration in Flink:

- **Scalability**: S3's virtually unlimited storage capacity allows Flink to scale elastically, accommodating data growth without the need for expensive hardware upgrades.

- **Durability and Availability**: Built-in redundancy within S3

178

ensures data integrity and availability; data is stored across multiple facilities and devices.

- **Cost-Efficiency**: S3 enables savings through flexible pricing based on actual storage and data transfer usage, paired with lifecycle management policies for optimizing storage costs over time.

Configuring and Using Google Cloud Storage with Flink:

Google Cloud Storage offers similar capabilities and integrates well with Flink, using GCS's excellent data availability and consistency. To set up connection between Flink and GCS, service accounts are typically used to authenticate requests, and the GCS connector (provided in the 'flink-gcs-connector' jar) leverages this authentication mechanism to interact with GCS buckets.

```
// Example of setting up Google Cloud Storage access through configuration
fs.gs.impl -> com.google.cloud.hadoop.fs.gcs.GoogleHadoopFileSystem
fs.AbstractFileGcsRootProtocolSupport
fs.gs.auth.service.account.enable -> true
google.cloud.auth.service.account.json.keyfile -> /path/to/my-service-account.json
```

After GCS is appropriately configured, it is straightforward to utilize in a similar fashion as AWS S3:

```
// Writing Flink data to GCS
env.getConfig().setGlobalJobParameters(configuration);

StreamingFileSink<String> gcsSink = StreamingFileSink
    .forRowFormat(new Path("gs://my-gcs-bucket/my-folder"), new
        SimpleStringEncoder<String>("UTF-8"))
    .build();

myDataStream.addSink(gcsSink);
```

Advantages of Google Cloud Storage Integration:

- **Latency and Throughput**: Google Cloud's strong network infrastructure provides high throughput and low latency for data transfers.

- **Simplicity and Integration**: GCS easily integrates into multicloud environments and with other Google Cloud Services (GCS), such as BigQuery, providing added functionality for in-depth data analysis.

179

- **Data Security**: GCS offers robust security frameworks, including data encryption at rest and during transport, ensuring data privacy and compliance with global standards.

Cloud Storage Integration Challenges and Solutions:

Despite the benefits, integrating Flink with cloud storage services can present challenges such as security, data transfer optimization, and cost management:

- **Security and Access Control**: Control who can access the data, maintain permissions through granular IAM setups. Use VPC endpoints to secure data transfers.

- **Data Transfer Optimization**: Leverage parallelism and compression techniques for efficient data movement between Flink and cloud storage, minimizing latency.

- **Cost Management**: Utilize storage classes, such as S3's Intelligent-Tiering or GCS's Nearline and Coldline, along with lifecycle policies to manage costs effectively.

Considerations for Effective Cloud Storage Utilization:

- **Data Lifecycle Management**: Configure rules to transition objects between different storage classes based on frequency of access, reducing costs as data becomes less frequently accessed.

- **Object Versioning and Logging**: Enable versioning and access logs to maintain data history and track access patterns for auditing and optimization of data usage policies.

- **Reducing Egress Costs**: When possible, perform compute tasks in the same cloud region as the data storage, which may yield significant cost savings from reduced egress charges.

The integration of Apache Flink with AWS S3 and Google Cloud Storage is fundamental to realizing the full potential of cloud-powered data processing. When integrated thoughtfully, these powerful tools allow for the management and processing of data at massive scales with reliability, cost efficiency, and flexibility, pushing the boundaries of what is possible with modern cloud data architectures. These integrations provide critical support to use cases ranging from real-time analytics to long-term data warehousing and machine learning model training, making them essential for any organization aiming to thrive in today's data-intensive landscape.

7.5 Custom Connectors Development

Apache Flink's ecosystem of connectors encompasses numerous built-in solutions for interfacing with diverse data sources and sinks. However, some applications encounter edge cases that predefined connectors cannot optimally address, such as interacting with proprietary systems, non-standard protocols, or legacy architectures. Developing custom connectors in Flink can bridge these gaps, offering tailored solutions for specific integration challenges. This section delves into the nuances of creating custom connectors, elucidating the process through a detailed explanation and coding examples.

Understanding the Need for Custom Connectors:

Flink's built-in connectors handle many scenarios across relational databases, messaging systems, file and cloud-based systems, but they may not address:

- **Legacy Systems**: Communicating with outdated interfaces that require specialized handling for incompatible protocols.

- **Non-Standard APIs**: Engaging with APIs or services that do not conform to widely adopted structures and mechanisms.

- **Proprietary Protocols**: Ensuring data flow with systems that operate on proprietary or custom communication protocols.

- **Business-Specific Integrations**: Fulfilling unique business rules and logic that govern interactions with external systems.

When such situations arise, a custom connector becomes invaluable, providing a seamless data interchange channel tailored to specific requirements.

Essentials of Custom Connector Design:

To wrap data operations in a custom connector, developers must implement interfaces for data sourcing and sinking backed by logic aligned with the source's behavior. The connectors must also handle parallelism, backpressure, consistency, and fault tolerance in line with Flink's underlying processing guarantees.

Developing a Custom Source Connector:

Creating a custom source connector involves implementing the Source-Function or extending RichSourceFunction for handling stateful operations. Here's an example that highlights building a simplified source for a proprietary message queue:

```
public class CustomQueueSource implements SourceFunction<String> {

    private volatile boolean isRunning = true;
    private CustomQueueClient client; // Hypothetical external system client

    public CustomQueueSource(String serverAddress, int port) {
        this.client = new CustomQueueClient(serverAddress, port);
    }

    @Override
    public void run(SourceContext<String> ctx) throws Exception {
        while (isRunning) {
            String message = client.receive(); // Custom logic to fetch message
            if (message != null) {
                synchronized (ctx.getCheckpointLock()) {
                    ctx.collect(message);
                }
            }
            Thread.sleep(500); // Control polling delay
        }
    }

    @Override
    public void cancel() {
        isRunning = false;
        client.close(); // Clean up resources
    }
}
```

This snippet exemplifies a basic source implementation where a polling loop reads messages from a custom queue, triggering the context's collect method to emit fetched records into the Flink pipeline. For richer processing, RichSourceFunction would be incorporated to manage richer lifecycle events, such as initialization and teardown of resources.

Ensuring Fault Tolerance:

Achieving state consistency in custom sources necessitates careful synchronization, particularly with Flink's checkpointing system, which captures the source's state to recover from failures efficiently. Achieving exactly-once semantics usually involves transactionally syncing the source state with checkpoint barriers, necessitating a manageable method to snapshot and restore state.

Developing a Custom Sink Connector:

Similar to source development, building custom sink connectors requires implementing SinkFunction or RichSinkFunction, with considerations for buffering, transactionality, and state persistence. Here's a demonstration of a custom sink writing to an external proprietary system:

```
public class CustomQueueSink extends RichSinkFunction<String> {

    private CustomQueueClient client;

    @Override
    public void open(Configuration parameters) throws Exception {
        this.client = new CustomQueueClient("serverAddress", 8080); // Setup resource
    }

    @Override
    public void invoke(String value, Context context) throws Exception {
        client.send(value); // Custom logic to send data
    }

    @Override
    public void close() throws Exception {
        client.close(); // Clean up resources
    }
}
```

Here, the invoke method sends each element from the data stream to a proprietary queue, incorporating the open and close methods to handle resource initialization and release.

Handling Transactions and Backpressure:

Custom sinks necessitate explicit handling of transactions, especially when targeting systems sensitive to duplicates. Implement transaction logic to ensure atomic writes, recording consistent snapshots with Flink's checkpointing to support data recovery without inconsistency.

Mitigating backpressure involves employing buffering strategies, often mediated through batch collecting or throttling APIs when encountering downstream bottlenecks, ensuring systemic resilience in the face of high-throughput demands.

Testing and Validation:

Critical to deploying custom connectors is thorough validation to ensure correctness, efficiency, and robustness under various conditions. Tests should simulate real-world data flows, examining:

- **Performance Benchmarks**: Assess latency and throughput in diverse scenarios to capture potential bottlenecks.

- **Fault Scenarios**: Evaluate recovery mechanisms after failures, assessing whether connectors rollback states correctly.

- **Scalability**: Assess how connectors adapt to varying workloads, particularly with parallel writes or reads.

Deploying Custom Connectors:

Once validated, deploy custom connectors by packaging them within Flink jobs, ensuring compatibility with both development and production environments. Consider tailoring connectors for specific Flink versions, abiding by changes in API or runtime environments.

Documentation and Maintenance:

Well-documented connectors support maintainability and facilitate any necessary handover to operations teams or new developers. Documentation should cover connector configuration parameters, deployment processes, limitations, and usage examples, ensuring ongoing relevance and ease of use.

Incorporating access auditing and logging within connectors facilitates operational monitoring and insight into data flows, enabling developers and operators to troubleshoot issues proactively, aligning with broader observability frameworks implemented in data ecosystems.

Conclusion:

Custom connector development in Flink is a powerful methodology for integrating individual application instances with unique and proprietary architectures, thus enhancing Flink's applicability across varied enterprise landscapes. Successful custom connector implementations require a nuanced understanding of target systems, attention towards Flink's execution paradigms, and a commitment to sustaining performance and robustness across dynamic operational conditions. As organizations increasingly engage in digital transformations, the capacity to design and implement precise data integrations through custom connectors will emerge as a pivotal asset in capturing enterprise value through scalable, efficient, and resilient data processing architectures.

7.6 Best Practices for Connector Management

Effective management of connectors within Apache Flink environments is pivotal for ensuring robust, scalable, and efficient data pipelines. Connectors serve as the critical interface between Flink applications and external systems, managing diverse tasks such as data sourcing, data sinking, and seamless integration across heterogeneous data ecosystems. This section elucidates best practices for connector management, emphasizing configuration, monitoring, performance tuning, and reliability strategies vital for maintaining high-quality stream and batch processing operations.

Understanding Connector Configuration:

Correct configuration is foundational to successful connector management. Each connector comes with its own set of configuration parameters that need meticulous tuning to match the operational context of target systems. For instance, Kafka connectors require specifications like bootstrap servers, topics, and serialization schemas, while JDBC connectors necessitate connection strings and credentials.

Key considerations include:

- **Configuration Management:** Utilize configuration files, such as application.conf or flink-conf.yaml, to define parameters systematically, thereby enabling easy updating and version control.

- **Environment-Sensitive Parameters:** Implement

environment-specific configurations for development, staging, and production systems using templating solutions or configuration management tools like Consul or ZooKeeper.

- **Security:** Protect sensitive information by leveraging environment variables for secrets, and confine access credentials (e.g., API keys) to secure vaults such as AWS Secrets Manager or HashiCorp Vault.

Ensuring Correct Serialization Schemas:

Serialization is crucial for converting data structures into a consumable form during inter-system communication. Improperly configured serialization can lead to data integrity issues and interoperability failures. When handling Kafka or file-based data formats, selecting appropriate serialization (such as Avro, JSON, or Protobuf) is paramount, accompanied by schema evolution strategies to accommodate structural changes over time.

```
// Snippet: Configuring Avro serialization schema
AvroDeserializationSchema<MyEvent> deserializationSchema =
    AvroDeserializationSchema.forSpecific(MyEvent.class);
FlinkKafkaConsumer<MyEvent> kafkaConsumer = new FlinkKafkaConsumer<>(
    "my-topic",
    deserializationSchema,
    kafkaProperties
);
```

Monitoring and Observability:

The dynamic nature of data streaming necessitates diligent monitoring and observability practices for connectors, ensuring fast detection and resolution of any bottlenecks or issues that arise:

- **Metrics and Dashboards:** Leverage Flink's built-in metrics system to capture connector-specific data, such as record lag, failure rates, and throughput. Integrate with monitoring platforms like Prometheus and Grafana to visualize and alert on key metrics.

- **Logging:** Implement structured logging practices using tools such as Elastic Stack or Splunk, providing comprehensive logs to audit connector activity and trace anomalies.

186

- **Alerting:** Set up alert thresholds to notify teams of critical issues, ensuring timely intervention. Alerts can cover excessive consumer lag or elevated error messages.

Balanced Performance Tuning:

Performance tuning involves adjusting configurations to optimize throughput, minimize latency, and maintain resource efficiency without sacrificing reliability:

- **Parallelism and Resource Management:** Configure parallelism based on workload demands and cluster capabilities, evenly distributing tasks across nodes to exploit horizontal scaling.

- **Buffer Timeout:** Adapt buffer timeout settings to strike a balance between latency and throughput, critical for connectors handling high-velocity data streams.

- **Batch Size and Interval:** For systems such as Kafka or file-based connectors, calibrate batch size and network buffer intervals to optimize data transfer performance.

```
// Example: Balancing buffer size and timeout for Kafka
props.setProperty("fetch.min.bytes", "50000"); // Adjust as per typical message size
props.setProperty("fetch.max.wait.ms", "1000"); // Time to wait before sending batch
FlinkKafkaConsumer<String> consumer = new FlinkKafkaConsumer<>(topic,
    schema, props);
```

Ensuring Reliability and Fault Tolerance:

Reliable operations depend on implementing fault tolerance and recovery mechanisms tailored to the nuances of data systems and processing guarantees:

- **Checkpointing:** Employ Flink's checkpointing mechanism to store consistent state snapshots, enabling recovery from intermediate failures. Configure suitable intervals that balance performance and resource usage.

- **Exactly-Once Semantics:** Enable exactly-once semantics where required, particularly for financial or critical data transactions, to prevent data duplication or loss.

187

- **Resilience Tactics:** Develop strategies around partition reassignment, leader elections, and resource throttling to safeguard against disruptive failures affecting connector operations.

Security and Compliance:

Security is a linchpin for connector management, governing how data is transmitted and accessed between systems:

- **Data Encryption:** Encrypt data both in transit and at rest using TLS and appropriate encryption standards to guard against unauthorized access.

- **Access Control:** Strict access management policies should enforce least privilege principles, allowing minimal access to connectors for necessitated operations.

- **Audit Trails:** Maintain comprehensive audit logs capturing access and modification events, supporting compliance frameworks and forensic investigations.

Change Management and Versioning:

The synchronous update of connectors and dependent systems presents challenges, stressing the importance of carefully controlled change management processes:

- **Schema Evolution:** Use schema registries like Confluent's Schema Registry to manage and validate schema changes, ensuring backward and forward compatibility.

- **Deployment Strategies:** Employ CI/CD pipelines for controlled rollouts, automating testing to validate connector functionality before production deployment.

- **Rollback Protocols:** Prepare robust rollback mechanisms to undo connector configurations or deployments promptly if unexpected issues emerge after changes.

Documentation and Knowledge Transfer:

Strong documentation supports ongoing connector management, ensuring continued utility and adaptability:

- **Maintenance Guides:** Develop comprehensive documentation for each connector detailing configuration, dependencies, common troubleshooting scenarios, and update procedures.

- **Knowledge Sharing:** Conduct regular knowledge transfer sessions and build shared Confluence pages or wiki entries to ensure all team members understand the intricacies of connector operations.

Incorporating these best practices into Apache Flink connector management fosters an environment conducive to high-quality data processing. Given their pivotal role in data architectures, connectors warrant deliberate design and oversight, capable of achieving agile data transport setups reflective of contemporary and future operational requirements. As data ecosystems grow in complexity, enhanced connector management underpins the scalable and resilient execution of data-driven initiatives, galvanizing analytical capabilities and business insights across organizational units.

Chapter 8

Managing Flink Jobs on a Cluster

This chapter addresses the crucial aspects of managing Flink jobs in a clustered environment, essential for achieving scalability and high performance. It describes the deployment process of Flink applications across different cluster modes, including standalone, YARN, and Kubernetes, each offering unique scalability features. The chapter covers job submission techniques, along with monitoring tools to oversee job performance and resource usage effectively. Configuring high availability to ensure continuous job operation is also detailed, alongside strategies for managing resources, task slots, and scaling jobs to meet varying data processing demands. These elements are vital for optimizing Flink job management in production environments.

8.1 Deploying Flink Applications on a Cluster

Deploying Apache Flink applications on a cluster is a fundamental step for leveraging the full capabilities of distributed stream processing. A successful deployment ensures scalability, resilience, and efficient resource utilization. In a cluster environment, Flink jobs are distributed across multiple nodes, allowing the system to handle large-scale data processing tasks effectively. This section elaborates on the deployment process, including necessary configurations and best practices.

Deploying a Flink application typically involves several key steps: setting up the cluster, configuring necessary parameters, submitting the job to the cluster, and ensuring robust monitoring and management for effective execution.

Cluster Setup:

Before deploying Flink applications, a suitable cluster environment must be established. Apache Flink supports various cluster modes, including standalone, YARN, and Kubernetes, each providing distinct advantages based on the operational requirements.

- *Standalone Cluster:* The standalone mode involves manually starting the Flink cluster's JobManager and TaskManagers on configured nodes. This setup is straightforward and suitable for environments where full control over the resources is required. The primary consideration in a standalone setup is deploying Flink binaries to all nodes and configuring network connectivity.

- *YARN Cluster:* YARN (Yet Another Resource Negotiator) is a widely-used resource management system in Hadoop ecosystems, managing computing resources in clusters. Deploying Flink on YARN involves leveraging YARN's resource management capabilities, allowing dynamic allocation of resources tailored to Job requirements. This approach is highly beneficial in shared resource environments where YARN manages competing applications' resource demands.

- *Kubernetes Cluster:* Kubernetes is an orchestration platform providing automated deployment and scaling. Deploying Flink on Kubernetes enables leveraging containerization benefits, such as portability and resource isolation. This mode typically involves creating Kubernetes manifests for defining JobManager and TaskManager pods, with configurations finely tuned through ConfigMaps and PersistentVolumes for stateful storage.

Configuring Cluster for Flink:

Configuring a cluster is paramount to ensure performance, fault tolerance, and efficient resource utilization:

- *Resource Configuration:* The 'flink-conf.yaml' file is central for configuration, specifying parameters such as the number of TaskManager slots, memory allocation, and network settings. The correct configuration ensures that each TaskManager can efficiently utilize system resources while avoiding bottlenecks.

- *State Backends:* State backends store consistently maintained state data. Flink supports various backends like 'MemoryStateBackend', 'FsStateBackend', and 'RocksDBStateBackend', each suited for different scenarios. Choosing the correct backend based on latency and durability needs is crucial.

- *High Availability:* Configuring high availability ensures system resilience by having standby JobManagers ready to take over if the primary JobManager fails. This configuration typically involves external systems, such as Zookeeper, to manage leader election and coordination.

Job Submission:

Submitting a job to a Flink cluster entails several steps. Jobs can be submitted using the 'flink run' command, which specifies the JAR file and any additional parameters or configurations.

For instance, submitting a job in a standalone cluster might look like:

```
flink run -m <jobmanager-host>:<jobmanager-port> -p [parallelism] path/to/your-
    flink-job.jar --arg1 value1 --arg2 value2
```

In a YARN cluster, the submission would use:

```
flink run -m yarn-cluster -ytm <taskmanager-memory> -ys <taskmanager-slots> path
    /to/your-flink-job.jar
```

And for Kubernetes, the job can be submitted through:

```
kubectl apply -f flink-submit-job.yaml
```

This 'flink-submit-job.yaml' file specifies the job parameters and deployment settings.

Monitoring and Management:

Efficient deployment in a cluster necessitates ongoing monitoring and management of jobs to ensure optimal performance:

- *Flink Dashboard:* Flink provides a web-based dashboard that visually represents job performance, resource usage, task stats, and more. This tool is vital for real-time monitoring and debugging issues as they arise.

- *Metrics and Logging:* Flink's integration with monitoring systems such as Prometheus and logging with Log4j2 enables access to detailed metrics and logs. Custom metrics can be defined to track application-specific metrics during executions.

- *Checkpointing and Savepoints:* As a fault-tolerance mechanism, Flink supports checkpointing, which periodically saves application state. Savepoints are similar but manually triggered, useful for upgrades or scaling.

A properly deployed Flink application in a cluster environment exhibits robustness and efficiency. Handling failures through meticulously configured checkpoints, scheduling regular monitoring, and adjusting configurations as needed based on observed metrics are integral components of successful cluster management.

8.2 Understanding Cluster Modes and Deployment Types

Understanding the various cluster modes and deployment types is critical for effectively managing Apache Flink applications. Each mode offers distinct features suitable for different operational environments, resource management needs, and scaling capabilities. This section explores standalone, YARN, and Kubernetes cluster modes, examining their characteristics, advantages, and deployment considerations to guide optimal decision-making based on specific application requirements.

The choice between different cluster modes depends on the specific operational context—whether the focus is on ease of setup, resource elasticity, integration with existing ecosystems, or leveraging container orchestration benefits.

Standalone Cluster Mode:

The standalone mode is the simplest form of Flink cluster deployment, wherein JobManagers and TaskManagers are started manually on predefined nodes. This mode is straightforward, providing direct control over the nodes' resources and configurations.

- *Architecture:* In standalone mode, each node runs a Flink process, either as a JobManager or TaskManager. Communication between nodes is achieved through RPC, ensuring tasks are distributed according to the configuration set by the user in the Flink configuration files.

- *Advantages:*
  - Simplified setup without the need for additional resource management systems.
  - Full control over hardware resources and network configurations.
  - Ideal for smaller setups or environments with simplified resource requirements.

- *Considerations:*
  - Scalability is limited by physical resources and manual setup processes.
  - Lacks built-in resource elasticity and dynamic scaling capabilities found in other modes.

To deploy in this mode, the Flink binaries need to be distributed to all nodes, and necessary configuration changes are applied within the flink-conf.yaml. Nodes are then started manually, often using scripts such as:

```
# Start JobManager
$FLINK_HOME/bin/start-cluster.sh

# On each TaskManager node, initiate TaskManager
$FLINK_HOME/bin/taskmanager.sh start
```

YARN (Yet Another Resource Negotiator) Deployment:

YARN, as part of the Apache Hadoop ecosystem, provides robust resource management that dynamically allocates and manages system resources for applications running across the cluster.

- *Architecture:* YARN facilitates deploying Flink applications by spinning up containers for each TaskManager and the JobManager. Applications request resources (CPU, memory) from YARN's ResourceManager, which are granted based on availability.

- *Advantages:*

  - Supports dynamic resource allocation, allowing for flexible scaling as workload demands fluctuate.

  - Integrates smoothly within Hadoop environments, sharing resources effectively with other applications.

  - Provides resource isolation improving application performance and stability.

- *Considerations:*

  - Requires integration within a Hadoop ecosystem, which may complicate initial configurations.

  - Performance depends on YARN scheduler configurations and the environment's shared resource load.

Deploying a Flink job on YARN typically involves configuring the Flink client to use YARN and submitting jobs with the YARN deployment target:

```
# Submit a Flink job on a YARN cluster
flink run -m yarn-cluster -ynm JobName -yt /path/to/flink-yarn-session.sh -yn <
    number_of_containers> -yjm <master_memory> -ytm <task_memory> path/
    to/your-flink-job.jar
```

Kubernetes Deployment:

Kubernetes provides a container orchestration platform that is widely adopted for deploying distributed applications, thanks to its automated deployment, scaling, and management capabilities.

- *Architecture:* In a Kubernetes environment, Flink is deployed as pods, with configurations specifying the number of JobManager and TaskManager pods required. Flink jobs are defined using Kubernetes manifests, supporting detailed tuning of deployment parameters.

- *Advantages:*

    - Leverages Kubernetes' inherent capabilities for container orchestration, enabling easy scaling, application updates, and recovery.

    - Provides superior flexibility and resource isolation, container-level granularity for resource allocation.

    - Suitable for cloud-native applications with required orchestration features.

- *Considerations:*

    - Requires a Kubernetes environment, demanding familiarity with Kubernetes constructs and management tools.

    - Network configuration and persistence setup, such as PersistentVolumes, introduce added complexity.

The deployment of Flink applications on Kubernetes involves defining configurations in YAML files that are utilized by Kubernetes to manage application lifecycle:

```
apiVersion: v1
kind: Service
metadata:
  name: flink-jobmanager
```

197

```
spec:
  ports:
  - port: 8081
    targetPort: 8081
  selector:
    app: flink
# Define the pod configuration for the JobManager
apiVersion: apps/v1
kind: Deployment
metadata:
  name: flink-jobmanager
spec:
  replicas: 1
  selector:
    matchLabels:
      app: flink
  template:
    metadata:
      labels:
        app: flink
    spec:
      containers:
        - name: jobmanager
          image: flink:latest
          ports:
            - containerPort: 8081
```

Selecting an appropriate cluster mode and deployment type is indispensable for achieving desired performance characteristics in Flink applications. The advantages and limitations of each model must be weighed based on the application's scale, the existing infrastructure, and the anticipated load.

Attribute considerations are crucial, such as high availability in failover scenarios, network traffic management, and system integration challenges. Mastery of these deployment types enriches Flink deployment strategies, ensuring resilience, efficiency, and scalability tailored to organizational needs and environments.

8.3   Job Submission and Monitoring

The process of submitting jobs and monitoring their progress forms a critical component in managing Apache Flink applications. Effective submission and monitoring techniques enable developers to deploy Flink jobs with precision and oversee their performance to ensure operational efficiency. This section elaborates on the intricacies involved in job submission to a Flink cluster and highlights monitoring strategies essential for maintaining robust and high-performance data stream processing.

Job Submission Process:

Job submission in Apache Flink involves preparing your application for execution within the cluster's distributed environment. Flink jobs can be submitted through various interfaces, each offering unique features tailored to different user requirements.

1. Command Line Interface (CLI):

The CLI is the most straightforward method for job submission. It allows users to deploy Flink jobs directly from a shell environment using the flink run command. This method requires specifying the job JAR file, the JobManager's address (unless using a default configuration), and additional job-specific parameters.

Example of a basic job submission using the CLI:

```
flink run -m <jobmanager-host>:<jobmanager-port> path/to/your-flink-job.jar --arg1
    val1 --arg2 val2
```

This command sends the compiled Flink job to the JobManager, which orchestrates its execution across TaskManagers.

2. Flink Dashboard:

The Flink Dashboard provides a graphical interface for submitting, tracking, and managing jobs. Users can upload job JAR files and configure settings directly through the dashboard's submission interface. Moreover, it serves as an accessible platform for users who prefer visual interactions over command line operations.

3. REST API:

Flink provides a comprehensive REST API facilitating programmatic control over job submission and monitoring. This API enables developers to build automated workflows that fit seamlessly into CI/CD pipelines:

```
POST /jobs
Host: <jobmanager-host>:8081
Content-Type: application/json

{
  "programArgs": "--arg1 val1 --arg2 val2",
```

```
"jobName": "exampleFlinkJob",
"parallelism": 2,
"entryClass": "com.example.Main"
}
```

Using the REST API, applications can interact with the Flink cluster for automated deployment processes and configuration management.

Job Monitoring and Management:

Job monitoring is integral for ensuring that Flink applications run smoothly and can recover from failures efficiently. Flink provides several tools and mechanisms to facilitate comprehensive monitoring.

1. Understanding Flink Metrics:

Flink's metrics system provides insight into job performance and resource utilization. Metrics can be divided into several categories:

- *Task Metrics:* Include data on task processing times, throughput, and backpressure which indicate where bottlenecks may occur. For instance, high backpressure metrics might signal that downstream operations are unable to process incoming data quickly.

    ```
    Task Count: 100
    Average Throughput: 1,000 records/second
    Backpressure: 30%
    ```

- *Job Metrics:* Encompass overall job status indicators such as running versus failed jobs, latency, and checkpoint durations. Monitoring these metrics helps identify jobs that are not meeting SLAs (Service Level Agreements).

2. Flink Dashboard Use for Monitoring:

The Flink Dashboard visualizes job metrics and offers tools for tracking running application health status. It features real-time logs, task status, and accumulators, allowing developers to drill down into detailed job execution paths and performance characteristics.

Key sections of the dashboard include:

- *Job Details:* Displays job-level metrics including execution graphs showing operator chaining, latency, and processing bottlenecks.

200

- *Task Managers:* Shows insights into TaskManager performance, resource usage, and failures.

3. Integration with External Monitoring Tools:

Flink can be integrated with external systems like Prometheus or Grafana to provide sophisticated metrics visualization and alerting capabilities.

Prometheus integration setup:

```
# Edit flink-conf.yaml to enable Prometheus exporter
metrics.reporters: prom
metrics.reporter.prom.class: org.apache.flink.metrics.prometheus.PrometheusReporter
metrics.reporter.prom.port: 9249
```

With this setup, Prometheus can scrape metrics, and Grafana can visualize them, providing a powerful environment to monitor job health over time.

4. Logging and Alerting:

Flink's logging system, primarily using Log4j, captures execution logs and contextual error information. Careful configuration enables not only error logging but also detailed informational log collection. Configuring alert systems based on these logs through external services (e.g., ELK stack) aids in proactive troubleshooting.

Example configuration snippet for Log4j:

```
<Configuration status="WARN">
  <Appenders>
    <Console name="Console" target="SYSTEM_OUT">
      <PatternLayout pattern="%d{HH:mm:ss.SSS} [%t] %-5level %logger{36} - %
          msg%n"/>
    </Console>
  </Appenders>
  <Loggers>
    <Root level="info">
      <AppenderRef ref="Console"/>
    </Root>
  </Loggers>
</Configuration>
```

Incorporating automated alerts based on log data ensures rapid response to potential issues such as task stalls, failures, or excessive latency spikes.

Efficient job submission coupled with comprehensive monitoring maximizes Flink's capability to handle real-time data streams reliably and effectively. Continual enhancements in these domains support the complex requirements of modern data processing applications, making Flink an indispensable tool for large-scale data operation management.

8.4 Configuring High Availability

High availability is a critical feature for any distributed system, ensuring that even in the event of failures, the system remains operational with minimal disruption or data loss. Configuring high availability (HA) in Apache Flink involves setting up robust failover mechanisms, distributed coordination, and state recovery procedures to ensure continuous application availability and reliability. This section provides an in-depth look at strategies and best practices for configuring high availability in Flink clusters, including Zookeeper integration and checkpointing mechanisms.

Key Concepts in High Availability:

Implementing high availability in Flink primarily involves two areas: maintaining consistent leader election using a coordination service like Zookeeper and managing state recovery through persistence and checkpointing technologies.

1. Leader Election and Zookeeper:

Flink utilizes leader election to designate a primary JobManager responsible for coordinating tasks across the cluster. In the event of a JobManager failure, a new leader is elected from standby nodes, minimizing downtime and ensuring job continuation.

- *Zookeeper Coordination:* Apache Zookeeper is a distributed coordination service that facilitates high availability by managing metadata essential for leader election and coordination tasks. Flink clusters are configured to connect to a Zookeeper ensemble, which handles membership information and decides the JobManager leader.

Example configuration in 'flink-conf.yaml' for enabling Zookeeper HA:

```
high-availability: zookeeper
high-availability.zookeeper.quorum: zk1:2181,zk2:2181,zk3:2181
high-availability.zookeeper.path.root: /flink
high-availability.cluster-id: /cluster_one
```

This configuration instructs Flink to use Zookeeper nodes for maintaining state consistency and failover coordination, employing a specified root path for storing metadata.

2. State Recovery and Checkpointing:

State recovery is vital for restarting jobs post-failure without data loss. Flink achieves this through checkpointing, which periodically records operator state and position.

- *Checkpointing:* Flink's checkpointing mechanism is designed for minimal latency impact while recording state to durable storage systems. Checkpoints can be stored in distributed file systems, such as HDFS or Amazon S3, providing both accessibility and durability.

Sample checkpoint configuration in 'flink-conf.yaml':

```
state.backend: rocksdb
state.checkpoints.dir: hdfs://namenode:port/flink/checkpoints
state.backend.rocksdb.memory.managed: true
execution.checkpointing.interval: 30000 # 30 seconds
execution.checkpointing.timeout: 600000 # 10 minutes
```

This configuration specifies RocksDB as the state backend and defines the directory location for checkpoints, interval settings for checkpoints, and associated timeouts.

Detailed High Availability Setup:

Configuring high availability in Flink consists of orchestrating multiple components into a seamless system.

1. Distributed Coordination with Zookeeper:

In a high availability setup, Apache Zookeeper acts as a centralized coordination hub, handling JobManager failovers, configuration metadata, and distributed locks:

- *Ensemble Setup:* A Zookeeper ensemble typically consists of an odd number of nodes (minimum three) to ensure quorum-based decisions, sustaining availability during node failures.

- *Service Registration:* Flink services register themselves with Zookeeper, where they track leader states, configuration data, and JobMaster/TaskManager processes. An established session with Zookeeper allows rapid detection of failures and seamless failover transitions.

- *Failover Logic:* Upon detecting a JobManager failure, Zookeeper triggers an automatic election of a new leader from available backups, which read the last state from persistent storage and continue execution seamlessly.

2. Persistence and Reliability in State Storage:

Durable storage systems ensure that operator states are reliably stored and can be retrieved even if the cluster experiences failures:

- *State Backends:*

  - FsStateBackend stores states as files, supporting simple and robust small-state scenarios.

  - RocksDBStateBackend is more suited for handling large states, operating with persistent on-disk storage ensuring durability.

- *Checkpoint Storage:* Centralized storage systems like HDFS or cloud storage solutions (AWS S3, Azure Blob Storage) provide scalable, redundant storage for checkpoint data crucial for disaster recovery.

- *Incremental Checkpointing:* Leveraging incremental checkpointing minimizes the size of state snapshots by only persisting changed states, leading to faster checkpoint completion and reduced storage overheads.

Sophisticated Resilience Mechanisms:

To further enhance the reliability of a Flink cluster, advanced techniques and practices can be applied:

- *Savepoints:* Beyond checkpoints, savepoints are manually-triggered snapshots ensuring a consistent application state, useful for upgrades or migrations without intermediate state loss.

- *Restart Strategies:* Configurable restart strategies determine how Flink handles task failures:

  - *Fixed Delay Restart:* Tasks restart after a specified delay, beneficial in handling transient failures with set retry attempts.

  - *Failure Rate Restart:* Limits the frequency of restarts over a time window, protecting against job thrashing and resource wastage.

Example restart strategy configuration:

```
restart-strategy: fixed-delay
restart-strategy.fixed-delay.attempts: 3
restart-strategy.fixed-delay.delay: 10s
```

Continuous Monitoring and Analysis:

Maintaining high availability mandates continuous health monitoring and analysis of cluster components:

- *Monitoring Tools Integration:* Integrate Flink with tools such as Prometheus, Grafana, or ELK for monitoring Zookeeper ensemble stats, JobManager/TaskManager performance, and system-level health metrics.

- *Automated Alerting:* Setup automated alert systems for critical errors, node failures, or increasing checkpoint latencies using real-time monitoring data, reducing mean time to recovery (MTTR).

Implementing high availability in Flink not only ensures system resilience against failures but also reinforces the capability to manage large-scale data stream processing with confidence. The modularity and adaptability of Flink's HA mechanisms support varied deployment scenarios, offering flexibility and robustness crucial for modern data-driven applications.

8.5 Managing Resources and Slots

In distributed stream processing, managing resources judiciously is fundamental to optimizing the performance and scalability of Apache Flink applications. A core aspect of this management involves understanding the concepts of TaskManager resources and task slots—these define how computational workload is distributed and executed within a Flink cluster. Effective resource and slot management lead to enhanced system efficiency, balanced load distribution, and improved throughput. This section delves into the details of managing these components, providing insights into configurations, strategies, and best practices.

Core Concepts of Resource Management:

Understanding the allocation and management of resources in a Flink cluster revolves around configurations stipulated within TaskManagers, which are the worker nodes responsible for executing subtasks of a Flink job.

1. TaskManager Memory:

Memory management complements CPU allocation in ensuring efficient task processing. Flink's memory model is highly customizable, allowing developers to tailor memory configurations to fit job-specific requirements.

- *Managed Memory:* Used for internal operations such as sorting and hash tables, managed memory is crucial for performance optimization.

- *JVM Heap Memory:* Reserved for heap-consuming operations, which include object allocations, task code execution, and runtime metadata.

- *Off-Heap Memory:* Utilized for reducing garbage collection overhead and working with direct byte buffers, particularly beneficial for memory-intensive operations.

Sample memory configuration snippet:

```
taskmanager.memory.process.size: 1024m
taskmanager.memory.framework.off-heap.size: 128m
taskmanager.memory.managed.size: 256m
```

2. Task Slots:

Task slots are Flink's mechanism for allocating computational resources within a TaskManager. Each task slot represents a slice of the TaskManager's computational capacity, aggregated from its core CPU and memory resources.

- *Slot Sharing:* By allowing multiple subtasks to share the same task slot if they do not compete for resources, Flink optimizes the use of available slots, reducing resource fragmentation and improving job throughput.

- *Configuration:* The number of task slots per TaskManager is defined in the configuration, representing an upper bound on the parallelism afforded by the TaskManager. A thorough understanding of workload and system capabilities is necessary to configure this effectively.

Configuration example for task slots:

```
taskmanager.numberOfTaskSlots: 4
```

This configuration implies that a single TaskManager can carry out four parallel task operations simultaneously, offering a balanced trade-off between resource allocation and parallelism for task execution.

Strategies for Optimal Resource Management:

Optimizing resource allocation requires a nuanced understanding of workload demands and system characteristics. Below are strategies to achieve efficient resource management:

1. Parallelism Configuration:

Parallelism determines the distribution of task processing across available slots, playing a critical role in resource management and job execution.

- *Granularity:* Choosing the right granularity for parallelism is crucial. Finer granularity enhances processing flexibly at the cost of increased resource demands per task. Conversely, coarser granularity simplifies resource demands but may lead to bottlenecks.

- *Dynamic Parallelism:* In environments with dynamic workloads, adjusting parallelism at runtime can optimize resource utilization, aligning processing capacity with current workload intensity.

2. Load Balancing and Resource Isolation:

Balanced resource utilization across TaskManagers induces efficient processing, preventing some nodes from becoming overloaded while others remain underutilized.

- *Resource Constraints:* Defining constraints and assigning priorities ensures critical tasks have guaranteed access to necessary resources, thereby stabilizing job execution during peak loads.

- *Node Affinity and Anti-Affinity:* Ensure resource distribution by defining affinity rules to collocate related tasks and anti-affinity rules to distribute load evenly across the cluster.

Example affinity rule configuration:

```
node-type-affinity:
  frontend:
    - high_priority_task
  backend:
    - low_priority_task
```

3. Resource Versatility with Docker and Kubernetes:

Containerized deployments enhance resource management versatility due to their inherent isolation and orchestration capabilities.

- *Kubernetes Pod Configurations:* Fine-tune resource allocation by defining 'limits' and 'requests' in Kubernetes deployments, ensuring reserved capacity and bounding maximum resource usage.

Example Kubernetes resource configuration:

```
resources:
  requests:
    memory: "512Mi"
    cpu: "500m"
  limits:
    memory: "1024Mi"
    cpu: "1"
```

Monitoring and Tuning Resources:

Ongoing monitoring helps identify resource bottlenecks and provides data for continual optimization of configurations.

1. Metric Integration with Monitoring Tools:

Integrating with tools like Prometheus and Grafana enables visualization of resource-related metrics such as memory usage, CPU load, and slot utilization. These metrics support identifying inefficiencies and guiding tuning decisions:

- *Memory Usage Metrics:* Track how memory is allocated and utilized across the cluster, identifying tasks that exceed expected usage patterns.

- *Task Slot Metrics:* Monitor slot occupancy rate and slot sharing efficiency to enhance task distribution and resource utilization.

2. Alerting and Automated Adjustments:

Set alerts for critical metrics reaching threshold values, prompting automated responses or alerts for human intervention to reconfigure task slots, parallelism, or resource limits.

Optimized resource and slot management within a Flink cluster can significantly impact the overall system efficiency, improving throughput and latency. By deploying strategic configurations drawing from workload dynamics, infrastructure characteristics, and system monitoring insights, organizations can fully leverage Flink's robust data processing capabilities.

8.6 Scaling Flink Jobs

Scaling Apache Flink jobs is essential for adapting to varying data loads and meeting performance requirements in stream processing applications. Scalability ensures that applications can efficiently handle increasing amounts of data without significant degradation in performance. This section explores numerous strategies and best practices for scaling Flink jobs, emphasizing horizontal and vertical scaling techniques, dynamic scalability, and the integration of state management and performance metrics to achieve optimal scalability.

Understanding Flink Job Scaling:

Scaling in Flink involves adjusting the resource allocation to the jobs, which can be done horizontally by increasing the number of physical or virtual machines, or vertically by enhancing the resources (CPU, memory) within existing nodes.

1. Horizontal Scaling:

Horizontal scaling, or scaling out, involves adding more TaskManagers to a cluster, which increases the available compute resources and task slots. This form of scaling is particularly effective in distributed environments where workloads can be parallelized across a greater set of resources.

- *TaskManager Addition:* By increasing the number of TaskManagers, you distribute tasks across more nodes, thereby improving processing speed and throughput. This is especially useful in stateless stream processing where tasks can be easily distributed without concerns of shared state consistency.

- *Stateless vs. Stateful Scaling:* While stateless jobs benefit directly from horizontal scaling, stateful jobs require careful consideration due to the need for state repartitioning and preservation across nodes. State must be redistributed appropriately without loss or inconsistency.

```
# Launch an additional TaskManager
$FLINK_HOME/bin/taskmanager.sh start
```

2. Vertical Scaling:

Vertical scaling, or scaling up, enhances the resources of existing TaskManagers by increasing CPU power, memory, or I/O capacity. This approach is often a faster alternative to hardware changes but includes limits based on the maximum capacity of a single node.

- *Resource Augmentation:* Increasing available resources per node allows an existing job to handle more tasks concurrently within a single TaskManager. This method is often more straightforward but less flexible than horizontal scaling once single-node limits are reached.

```
# Example to increase memory allocation in flink-conf.yaml
taskmanager.memory.process.size: 2048m
```

Dynamic Scaling:

Dynamic scaling refers to the ability to adjust resources in real-time based on current workload demands. This approach is vital for maintaining performance and cost-efficiency in environments with fluctuating data processing requirements.

1. Reactive Scaling:

Reactive scaling involves scaling the cluster as a response to specific triggers or performance metrics. Common triggers include CPU usage, latency metrics, or task queue lengths reaching predefined threshold levels.

- *Autoscaling Mechanisms:* Implement autoscaling tools and scripts that automatically adjust parallelism based on workload metrics collected through monitoring systems.

Example of a simple autoscaler script outline:

```
def adjust_parallelism():
    cpu_usage = get_cpu_usage()
    if cpu_usage > THRESHOLD_HIGH:
        increase_parallelism()
    elif cpu_usage < THRESHOLD_LOW:
        decrease_parallelism()
    else:
        maintain_current_state()
```

2. Predictive Scaling:

Predictive scaling utilizes historical data and analytics to forecast load patterns, enabling proactive resource adjustments before demand spikes. This method leverages machine learning models or statistical techniques to predict future loads and manage resource allocation effectively.

3. Stateless vs. Stateful Jobs:

Dynamic scaling of stateful jobs requires careful state management to ensure seamless scaling actions. Ensure that scaling operations preserve state integrity across task repartitions, leveraging Flink's state backend configurations and mechanisms.

Balancing Through Parallelism:

Optimizing parallelism—the number of task instances—helps in distributing the workload evenly across nodes, enhancing processing capabilities and reducing bottlenecks.

1. Setting the Right Degree of Parallelism:

Parallelism is a core attribute that defines how tasks are distributed and processed across the cluster. The parallelism level can be statically configured or dynamically adjusted, balancing resource usage against computational needs.

Example of setting job-level parallelism:

```
flink run -p 6 path/to/your-flink-job.jar
```

2. Over- and Under-provisioning Risks:

Proper scaling requires avoiding over-provisioning (excess resources leading to inefficiency) and under-provisioning (insufficient resources causing performance bottlenecks). Continuous monitoring and recent workload assessments help maintain optimal parallelism settings.

Advanced State Management for Scalability:

Effective state management enables the stateful scaling of jobs, ensuring the continuity of complex data transformations that require consistency and fault tolerance.

1. Role of State Backends:

Choosing an appropriate state backend is crucial for managing state in scalable applications. Flink supports several backends such as MemoryStateBackend, FsStateBackend, and RocksDBStateBackend, each offering different trade-offs in terms of performance and durability.

Example configuration for RocksDB backend for large-scale applications:

```
state.backend: rocksdb
state.backend.rocksdb.memory.managed: true
state.checkpoints.dir: hdfs://namenode:port/flink/checkpoints
```

2. Efficient State Handover:

Efficiently managing state during scaling up or down ensures that state is not lost and jobs continue seamlessly without data disruptions. Implement state migration strategies that redistribute state transparently among available TaskManagers during scaling operations.

212

Monitoring and Alert Systems:

Scalable Flink jobs benefit from robust monitoring and alerting systems to track performance metrics and predict scaling needs.

1. Integrating with Monitoring Tools:

In real-time data streams, integrating Flink with monitoring systems like Prometheus, Grafana, or Elasticsearch provides valuable insights into system performance, helping identify when and how to scale:

- *Metric Tracking:* Collect key metrics like throughput, latency, and task load distribution to inform scaling decisions.

- *Performance Dashboards:* Create visualization dashboards that highlight inconsistencies or bottlenecks, supporting in-depth analysis of job performance in real time.

2. Automated Alerts and Actionable Insights:

Develop automated alert systems to notify administrators of potential scaling triggers, supported by actionable analytics enabling quick decision-making to adapt resources appropriately.

Scaling Flink jobs efficiently involves leveraging varying scaling techniques, optimizing task parallelism, and ensuring reliable state management. By employing dynamic and predictive scaling strategies in conjunction with comprehensive monitoring, Flink applications can adapt seamlessly to fluctuating workloads, ensuring high performance and operational resilience in complex data processing ecosystems.

Chapter 9

Advanced Concepts: Flink's CEP and SQL

This chapter explores advanced concepts in Apache Flink, focusing on Complex Event Processing (CEP) and SQL functionalities that enhance its analytical capabilities. It delves into the principles of CEP, which enable the detection of patterns across data streams, allowing for real-time insights and decision-making. The use of Flink's Pattern API in defining complex event sequences is examined, highlighting its role in capturing intricate data relationships. Furthermore, the chapter covers the integration of Flink SQL, providing a structured approach to querying streaming data with SQL-like syntax. This integration facilitates sophisticated stream analytics, with discussions on writing and optimizing SQL queries for improved performance in dynamic data environments.

9.1 Complex Event Processing with Flink CEP

Complex Event Processing (CEP) in Apache Flink enables real-time pattern recognition over streaming data, facilitating the identification of meaningful event patterns within continuous data flows. This capability is central to applications requiring immediate detection and response actions, such as fraud detection, monitoring, and alerting systems. At its core, CEP in Flink is designed to sift through high volumes of data and to distill complex events from simpler ones by correlating multiple events over determined patterns.

Flink CEP is built upon a powerful API that allows developers to expressively define event patterns through a DSL (Domain Specific Language) and supports event matching based on these patterns. A pattern in CEP is essentially a blueprint that describes how a sequence of incoming events should be inspected and matched against a pre-defined sequence or structure. This section provides an in-depth analysis of Flink CEP's components, mechanisms, and applications while offering practical guidance on utilizing its API.

In a typical stream processing environment, events are time-stamped data points representing dynamic occurrences over time. The ability to accurately model and detect specific sequences of these events is critical in generating real-time insights. Flink's CEP library provides a means to define complex event patterns and match them against a stream of incoming events by leveraging seamless integration with its underlying dataflow execution model.

- To employ CEP with Flink, users need to define patterns using the Pattern API. This begins by identifying the fundamental elements that constitute a pattern. A simple pattern might involve detecting a sequence of events occurring in rapid succession, such as multiple failed login attempts in a security system.

The basic building block in Flink CEP is the Pattern class, which allows the user to define operations like sequence (next), loop (oneOrMore), optional (optional), and Kleene star (zeroOrMore). Below is an example of how to use Flink CEP to define a simple pattern to detect three

216

consecutive events of the same type:

```
import org.apache.flink.cep.pattern.Pattern;
import org.apache.flink.cep.scala.CEP;

Pattern<Event, ?> pattern = Pattern.<Event>begin("start")
    .where(new SimpleCondition<Event>() {
        @Override
        public boolean filter(Event event) throws Exception {
            return event.getType().equals("LOGIN_FAIL");
        }
    })
    .next("middle").where(new SimpleCondition<Event>() {
        @Override
        public boolean filter(Event event) throws Exception {
            return event.getType().equals("LOGIN_FAIL");
        }
    })
    .next("end").where(new SimpleCondition<Event>() {
        @Override
        public boolean filter(Event event) throws Exception {
            return event.getType().equals("LOGIN_FAIL");
        }
    });
```

In this snippet, we define a sequence of three consecutive "LOGIN_-FAIL" events. The method where is used to analyze the properties of incoming events and determine if they meet the specified criteria. The begin method initiates the pattern, while the next method chains further constraints or steps in the pattern sequence.

Once a pattern is defined, it is applied to an incoming stream. In using the Flink CEP library, a PatternStream is created by applying the defined pattern against a source stream of events. This stream captures all matched event sequences and can be processed for further actions. Below we illustrate pattern stream creation with the previously defined pattern.

```
DataStream<Event> inputEventStream = // source DataStream of events

PatternStream<Event> patternStream = CEP.pattern(inputEventStream, pattern);
```

By applying CEP.pattern, we can seamlessly transition from a basic event stream to a PatternStream that monitors the events for the outlined sequence. This transformation allows users to extract matched sequences while applying time constraints or condition-based filters.

A crucial aspect of CEP is the ability to apply temporal constraints during pattern matching. Time constraints allow patterns to be matched only when the events occur within a specified timeframe, thereby distinguishing meaningful event sequences from simple coincidental occurrences.

Flink CEP supports time windows using either processing time or event time. When using event time, Flink ensures that patterns respect the timestamps of the incoming data, making it vital in applications where the timing of events is critical. Below is an extended example, incorporating a time constraint:

```
Pattern<Event, ?> timeConstrainedPattern = Pattern.<Event>begin("start")
    .where(new SimpleCondition<Event>() {
        @Override
        public boolean filter(Event event) throws Exception {
            return event.getType().equals("LOGIN_FAIL");
        }
    })
    .next("middle").where(new SimpleCondition<Event>() {
        @Override
        public boolean filter(Event event) throws Exception {
            return event.getType().equals("LOGIN_FAIL");
        }
    })
    .within(Time.minutes(10)); // Events must occur within 10 minutes
```

In this updated pattern, the use of the within method specifies that the meaningful event series must complete in no more than 10 minutes, enhancing the accuracy of incident detection.

After pattern matching, the results are accessed using a pattern selection function, translating matched events into actionable insights. This is implemented in Flink by defining a select function, which processes the results of matched pattern sequences. For instance, an alarm could be triggered in response to the detected patterns:

```
patternStream.select(new PatternSelectFunction<Event, String>() {
    @Override
    public String select(Map<String, List<Event>> pattern) throws Exception {
        Event startEvent = pattern.get("start").get(0);
        Event middleEvent = pattern.get("middle").get(0);

        return "Detected sequence of login failures: " +
            startEvent.getUser() + ", " +
            middleEvent.getUser();
    }
}).print();
```

In this example, the pattern selection function compiles the matched events into a string message once a suspicious sequence of events has

218

been identified. The output can be routed to logs or alerting systems dedicated to handling security breaches.

The applications for CEP within Apache Flink are numerous and varied. Industries adopt this technology for tasks such as fraud detection in banking, monitoring IoT sensor data, tracking user engagement patterns, and real-time recommendations in e-commerce platforms.

In fraud detection, for example, CEP can help identify suspicious financial transactions by detecting unusual patterns of behavior like multiple withdrawals within a short frame, which may signify unauthorized access. With IoT, CEP is employed to aggregate and analyze sensor streams, triggering alerts when certain conditions are met, such as a significant temperature increase or unexpected machine behavior.

Flink CEP's ability to manage complex patterns efficiently and at scale renders it indispensable for real-time event processing requirements where latency is a significant factor. As streaming data continues to expand its presence across various sectors, the adoption of CEP within Flink will advance, empowering organizations to make informed and timely decisions based on streaming event data.

Understanding and utilizing Flink's CEP thus involves mastering the concepts of pattern definition, time constraints, and pattern selection—the details of which play a crucial role in exploiting the full potential of Flink's stream processing prowess. Appending this with practical coding exercises and real-world scenarios ensures a comprehension not just of the technical capabilities, but also of the strategic importance of integrating CEP in modern-day stream processing solutions.

9.2 Defining Patterns and Pattern API

Defining patterns within Apache Flink's Complex Event Processing (CEP) framework involves specifying the sequences and relationships between events that users wish to detect. Flink's Pattern API is an expressive tool designed to facilitate this process, enabling developers to write detailed and complex event patterns with ease. The purpose of utilizing such an API is to enable real-time analysis and reaction based on the recognition of non-trivial temporal event relationships within the data streams, which are otherwise difficult to capture using traditional query methods.

A pattern is essentially a declarative specification of the events or series of events one seeks to match within a data stream. Flink's Pattern API is structured to define and manage these patterns through a sequence of constructs, enhancing the recognition capabilities of stream processing applications.

Understanding Pattern Structure

The foundation of pattern definition in Flink CEP lies in the Pattern class. This class includes methods to define initial states, the conditions that must be met for these states to transition, and eventual pattern termination. The Pattern API lets users define simple to highly complex scenarios using a chain of method calls.

Below is a basic example illustrating how a sequence to detect three consecutive increases in stock prices might be set up:

```
import org.apache.flink.cep.pattern.Pattern;
import org.apache.flink.streaming.api.windowing.time.Time;
import org.apache.flink.cep.pattern.conditions.SimpleCondition;

Pattern<StockEvent, ?> pattern = Pattern.<StockEvent>begin("first")
    .where(new SimpleCondition<StockEvent>() {
        @Override
        public boolean filter(StockEvent event) throws Exception {
            return event.getPrice() > 0;
        }
    })
    .next("second").where(new SimpleCondition<StockEvent>() {
        @Override
        public boolean filter(StockEvent event) throws Exception {
            return event.getPrice() > previousPrice;
        }
    })
    .next("third").where(new SimpleCondition<StockEvent>() {
        @Override
        public boolean filter(StockEvent event) throws Exception {
            return event.getPrice() > previousPrice;
        }
    });
```

In this illustration, the Pattern API initiates with begin, setting a point of reference, before moving through next methods that add further events to the sequence requirement. The SimpleCondition encapsulates the logic for each event, defining the constraint that selects events based on characteristics such as price in this case.

Pattern Sequence and Iteration Constructs

Flink provides several methods to append additional complexity and nuance into event sequences:

- next(String): Captures events that occur directly after the previous event.

- followedBy(String): Allows for events that do not directly follow but are still sequential.

- followedByAny(String): Matches any pattern in between, if intervening patterns are not important.

- oneOrMore(): Indicates the occurrence of one or more events in sequence, achievable in multiple patterns.

- zeroOrMore(): Supports matching for zero or more occurrences.

Let's extend our previous sequence to ensure robustness by accommodating variations:

```
Pattern<StockEvent, ?> pattern = Pattern.<StockEvent>begin("start")
    .where(new SimpleCondition<StockEvent>() {
        @Override
        public boolean filter(StockEvent event) throws Exception {
            return event.getPrice() > 0;
        }
    })
    .followedByAny("increase").where(new SimpleCondition<StockEvent>() {
        @Override
        public boolean filter(StockEvent event) throws Exception {
            return event.getPrice() > previousPrice;
        }
    }).oneOrMore()
    .followedBy("last").where(new SimpleCondition<StockEvent>() {
        @Override
        public boolean filter(StockEvent event) throws Exception {
            return event.getPrice() > previousPrice;
        }
    });
```

Incorporating followedByAny and oneOrMore enforces flexibility within our detection pattern, making it adaptable to different observational data points while maintaining the core logic.

Complex Pattern Combinations and Iterations

Patterns often involve combinations of multiple events that interlink in complex ways. The API facilitates this through Kleene patterns and optional patterns:

- within(Time): **Adds a time constraint to limit the sequence duration.**

- optional(): **Adds flexibility, making certain events optional yet part of the valid pattern.**

- times(int min, int max): **Specifies an exact or a range of occurrences for more precise iteration.**

For example, should a scenario require detecting sequences with optional periodic notifications and bounded by time, the pattern definition might resemble the following:

```
Pattern<NotificationEvent, ?> notificationPattern = Pattern.<NotificationEvent>
    begin("initial")
  .where(new SimpleCondition<NotificationEvent>() {
      @Override
      public boolean filter(NotificationEvent event) throws Exception {
        return "ALERT".equals(event.getType());
      }
  })
  .optional() // Optional alert event
  .followedBy("periodic")
  .where(new SimpleCondition<NotificationEvent>() {
      @Override
      public boolean filter(NotificationEvent event) throws Exception {
        return "NOTIFY".equals(event.getType());
      }
  })
  .times(3, 5) // Match between 3 and 5 notifications
  .within(Time.minutes(5)); // Events must occur within 5 minutes
```

This scenario anticipates an event sequence where optional initial alerts precede a series of mandatory notifications, all bound within a five-minute interval, to enforce timely patterns typical in periodic alerting systems.

Advanced Conditions: Rich Pattern API

Flink's CEP library supports custom condition expressions using Java Lambda or anonymous classes to add business logic into the evaluation of each element:

```
Pattern<Event, ?> advancedPattern = Pattern.<Event>begin("start")
  .where(new IterativeCondition<Event>() {
      @Override
      public boolean filter(Event event, Context<Event> context) throws Exception {

        for (Event previousEvent : context.getEventsForPattern("previous")) {
          if (someComplexCheck(previousEvent, event)) {
```

```
            return true;
        }
    }
    return false;
    }
});
```

Here, we employ IterativeCondition to iterate over previously matched events in context, encompassing sophisticated conditions such as cross-referencing against past entries, reinforcing comprehensive pattern logic.

Applying Conditions in Real-Time Systems

The concept of real-time processing necessitates exact yet fluid detection capabilities that adapt to variable data flows and unpredictable temporal patterns. Consider networks or telecommunications systems that monitor live data to preemptively identify outages and performance bottlenecks. By using sequential, Kleene, or range patterns, organizations can define criteria to detect gradual performance degradation followed by sudden outage events, enabling rapid and informed interventions.

When developing a CEP rule in Flink, acknowledging the network characteristics (e.g., jitter, burstiness, latency), configure sequence time boundaries and optionality. Adjustments and optimizations in patterns reflect an understanding of both the application's operational constraints and qualitative user guarantees.

Defining patterns and leveraging the Pattern API in Flink CEP is not just an armchair exercise in code parsing. It is the science of orchestrating data in choreographed, deterministic, and optimized sequences, transforming the abstract flow of information into tangible and actionable insights. Through iterative examples, intrinsic pattern functions, and novel applications, you harness the full analytical power of stream processing, expanded through Flink's sophisticated CEP arsenal.

9.3 Handling Time and Event Constraints

Efficient handling of time and event constraints is a pivotal aspect of designing robust Complex Event Processing (CEP) systems in Apache Flink. Time plays a critical role as data streams are inherently temporal. Properly capturing and interpreting time-related aspects, including event lifecycles, intervals, and synchronization, enables the accurate delivery of results and insights. Flink provides out-of-the-box capabilities to integrate, synchronize, and optimize time and event constraints within its CEP framework.

Understanding the temporal relationships among events is essential for developing applications that require real-time data processing. This includes temporal operators for handling out-of-order events and synchronizing events concerning defined constraints. Flink's event-time and processing-time semantics provide strong foundations upon which sophisticated time-based windows and conditions are constructed.

Event Time vs. Processing Time

In stream processing, two predominant concepts govern time handling: event time and processing time. Choosing the correct approach directly influences the effectiveness of the patterns and the accuracy of the results produced by the CEP engine.

Event Time refers to the time at which the event actually occurred, as recorded in the data itself. This approach is crucial for scenarios where deterministic event ordering, independent of the processing schedule, is necessary. Conversely, **Processing Time** represents the system's notion of time, i.e., the time at which the event is being processed.

For applications that prioritize accuracy and consistency, particularly in environments where the data may arrive out-of-order, event time offers distinct advantages. It allows the system to use the inherent event timestamps to establish the sequence rather than relying on when they are processed in the Flink system.

Handling Timestamps and Watermarks

Event time relies on an additional concept: watermarks. Watermarks are markers that signal the progress of event time in the stream. They indicate the point beyond which Flink assumes no earlier events will arrive, enabling the framework to process events deterministically even with late data arrivals.

Below is a snippet showing how to assign timestamps and watermarks to a stream:

```
import org.apache.flink.api.common.eventtime.WatermarkStrategy;
import org.apache.flink.api.common.eventtime.WatermarkGeneratorSupplier;
import org.apache.flink.api.common.eventtime.WatermarkGenerator;

DataStream<Event> stream = ...

WatermarkStrategy<Event> strategy = WatermarkStrategy
    .<Event>forBoundedOutOfOrderness(Duration.ofSeconds(5))
    .withTimestampAssigner((event, timestamp) -> event.getTimestamp());

DataStream<Event> timestampedStream = stream.assignTimestampsAndWatermarks
    (strategy);
```

Here, a WatermarkStrategy is defined with a forBoundedOutOfOrderness watermark generator which allows for late events with up to five seconds of lateness to still be included in the computed results. The timestamp is extracted from the event timestamps, ensuring the event time alignment.

Incorporating Time Constraints in Patterns

The inclusion of time constraints within event patterns can significantly enhance pattern specificity. Flink uses the within method in the Pattern API to embed such constraints, setting a time window in which the defined pattern must be detected and completed.

Consider a scenario in a streaming analytics application that requires detecting a user login sequence comprising multiple phases within a specific timeframe, leveraging within-time constraints:

```
Pattern<LoginEvent, ?> pattern = Pattern.<LoginEvent>begin("start")
    .where(new SimpleCondition<LoginEvent>() {
        @Override
        public boolean filter(LoginEvent event) throws Exception {
            return "LOGIN_ATTEMPT".equals(event.getType());
        }
    })
    .next("middle").where(new SimpleCondition<LoginEvent>() {
        @Override
        public boolean filter(LoginEvent event) throws Exception {
            return "PASSWORD_ENTERED".equals(event.getType());
        }
```

```
})
   .next("end").where(new SimpleCondition<LoginEvent>() {
      @Override
      public boolean filter(LoginEvent event) throws Exception {
         return "LOGIN_SUCCESS".equals(event.getType());
      }
   })
   .within(Time.minutes(2)); // Must occur within 2 minutes
```

This pattern ensures that the sequence starting from a login attempt through to a successful login must occur within two minutes. If the sequence cannot be completed in this timeframe, it is considered invalid, allowing businesses to monitor and track session anomalies effectively.

Handling Late Arriving Events

Handling late events is an essential component of a cohesive streaming strategy, particularly in distributed systems where network delays and variable latencies are common. Flink provides the capability to process such events without losing critical data by using varying watermark strategies and customized event windows with permissible lateness.

Define window functions that accommodate late data by using the AllowedLateness attribute. This specifies the amount of time a window remains open to incorporate late arrivals:

```
import org.apache.flink.streaming.api.windowing.assigners.
      TumblingEventTimeWindows;
import org.apache.flink.streaming.api.windowing.time.Time;

DataStream<Event> lateAwareStream = timestampedStream
   .keyBy(event -> event.getUserId())
   .window(TumblingEventTimeWindows.of(Time.minutes(5)))
   .allowedLateness(Time.minutes(1))
   .apply(new WindowFunction<Event, Summary, String, TimeWindow>() {
      @Override
      public void apply(String key, TimeWindow window, Iterable<Event> input,
            Collector<Summary> out) {
         // Processing logic for late events
      }
   });
```

By specifying an allowedLateness, this window function ensures to consider events arriving up to one minute late, allowing the window to update results accordingly. This shows flexibility in scenarios such as financial transactions processing, where data may trickle in over varying intervals.

Time-Based Pattern Selection Strategies

Sophisticated CEP applications often require more than mere event occurrence matching; they demand careful selection and correlation strategies based on time constraints. This includes managing windows and temporal joins appropriately, considering both event timing and ordering.

Flink CEP supports enhanced event correlation by exploiting time constraints alongside event conditions to refine detected complex patterns. Advanced strategies can involve causal relationship detection, rate-based event detection, or even concurrency checks between processes.

In a more elaborate example, assume a retail scenario where order and shipping events must be tracked across multiple channels. We may apply pattern correlation to ensure order confirmation quickly leads to shipping dispatch within a narrow time-gap:

```
Pattern<OrderEvent, ?> orderPattern = Pattern.<OrderEvent>begin("confirmed")
    .where(new SimpleCondition<OrderEvent>() {
        @Override
        public boolean filter(OrderEvent event) throws Exception {
            return "ORDER_CONFIRMED".equals(event.getStatus());
        }
    })
    .followedBy("shipped").where(new SimpleCondition<OrderEvent>() {
        @Override
        public boolean filter(OrderEvent event) throws Exception {
            return "ORDER_SHIPPED".equals(event.getStatus());
        }
    })
    .within(Time.hours(1)); // Order shipped within 1 hour of confirmation
```

Here, a relationship is drawn between the ordering process and shipping fulfillment under a predetermined hour. This pattern ensures that business rules regarding prompt order fulfillment are enforced and adhered to.

The role of time management and constraints in Apache Flink's CEP extends beyond simple timestamp verification. It encompasses designing meticulous pattern-matching strategies that are informed by practical use cases, business requirements, and real-world variabilities. By doing so, users of Flink CEP transform temporal streams from noisiness into meticulous, insightful, and actionable intelligence, furthering both data accuracy and decision-making quality through temporal precision. Engaging exhaustively with timestamps, patterns, watermarks, and event constraints ultimately yields streamlined, reliable stream processing applications — in sync with time itself.

9.4 Integrating Flink SQL for Stream Analytics

Integrating Flink SQL into Apache Flink's architecture enriches its stream processing capabilities by introducing a structured, SQL-like interface to query and manipulate streaming data. This integration serves as a powerful tool for analysts, allowing them to leverage established SQL knowledge to engage directly with real-time data streams, execute complex queries, and derive insights without delving into lower-level programming.

Flink SQL caters to a broad range of applications, providing seamless transitions from traditional batch-processing databases to dynamic, real-time environments where timeliness and immediacy are paramount. This section explores the core concepts of Flink SQL integration, highlighting the mechanics of data streaming as tabular series, query execution, and performance considerations that come into play when operating within continuous data streams.

Apache Flink functions natively as a stream-processing engine with sources, operators, and sinks forming the backbone of its application logic. Flink SQL fits into this architecture by transforming streams into a tabular abstraction, similar to relational database tables. This shift allows users to perform structured queries using SQL statements over these relational views.

The essential task of Flink SQL is facilitating SQL queries over both bounded (batch) and unbounded (stream) datasets. Through a coherent layer called Table API, Flink represents streaming data as dynamic tables. Whenever an event changes, the corresponding rows in the table are updated, amended, or removed, ensuring that the streams perpetually reflect the current state of the underlying data.

Consider an analytical challenge of monitoring a continuous stream of transaction events for fraudulent activity by leveraging SQL queries:

```
SELECT userId, SUM(amount) as totalSpending
FROM Transactions
GROUP BY userId
HAVING SUM(amount) > 10000
```

This query processes a dynamic transactions table continuously to aggregate transactions per user ('userId'), calculating total spending and flagging accounts where aggregate spend exceeds a threshold—in this case, detecting potential fraud.

In Flink SQL, streams are presented as evolving tables where changes propagate in real-time. This flows out of a need to simulate continuous SQL operations over transient datasets. Flink materializes streams dynamically, making SQL operations suitable for control logic applications, real-time business intelligence, and operational analytics.

Flink supports two fundamental table operations:

- **Append Table** operations: Suitable for streams where only new rows are introduced, typically for static event data augmentations.

- **Retract Table** operations: Necessary for mutable state scenarios where rows may undergo inserts, updates, and deletions, applicable for complex analytics.

Transformation between streams and tables is accomplished through connectors, which support source and sink interactions by interfacing with databases, message queues, or file systems. The connectors select their operation modes based on the nature of incoming events.

For instance, when handling purchase data, events may arrive with updating quantities, requiring the use of retract streams.

```
CREATE TABLE Purchases (
    productId STRING,
    userId STRING,
    quantity INT,
    transactionTime TIMESTAMP(3)
) WITH (
    'connector' = 'kafka',
    'topic' = 'purchases',
    'properties.bootstrap.servers' = 'localhost:9092',
    'format' = 'json'
)
```

SQL DDL statements such as this configure how incoming Purchase data is established, enabling SQL operators to engage with the Kafka topic purchases containing event transactions.

Time aspects are foundational in Flink SQL, enabling explicit definition of event and processing time characteristics influencing query ex-

229

ecution. Time attributes can be defined directly within SQL schema setups, introducing the capability to establish time-based window functions in queries.

```
CREATE TABLE Clicks (
    userId STRING,
    url STRING,
    clickTime TIMESTAMP(3),
    WATERMARK FOR clickTime AS clickTime - INTERVAL '5' SECOND
) WITH (
    'connector' = 'filesystem',
    'path' = 'path/to/clicks',
    'format' = 'csv'
)
```

The inclusion of 'WATERMARK' ensures Flink understands expected event time delays, accommodating the potential arrival of late data.

Windowing aggregate functions afford additional dimensions to Flink SQL's expressiveness:

- **Tumble Window** aggregates operate in fixed interval windows.

- **Hop Window** provide sliding window-support using overlapping segments.

- **Session Window** aggregate by session activity, framed by inactivity timeouts.

Example of incorporating a tumbling window to compute hourly click counts:

```
SELECT TUMBLE_START(clickTime, INTERVAL '1' HOUR) as windowStart,
       COUNT(url) as clickCount
FROM Clicks
GROUP BY TUMBLE(clickTime, INTERVAL '1' HOUR)
```

The 'TUMBLE' function delineates non-overlapping windows, ensuring periodic analysis of data slices.

Flink SQL extends beyond standard event stream operations, granting join capabilities that allow dynamic relations across disparate streams and temporal tables. These joins enrich Flink SQL queries with dimensions from diverse data sources reflecting real-time contextualizations.

Temporal table joins, in particular, provide a snapshot mechanism that showcases reference data, calculated as a function of time-dependent dimensional attributes for historical or lookup enrichments:

```
SELECT o.orderId, o.orderTime, e.exchangeRate, o.price * e.exchangeRate as
    totalPrice
FROM Orders AS o
    JOIN ExchangeRates FOR SYSTEM_TIME AS OF o.orderTime AS e
    ON o.currency = e.currency
```

In this scenario, the 'ExchangeRates' table adapts in real-time, factoring in time-centric exchange rate calculations at each order moment, amplifying analytic depth.

While Flink SQL lays an intuitive foundation, optimizing queries ensures operational scalability and resource-efficient execution. Strategic approaches such as indexing equivalent to those in traditional databases, query reordering, and pruning guarantee expected performance levels:

- **Indexing and Partitioning**: Organizes data for fast lookups while logical partitioning groups related data, minimizing full-table scans.

- **Federation with Data Lakes and Warehouses**: Used for extensive dataset interactions, integrating Flink SQL with systems like Apache Hive or AWS S3 extends reach and processes large volumes with distributed efficiency.

- **Query Estimations**: Use explain statements to determine the logical execution plan, allowing adjustments based on data size and distribution.

Implementing query plans in alignment with infrastructure capabilities profoundly impacts resource consumption and, by extension, application effectiveness.

The integration of Flink SQL into streaming platforms creates competitive advantages by accelerating the transformation of real-time data into business outcomes:

- **Financial Services**: Monitor compliance with real-time transaction analysis covering fraud detection and portfolio management tasks.

231

- **E-commerce**: Enhance recommendation systems by capturing and reacting to user behavior streams instantaneously.

- **Telecommunications**: Track network performance in real-time, offering predictive maintenance and operational insights.

Flink SQL's design principles effectively balance user familiarity with robust stream processing mechanisms, democratizing sophisticated stream analytics while maintaining the scalability and timeliness demanded by modern stream applications. Through methodical schema definitions, customized queries, and calculated joins, Flink SQL consolidates itself as an indispensable methodology in evolving data paradigms and analytics.

9.5 Writing SQL Queries for Streams

Writing SQL queries for streams in Apache Flink enables users to process and analyze streaming data using declarative SQL. This capability brings SQL's expressive power and familiarity to the domain of real-time stream processing. Flink SQL offers a seamless framework that treats streams as continuously updating tables, allowing users to perform complex transformations and analyses as if working with relational databases.

With Flink SQL, you can execute SQL queries that operate on live data, perform real-time aggregations, join streams, and apply windowing functions. These capabilities make it possible to gain insights from data in motion and perform on-the-fly analytics without sacrificing the declarative simplicity of SQL.

The Basics of Flink SQL Queries

Flink SQL queries bear resemblance to traditional SQL, but with special constructs to accommodate continuous streams and time-based operations. The foundational blocks include selecting fields, filtering, and aggregating data.

```
SELECT userId, COUNT(*) AS loginCount
FROM Logins
GROUP BY userId
```

This basic query counts login events per user in real-time, updating counts as new data arrives. Real-time execution is possible because the 'Logins' table is a representation of the continuous stream.

To use Flink SQL, one must first define tables that represent streams, often done using DDL (Data Definition Language):

```
CREATE TABLE Logins (
    userId STRING,
    loginTime TIMESTAMP(3),
    WATERMARK FOR loginTime AS loginTime - INTERVAL '5' SECOND
) WITH (
    'connector' = 'kafka',
    'topic' = 'logins_topic',
    'properties.bootstrap.servers' = 'localhost:9092',
    'format' = 'json'
);
```

Here, the table 'Logins' is associated with a Kafka topic and JSON format, establishing a linkage between source data and SQL operations. The definition also sets up a watermark strategy to handle late-arriving events, essential for maintaining temporal accuracy.

Advanced Query Features

Filtering is among the simplest yet most powerful operations in SQL, enabling users to extract relevant data points from a vast stream. Using WHERE clauses, users isolate data according to specified conditions:

```
SELECT userId, url
FROM Clickstream
WHERE url LIKE 'https://flink.apache.org%'
```

In this case, the query selects entries from a clickstream where users visit URLs related to Apache Flink, filtering noise from irrelevant domains. This filtration helps focus analytical efforts on pertinent records, optimizing downstream data handling.

Data transformation in SQL leverages functions to derive new columns or modify existing data. Consider converting timestamps to readable formats:

```
SELECT userId,
    TO_TIMESTAMP(clickTime) AS formattedTime
FROM Clickstream
WHERE url IS NOT NULL
```

Such transformations improve comprehensibility, facilitate integra-

233

tion with other systems, and allow for more intuitive reporting.

Joining Streams and Tables

Joins in streaming SQL entail synchronizing disparate streams or combining streams with static datasets. Flink SQL supports various join types, enhancing its ability to adapt to diverse data scenarios.

```
SELECT o.orderId, u.userName
FROM Orders AS o
JOIN Users AS u
ON o.userId = u.id
WHERE o.timestamp BETWEEN u.startMembership AND u.endMembership
```

This query demonstrates a temporal join where orders are matched to user details for the membership period. Temporal precision is critical when pairing dynamic streams with tables, ensuring data integrity.

Aggregations and Grouping

Aggregation queries empower analysts to summarize data, offering immense value in trend detection and evaluation. Aggregating streaming data necessitates careful use due to the infinite nature of streams, thus employing windows to localize computations over bounded temporal frames.

Example of counting events by window:

```
SELECT TUMBLE_START(eventTime, INTERVAL '10' MINUTE) AS windowStart,
       COUNT(eventId) AS eventCount
FROM Events
GROUP BY TUMBLE(eventTime, INTERVAL '10' MINUTE)
```

The 'TUMBLE' window function allows aggregation over defined intervals, yielding periodic snapshots of activity which analysts can interpret for periodic patterns.

Windowing Functions for Stream Processing

In stream processing, window functions partition data streams into finite chunks over which SQL operations can be applied. Window types include tumbling, sliding, and session windows, each serving particular analytical needs.

- Tumbling Windows: Fixed-size, non-overlapping windows that align transformations to regular intervals.

234

- Sliding Windows: Overlapping windows moving in steps, offering overlapping insights for trend observation.

- Session Windows: Defined by periods of idleness, ideal for analyzing user sessions characterized by bursty behavior.

Example using sliding windows to calculate moving averages:

```
SELECT
    HOP_START(transactionTime, INTERVAL '5' MINUTES, INTERVAL '1' HOUR)
        AS windowStart,
    userId,
    AVG(transactionAmount) AS avgTransaction
FROM Transactions
GROUP BY userId, HOP(transactionTime, INTERVAL '5' MINUTES, INTERVAL '1'
    HOUR)
```

These overlapping windows analyze transactions every five minutes over a one-hour sliding window, capturing refined temporal insights.

Temporal and Complex Pattern Recognition

Temporal tables and complex pattern recognition features offer expansive SQL capabilities for identifying rich patterns and behaviors in real-time.

Temporal SQL functions inductively consider time aspects for creating running totals or decay functions, keeping historical data context succinctly connected to present evaluations.

For recognizing complex patterns, DASQL enriches pattern identification by applying iterative strategies or conditional expressions. Consider detecting fraud through irregular sequence patterns:

```
SELECT f.accountId
FROM (SELECT accountId,
        CEIL(paymentAmount/avgPaymentAmount) as alertLevel
    FROM PaymentStream
    GROUP BY accountId)
WHERE alertLevel > 2
```

In this example, the query identifies accounts with unusually high payment activities, potentially signaling fraud.

Operational Considerations and Optimization

Scalable stream query performance hinges on tailored execution plans matching application demands. Flink SQL empowers data scientists to

235

align such plans through optimizations:

- Parallelization: Optimize query execution by adjusting parallelism levels, facilitating faster data ingress and processing.

- Resource Allocation: Utilize Flink's cluster management to provision appropriate resource quotas for streams based on complexity and data velocity.

- Custom Connectors: Develop bespoke connectors to ensure seamless data integration between diverse systems.

Realizing high-throughput and low-latency queries requires a balance between computational efficiency, data partitioning strategies, and the physical topology of the processing infrastructure.

Harnessing Flink SQL for Real-Time Analytics

Leveraging Flink SQL for real-time stream analytics allows organizations to craft responsive and scalable data-driven solutions. Industries harness these capabilities to:

- Monitor and respond to financial market fluctuations amidst volatile conditions.

- Engage users with dynamic content personalization informed by live interaction contexts.

- Enhance system failover mechanisms by detecting operational anomalies proactively.

Introducing Flink SQL in an organization's data stack enhances agility, facilitating real-time decision-making through relational paradigms. This enables both strengthened historical learnings and responsive foresight into emerging trends.

In summary, writing SQL queries for streams with Flink bridges legacy SQL insights with the dynamism of modern streaming data, transforming ephemeral event streams into enduring knowledge repositories awake to perpetual change. Through structured tables, robust windowing techniques, and informed temporal analysis, industries enrich their ability to act proactively to data developments, tailoring insights to meet nuanced business objectives amid an ever-shifting landscape.

9.6 Optimizing Flink SQL Queries

Optimizing Flink SQL queries is essential to achieving high performance and efficiency in stream processing environments. As the volume and velocity of data increase, the ability to execute queries efficiently can significantly impact application responsiveness and resource utilization. Effective optimization involves understanding query plans, utilizing specific SQL features and constructs, and configuring Flink's execution environment to suit the specific characteristics of your workloads.

This section delves into various strategies and considerations for optimizing Flink SQL queries to ensure that systems can scale effectively while maintaining low latency and precise data processing.

Understanding the underlying execution plan of a SQL query is the foundation of optimization. Flink SQL translates SQL queries into execution plans that detail each step from source data retrieval to final result computation. Using the EXPLAIN statement, developers can gain insights into these plans:

```
EXPLAIN PLAN FOR
SELECT productId, SUM(sales) AS totalSales
FROM Sales
GROUP BY productId
```

The EXPLAIN output provides a logical plan detailing the sequence of operations—such as filters, joins, and aggregations—that Flink will execute. By examining this plan, you can identify redundant operations, inefficient join orders, or unnecessary data shuffles and adjust your queries or data structures accordingly.

Indexing is a cornerstone of SQL optimization, accelerating query processing by enabling efficient data retrieval. While Flink SQL does not directly support traditional database indexing, strategic data partitioning serves a similar purpose, distributing data across nodes to expedite query execution.

Partitioning data by frequently queried fields can reduce the data scanned during query execution. An example of partitioning a large dataset by date might involve:

237

- Creating Partitioned Tables:

```
CREATE TABLE Sales (
    productId STRING,
    saleAmount DECIMAL(10, 2),
    salesDate DATE
) PARTITIONED BY (salesDate);
```

- Defining Data Schemas to Reflect Partitions:

Partition strategies should align with typical query access patterns to minimize data skew and localized resource contention. This leads to improved parallel processing efficiency, reducing latency and enhancing throughput.

Joins are inherently resource-intensive operations, especially in streaming contexts with high data concurrency and volume. Flink SQL supports various join types, including inner, outer, and temporal joins, each suited to specific data scenarios.

- Reorder Join Sequences:

The order in which tables are joined can affect performance. Prioritize joining smaller datasets first to reduce intermediate data sizes and enable operations to complete faster.

- Using Appropriate Join Techniques:

For instance, use temporal joins to correlate time-critical streams with reference data in a way that maintains causality and reduces state requirements:

```
SELECT t.transactionId, r.discount
FROM Transactions AS t
LEFT JOIN LATERAL TABLE (discounts_at(t.transactionTime)) AS r
ON t.productId = r.productId
```

This temporal join correlates the Transactions stream with a historical discount table, dynamically assigning discounts relevant at the transaction time.

238

Window functions are compelling, allowing complex calculations over streaming data segments. However, improper use, especially in high-frequency data streams, can lead to resource bloat and inefficiency.

- Choose Appropriate Window Sizes:

Tuning window sizes can balance freshness against computation cost. Using excessively small windows leads to high overhead from frequent aggregations, while too large windows increase state size and reduce result timeliness.

- Streaming Aggregation Optimizations:

Apply aggregation functions wisely by computing aggregates for only the necessary fields and optimizing time windows based on business relevance.

```
SELECT userId,
       SUM(transactionValue) AS totalSpent
FROM Transactions
GROUP BY userId, TUMBLE(transactionTime, INTERVAL '1' HOUR)
```

- Expanding Windows with Flink's Incremental Calculations:

Incremental calculations can reduce overhead by maintaining and updating running totals over time rather than recalculating aggregates iteratively.

Filter pushdown involves executing filter operations as early as possible in the query plan to minimize unnecessary data processing and transmission.

- Move Predicates Closer to Data Sources:

Prioritize simple queries and precise predicates early in the execution plan to reduce the dataset that subsequent operations must manage.

- Integrate Predicate Logic into Data Connectors:

239

Some connectors support native predicate pushdown, reducing the volume of data Flink SQL must import when connected to external systems:

```
SELECT * FROM Orders WHERE orderDate > '2023-01-01'
```

- Leveraging Connector-specific Optimizations:

For data sources like JDBC tables or HBase, utilize connectors that apply backend optimizations, reducing Flink's need to process irrelevant data in aggregations or joins.

Effective resource configuration and parallel data processing are cornerstones of optimizing Flink SQL queries, especially for broader workloads.

- Tuning Slot Counts and Resource Allocation:

Configuring job parallelism correctly using execution slots can absorb data burstiness and balance workload across cluster nodes. Flink task managers can be scaled horizontally to handle parallel SQL operations, improving latency and robustness.

- Exploit Stateful Stream Processing:

Ensure stateful operations are carefully managed through checkpoints, avoiding redundant state accumulation beyond essential result domains. Employ large-enough state backends that sustain expected data load:

```
env.getCheckpointConfig().setMinPauseBetweenCheckpoints(500);
```

The above sets a minimum pause between checkpoints to balance system performance with fault tolerance.

Bottlenecks manifest when resource demand outpaces supply, impacting data latency and throughput. Profiling and debugging Flink SQL queries to expose choke points facilitate performance tuning measures:

- Utilizing Flink's Monitoring and Profiling Tools:

Flink provides a range of CLI tools and dashboards to monitor execution metrics and detect potential performance inhibitors in real-time data flows.

- Iteratively Optimize and Refine Query Logic:

Profile complex query components, isolate costly operations, and explore alternate query formulations that preserve semantics while reducing execution time.

- Adopt a Continuous Integration and Testing Strategy:

Dynamic load testing environments should mimic production data characteristics, offering perspectives on query adaptability to envisioned workloads.

Applying these optimization techniques manifests in tangible benefits across industries engaging in real-time analytics and decision-making:

- Financial Analysis and Trade Execution:

Latency reduction strategies yield faster trading decisions and compliance reporting, empowering rapid response to market conditions without undermining regulatory adherence.

- Digital Advertising and Marketing Optimization:

Efficient Flink SQL queries generate insights into consumer behaviors in milliseconds, timing ad placements with user interactions dynamically and accurately.

- Industrial IoT and Smart Manufacturing:

Seamless interoperation between streaming sensors enhances predictive models and operational diagnostics, supporting timely maintenance and optimized resource allocation.

In summation, optimizing Flink SQL queries is a multidimensional endeavor that brings together query execution understanding, tuned resource allocation, and strategic data handling. This ensures that Flink

SQL not only manages real-time data effectively but elevates it into agile streams of insights, steering towards an enterprise's broader strategic mandates. Through an articulate blend of theoretical best practices and practical implementations, Flink SQL emerges as a definitive platform for real-time operational intelligence.

Chapter 10

Performance Tuning and Best Practices

This chapter provides insights into performance tuning and best practices for optimizing Apache Flink applications. It covers strategies for efficient resource allocation and the tuning of configuration parameters to enhance system performance. Techniques for increasing data throughput while minimizing latency are discussed, focusing on achieving high efficiency in data processing streams. The chapter also highlights best practices in checkpointing and state management to balance fault tolerance with performance. Additionally, tools and methods for monitoring and profiling Flink applications are explored, allowing for the identification and resolution of bottlenecks. Common pitfalls are addressed with practical solutions, equipping developers with the knowledge to deploy robust and effective Flink applications.

10.1 Optimizing Resource Allocation

Efficient resource allocation serves as a cornerstone in enhancing the performance and scalability of Apache Flink applications. By optimizing resource allocation, we can significantly improve job performance and reduce latency, leading to more responsive and efficient stream processing. Here, we delve into best practices and methodologies for effectively allocating resources in Apache Flink jobs to achieve optimal results.

Resource allocation in Flink comprises several elements, including task slots, task managers, and the parallelism of operations. Each of these components affects the performance of Flink jobs and their ability to utilize distributed systems efficiently. Understanding the interplay between these elements is crucial in determining how resources can be allocated optimally.

- **Task Slots and Task Managers**

In Flink, a Task Manager is a JVM process responsible for executing portions of a job. Each Task Manager is allocated a fixed number of task slots, which determine the degree of parallelism and concurrency for the execution of tasks. In managing task slots, an essential consideration is ensuring that they are neither over-subscribed nor under-utilized. Over-subscription can lead to increased contention for CPU and memory resources, while under-utilization can waste available capacity.

The number of task slots per Task Manager can be configured in the flink-conf.yaml file. A general approach is to align the number of task slots with the number of CPU cores available on a node, thus ensuring efficient CPU utilization.

```
taskmanager.numberOfTaskSlots: 4
```

In high-throughput scenarios, it might be beneficial to allocate fewer slots per Task Manager, with each slot assigned more resources. This configuration can help mitigate the overhead associated with context switching and reduce the impact of garbage collection pauses.

- **Parallelism Considerations**

Parallelism in Flink determines how tasks are distributed among the available task slots. A higher level of parallelism can lead to better throughput as more operations are performed concurrently. However, this must be balanced against the resource constraints of the environment and the complexity introduced by increased coordination among parallel tasks.

To configure the default parallelism, adjust the parameter in the configuration file:

```
parallelism.default: 8
```

When tuning parallelism:

- Consider the nature of the operations: CPU-bound operations such as sorting may benefit from higher parallelism, while I/O-bound operations might not.

- Observe the input data size: Larger datasets naturally demand higher parallelism to process in a timely manner.

- Utilize Flink's auto-scaling features to dynamically adjust parallelism in response to workload changes.

- **Memory Management**

Efficient memory management is fundamental in optimizing resource allocation. Flink's memory model divides memory into different regions: JVM Heap, Off-Heap Memory, and Network Buffers. Properly configuring these regions can significantly impact performance:

- **JVM Heap**: This is reserved for task-specific data such as operators' state. Configurations of JVM heap space should avoid excessive garbage collection. The JVM options can be set using:

  ```
  taskmanager.heap.mb: 1024
  ```

- **Off-Heap Memory**: Used for storing large state and managing buffer pools. Minimizing the use of heap-based state storage reduces the pressure on garbage collection and can enhance throughput.

245

- **Network Buffers**: Default buffer settings should be increased in environments with high network throughput demands. Network buffers are configured via:

```
taskmanager.network.memory.buffers-per-channel: 4
taskmanager.network.memory.fraction: 0.1
```

- ## Resource Scheduling and Cluster Modes

Choosing the appropriate cluster mode and resource scheduling strategy is vital for efficient resource use. Flink supports several deployment modes, including Standalone, YARN, and Kubernetes. Each mode provides unique capabilities for resource scheduling:

- **Standalone Mode**: Ideal for small-scale or testing scenarios where manual control over resources is preferred.

- **YARN Mode**: Provides dynamic resource allocation, making it suitable for workloads with varying demands. YARN's fine-grained resource management allows scaling resources up or down based on job needs.

- **Kubernetes Mode**: Offers container orchestration with the ability to define CPU and memory limits for containers, allowing elastic scaling and resource usage optimization.

For Kubernetes deployments:

```
kubectl set resources deployment flink-taskmanager --limits=cpu=2,memory=4096Mi --
    requests=cpu=1,memory=2048Mi
```

- ## Analyzing and Adjusting Job Characteristics

Understanding the nature of the Flink job itself can help in allocating resources optimally. Data skew, for instance, can lead to inefficient resource usage if certain tasks become bottlenecks due to uneven data distribution. Flink's partitioning strategies should be employed to evenly distribute data across operators.

Flink provides a variety of partitioning options such as key-based, random, and custom partitioning. Select the strategy that best matches the workload characteristics, ensuring even utilization of task slots and reducing latency.

Analyzing transformations that are stateful is also imperative since they have different resource needs compared to stateless operations. Stateful operations often require additional memory and CPU resources and may benefit from distributed state backends such as RocksDB for more efficient state storage and retrieval.

- **Performance Monitoring and Feedback Mechanisms**

Continuous performance monitoring assists in identifying bottlenecks and under-utilized resources. Flink's built-in metrics and logging provide a wealth of data on job execution, which can be leveraged to fine-tune resource allocation. Utilizing tools such as Grafana and Prometheus for visualizing metrics, or logging frameworks for detailed error analysis, can aid in maintaining an optimal configuration.

Flink's metric configuration, enabled via the flink-conf.yaml, facilitates the integration with monitoring systems:

```
metrics.reporter.prom.class: org.apache.flink.metrics.prometheus.PrometheusReporter
metrics.reporter.prom.port: 9249
```

Through careful analysis of metrics, adjustments in parallelism, task slot configuration, and memory settings can be iteratively improved.

Ultimately, achieving optimal resource allocation in Flink is a dynamic, ongoing process that demands a comprehensive understanding of both the application requirements and the execution environment's capabilities. By combining strategic configuration adjustments with real-time data insights, Flink jobs can be tuned to deliver the highest levels of performance, responsiveness, and efficiency.

10.2 Tuning Flink's Configuration Parameters

Apache Flink's performance and efficiency in processing data streams are significantly influenced by its configuration parameters. Fine-tuning these parameters allows users to exploit Flink's capabilities fully, ensuring effective resource utilization and achieving desired processing goals. This section delves into the critical configuration parameters in Flink and offers guidance on adjusting these settings to maximize performance.

At the core of Flink's configuration is the flink-conf.yaml file, where various parameters controlling the runtime environment and job execution are specified. Through meticulous adjustment of these parameters, one can effectively manage system resources, optimize execution performance, and tailor the Flink environment to meet specific workload requirements.

Key entries include:

- taskmanager.memory.process.size: 2048m - Sets the total memory for a task manager process, impacting how much data can be handled in memory. Efficiently setting memory limits is crucial for high-throughput operations.

```
taskmanager.memory.flink.size: 1024m
taskmanager.memory.off-heap.size: 512m
```

- parallelism.default: 1 - Determines how many parallel tasks Flink should launch if not specified per job. It influences task distribution and scheduling:

```
parallelism.default: 4
```

- rest.port: 8081 - Configures the port for the REST server, which supports Flink's web-based user interface for task monitoring.

Efficient task execution is heavily dependent on the proper configuration of task slots and memory, balanced against resource availability and job requirements.

- **Task Slots**: Defined as:

```
taskmanager.numberOfTaskSlots: 8
```

The number of task slots affects how tasks are executed concurrently. By increasing the number of slots, parallelism can be expanded, but only to the extent that network and memory resources allow.

248

- **Slot Sharing**: In scenarios with jobs that have varying load characteristics, enabling slot sharing allows the optimizer to determine an efficient execution strategy by co-locating tasks within the same slot when beneficial.

```
slotmanager.slot-sharing: true
```

State management is a pivotal feature in Flink, enabling robust fault tolerance and consistent application state even following failures.

- **State Backend**: Selecting the appropriate state backend can drastically influence performance. The default memory state backend is suitable for testing and small jobs, whereas the RocksDB state backend is better for large stateful jobs.

```
state.backend: rocksdb
state.checkpoints.dir: file:///checkpoints/
```

- **Checkpoint Configuration**: Frequency and settings for checkpoints balance between performance and fault tolerance. Lower checkpoint intervals may increase latency but improve fault tolerance.

```
execution.checkpointing.interval: 5000
execution.checkpointing.mode: EXACTLY_ONCE
```

Efficient networking is critical for the performance of distributed data processing:

- **Network Buffers**: Increase these buffers to enhance throughput, particularly for network-heavy applications:

```
taskmanager.network.memory.fraction: 0.2
taskmanager.network.memory.min: 64mb
```

Adjusting network buffers carefully is essential, as setting this too high might lead to insufficient memory for other tasks, while too low might cause network bottlenecking.

Flink's execution model is controlled by configuring how tasks are scheduled and executed. Properly setting these parameters enhances parallelism and resource utilization:

- **JobManager Configuration**: Controls the number of slots and resource allocations in the Job Manager:

```
jobmanager.memory.process.size: 1024m
```

- **Restart Strategy**: Defines how Flink jobs recover from failures. Choosing an appropriate strategy ensures minimal downtime:

```
restart-strategy: fixed-delay
restart-strategy.fixed-delay.attempts: 3
restart-strategy.fixed-delay.delay: 10000ms
```

For scenarios requiring advanced performance considerations, diving deep into Flink's threading and parallelism options can yield additional gains:

- **Task Chaining**: Implicitly or explicitly chain tasks within an operator, reducing serialization/deserialization overhead:

```
taskmanager.chain-tasks: true
```

  Task chaining is especially beneficial when there are multiple operations that consume a shared data flow or window.

- **Latency Tracking**: Use latency tracking to tune applications against end-to-end latency constraints by examining buffer occupancy and processing rates:

```
taskmanager.latency-tracking.enabled: true
```

  Enabling latency tracking can help reveal bottlenecks in operator chains and network exchange phases.

While default configurations may suffice for generic use cases, specific applications will often have unique requirements that necessitate additional tuning:

- **Time Characteristics**: Configuring event time or processing time can significantly influence window semantics and lateness handling.

```
time.characteristic: EventTime
```

- **Watermarks**: Configure custom watermark emissions for applications sensitive to time alignment or event order:

```
watermark.frequency: 200ms
```

Finally, continuous monitoring provides the feedback necessary for adaptive tuning—making iterative adjustments to the parameters as workload demands change.

- **Use Metrics and Logs**: Instrument applications with key metrics and use logging for process insight:

```
metrics.reporter.slf4j.class: org.apache.flink.metrics.slf4j.Slf4jReporter
metrics.reporter.slf4j.interval: 60 SECONDS
```

By continuously gathering runtime statistics and job performance metrics, it becomes possible to identify areas for improvement and execute an agile, adaptive tuning process that ensures optimal performance over time.

In systematically scrutinizing and adjusting Flink's configuration parameters, developers and operators can fine-tune the performance characteristics to meet specific quality of service requirements and operational objectives. Such nuanced understanding and application of these settings enhance Flink's ability to process large volumes of data efficiently and reliably within diverse processing ecosystems.

10.3 Enhancing Data Throughput and Reducing Latency

In the domain of real-time data processing, achieving high data throughput while maintaining low latency is imperative for the performance of Apache Flink applications. This section explores comprehensive strategies, optimizations, and configurations designed to enhance data throughput and minimize latency in Apache Flink environments.

Optimizing throughput involves maximizing the volume of data processed within a unit of time, while reducing latency refers to minimizing the delay from data ingestion to result output. Balancing these two objectives is challenging and requires an understanding of Flink's architecture and operational parameters.

Understanding Throughput and Latency in Flink

Before delving into optimization strategies, it's crucial to understand the inherent characteristics of throughput and latency.

- **Throughput** is the rate at which Flink processes incoming data streams, often dictated by factors like parallelism, task slot configuration, and data serialization/deserialization efficiency.

- **Latency** is the measure of delay from the point of data entry in the stream to when results are produced, influenced by factors such as processing delays, network congestion, and checkpointing overhead.

While increased parallelism typically improves throughput, it can occasionally exacerbate latency due to the added complexity of task coordination and potential for backpressure in network exchanges.

Optimization of Parallelism and Resource Utilization

One of the most direct methods to impact throughput and latency is via tuning parallelism:

- **Task Parallelism and Slot Configuration**:
  Aligning task parallelism with the number of CPU cores available can reduce contention and maximize resource usage. This alignment ensures tasks are distributed efficiently without overloading the Flink cluster nodes.

  ```
  parallelism.default: 16
  taskmanager.numberOfTaskSlots: 4
  ```

  It is advantageous to experiment with parallelism settings specific to each job's needs, balancing the workload across available resources to prevent any single task from becoming a bottleneck.

Efficient Serialization and Deserialization

Serialization formats and schemas have a significant impact on both throughput and latency:

- **Selecting Optimal Data Formats**:

  Use binary serialization formats like Avro or Protocol Buffers instead of JSON or XML to reduce data size and improve read-
  /write speeds.

  ```
  // Using Avro for serialization
  SpecificDatumWriter<User> writer = new SpecificDatumWriter<>(User.
      class);
  ByteArrayOutputStream out = new ByteArrayOutputStream();
  DataFileWriter<User> dataFileWriter = new DataFileWriter<>(writer);
  dataFileWriter.create(user.getSchema(), out);
  ```

- **Schema Evolution Handling**:

  Efficient handling of schema evolution in stream processing
  can minimize the performance loss incurred during data format
  changes.

Data Partitioning and Sharding Techniques

Partitioning strategies directly impact the distribution of workload
across the cluster, significantly influencing throughput and latency.

- **Keyed Streams**:

  The use of keyed streams to partition data among tasks based
  on the key reduces data skew and allows localized state management.

  ```
  dataStream.keyBy((KeySelector<MyType, String>) MyType::getKey)
          .process(new MyProcessFunction());
  ```

  However, care must be taken to avoid creating hotspots by selecting well-distributed keys.

- **Custom Partitioning**:

  Implementing custom partitioners can optimize data distribution patterns to better match application-specific demands.

  ```
  dataStream.partitionCustom(new CustomPartitioner(), (KeySelector<
      MyType, String>) MyType::getKey)
          .process(new CustomProcessFunction());
  ```

Utilizing Efficient State Management Practices

Flink's stateful processing capabilities are powerful for maintaining throughput while ensuring low latency:

- **RocksDB State Backend**:

  Use the RocksDB state backend for large state storage to benefit from its efficient memory usage and disk spill capabilities during memory-intensive operations.

  ```
  state.backend: rocksdb
  state.backend.rocksdb.checkpoint.transfer-thread-num: 4
  ```

  RocksDB optimally balances in-memory and on-disk states, reducing the need for frequent state serialization/deserialization.

- **Incremental Checkpoints**:

  Implement incremental checkpoints to minimize disruption to data flow and reduce the latency incurred during state storage.

  ```
  execution.checkpointing.incremental: true
  ```

Network Configuration and Buffer Management

Network configuration can dramatically affect both data throughput and the latency of data transfer:

- **Shuffle Service Settings**:

  Use Flink's data exchange mode to specify how records are shuffled between operators. Adjust from pipelined to batch shuffles based on network stability and resource availability:

  ```
  execution.batch-shuffle-mode: ALL_EXCHANGES_BLOCKING
  ```

- **Buffer Size and Management**:

  Configuring adequate network buffers ensures efficient data exchange and prevents delays incurred by I/O operations.

  ```
  taskmanager.network.memory.fraction: 0.15
  taskmanager.network.memory.min: 128mb
  ```

Leveraging Advanced Windowing Features

254

Windows define the boundaries of data streams processed together and significantly influence throughputs and latency:

- **Session Windows and Tumbling Windows**:
  Configure window sizes and types based on the application latency tolerance and throughput requirements.

  ```
  dataStream.windowAll(TumblingProcessingTimeWindows.of(Time.seconds
      (10)))
             .reduce(new ReduceFunction<MyType>() {...});
  ```

  Leverage session windows to handle bursty data patterns more effectively, adapting window size dynamically based on session gaps.

Backpressure Management and Flow Control

Balancing input rates with processing capacity is critical to maintaining low latency while achieving high throughput:

- **Backpressure Handling**:
  Analyze operator throughput via logging or metrics to identify backpressure sources. Employ buffer timeouts to increase resilience to sudden spikes in data volume.

  ```
  taskmanager.network.netty.flush.timeout.ms: 500
  ```

  This action assists in smoothing out fluctuations in data processing rates by controlling the rate at which network buffers are drained.

Continuous Configuration and Adaptive Tuning

Ultimately, a thorough understanding of workload characteristics, supported by active monitoring and adaptive tuning, contributes significantly to throughput and latency optimizations:

- **Automated Tuning Pipelines**:
  Consider using adaptive resource management tools to dynamically adjust task parallelism, network configurations, and even computational resources based on real-time workload insights.

Develop scripts to modify configuration files dynamically and redeploy configurations in response to observed patterns via Flink's REST API.

- **Monitoring Tools Integration**:

  Implement integrated monitors using Prometheus and Grafana to provide real-time feedback on latency and throughput metrics. Use these insights to adjust running configurations proactively and adaptively.

  ```
  metrics.reporter.promgateway.class: org.apache.flink.metrics.prometheus.
  PrometheusPushGatewayReporter
  ```

By employing these strategies, Flink's processing capabilities can be tuned for specific applications and environments, thereby maximizing throughput while minimizing latency. This tuning ensures robust and efficient handling of data streams, conducive to real-time processing objectives across various sectors and fields.

10.4   Checkpointing and State Management Best Practices

In Apache Flink, checkpointing and state management are critical components that enable fault tolerance and ensure consistency in streaming applications. This section delves into best practices for optimizing checkpoint intervals and managing state efficiently. These practices help balance the demands of fault tolerance against performance, providing robust guarantees even in the face of failures.

Flink's ability to recover from failures without losing state is one of its defining characteristics, offering exactly-once processing guarantees through its sophisticated checkpointing mechanism. Understanding and applying the correct checkpointing strategies is vital for maintaining system resilience and meeting performance objectives.

- **Understanding Flink's Checkpointing Mechanism**:

  Checkpointing in Flink creates consistent snapshots of an application's state distributed across all its tasks. These snapshots are stored in a reliable storage backend and can be used to restore the application state in case of a failure. The checkpointing frequency and configuration directly impact both performance and fault tolerance capabilities.

During checkpointing, a global snapshot is initiated by the Job-Manager, which instructs all participating tasks to take a snapshot of their in-memory state and buffers. The snapshots travel through the dataflow, coordinated by barriers that encapsulate checkpoints across parallel streams.

```
execution.checkpointing.interval: 10000
```

The choice of interval influences application performance: shorter intervals improve fault tolerance but incur higher performance costs due to increased IO and state persistence operations.

- **Choosing the Right State Backend**:

  The state backend configuration influences how states are stored and retrieved, impacting both resilience and performance:

  - **Memory State Backend**: Best suited for lightweight stateful computations with limited storage needs. This backend keeps states in the TaskManager's memory, providing fast access but risking data loss if the TaskManager fails.

  ```
  state.backend: memory
  ```

  - **Filesystem State Backend**: Stores state locally or in distributed filesystems, balancing speed with durability.

  ```
  state.backend.fs.checkpointdir: hdfs:///flink/checkpoints
  ```

  - **RocksDB State Backend**: Ideal for large-scale stateful applications. It offers more complex state serialization with disk-based durability, allowing large states without overwhelming memory resources.

  ```
  state.backend: rocksdb
  state.backend.rocksdb.localdir: /mnt/rocksdb/
  ```

257

- **Optimizing Checkpoint Intervals and Durability**:

  The frequency and durability settings for checkpoints must be adjusted per the fault tolerance requirements and the overhead they impose on throughput and latency.

  - **Checkpoint Interval**: Tweaking this interval affects the balance between throughput and resilience.

    Shorter intervals reduce data loss upon failure but can increase processing latency by introducing frequent state persistences. Longer intervals yield opposite effects.

    ```
    execution.checkpointing.interval: 5000
    execution.checkpointing.mode: EXACTLY_ONCE
    ```

  - **Asynchronous Checkpointing**: Allow checkpoints to happen asynchronously, minimizing disruptions to ongoing processing tasks.

    ```
    env.enableCheckpointing(5000, CheckpointingMode.
        EXACTLY_ONCE);
    env.getCheckpointConfig().enableExternalizedCheckpoints(
        CheckpointConfig.ExternalizedCheckpointCleanup.
        RETAIN_ON_CANCELLATION);
    ```

    This method allows processing to continue with minimal bottlenecks, particularly important in heavy-load scenarios.

- **State Size Management and Optimization**:

  Efficiently managing the state size is crucial for high-performance Flink applications:

  - **State TTL (Time-to-Live)**: Configure State TTL to ensure that state entries are automatically purged after their usefulness expires, thus reducing memory usage and improving performance.

    ```
    StateTtlConfig ttlConfig = StateTtlConfig
        .newBuilder(Time.hours(2))
        .setUpdateType(StateTtlConfig.UpdateType.
            OnCreateAndWrite)
        .build();

    ValueStateDescriptor<String> valueStateDescriptor =
        new ValueStateDescriptor<>("myState", String.class);
    valueStateDescriptor.enableTimeToLive(ttlConfig);
    ```

258

- **Reducing State Metadata**: Minimize metadata stored alongside state data to save space. Use compressed or optimized data formats when possible.

- **State Scaling and Repartitioning**: When application state grows too large, consider repartitioning or redistributing stateful operations. Use keyed streams wisely to ensure even state distribution across tasks.

• **Managing Checkpoint Storage and Cleanup**:

Efficient storage and cleanup of checkpoints are vital to prevent resource exhaustion:

- **Externalized Checkpoints**: Use externalized checkpoints to allow manual recovery and cleaning decisions post-application failures or restarts.

```
env.getCheckpointConfig().enableExternalizedCheckpoints(
    CheckpointConfig.ExternalizedCheckpointCleanup.
    DELETE_ON_CANCELLATION);
```

- **Using Distributed Object Stores**: Leverage reliable distributed stores like Amazon S3, Google Cloud Storage, or HDFS to persist state. Ensure storage policies and cleanup settings align with your application's data retention policies.

• **Reducing State I/O Overhead**:

Minimizing input/output operations during state access and updates improves performance:

- **Incremental Checkpoints**: Enable incremental checkpoints to snapshot only the state regions changed since the last checkpoint.

```
execution.checkpointing.incremental: true
```

This method greatly cuts down the amount of data written and transferred during checkpointing, ultimately speeding up state persistence.

- **Leveraging Off-Heap Memory**: For large, in-memory states, utilize off-heap memory to reduce garbage collection pressure and improve response times.

```
state.backend.rocksdb.ttl.compaction.filter.enabled: true
```

- **Advanced Fault Tolerance Strategies**:

Flink's resilience can be further fortified with advanced fault tolerance configurations and strategies:

  - **Savepoints**: Integrate savepoints for controlled application state captures, often used when upgrading jobs or redeploying with changes.

```
bin/flink savepoint <jobID> hdfs:///flink/savepoints/
```

  By initiating a savepoint, administrators can safely pause execution and conduct maintenance or upgrades.

  - **State Processor API**: Employ the State Processor API for programmatically manipulating snapshots to manage state changes or analysis retrospectively. This enhances flexibility when dealing with dynamic application topology or state schema modifications.

```
final ExecutionEnvironment bEnv = ExecutionEnvironment.
    getExecutionEnvironment();
bEnv.createInput(Savepoint.load(bEnv, "hdfs:///flink/savepoints",
    new MemoryStateBackend()))
    .readKeyedState("statefulOpUid", new ValueStateDescriptor<
        Integer>("state", Integer.class))
    .collect()
    .forEach(result -> System.out.println("State Entry: " + result)
        );
```

By adhering to these best practices, Flink applications can achieve the resilience and performance necessary for mission-critical, stateful, real-time data processing tasks. Mastery of checkpoint configurations and state management not only ensures system robustness but also maximizes efficiency, granting developers the confidence to meet stringent data processing demands.

10.5 Monitoring and Profiling Flink Applications

Monitoring and profiling are key practices for managing and optimizing the performance of Apache Flink applications. These processes provide insights into application behavior, resource usage, and bottlenecks, enabling developers to fine-tune performance and ensure reliability in real-time data processing. This section explores various tools, techniques, and best practices utilized in monitoring and profiling Flink applications.

Comprehensively understanding how Flink applications consume resources and process data is critical for maintaining a stable and efficient real-time data pipeline. Monitoring setups give real-time feedback regarding system health, while profiling identifies inefficiencies in code execution. Both practices combined can help rapidly diagnose and resolve performance issues.

- **Flink's Built-in Monitoring Tools**

  Apache Flink provides several built-in tools that facilitate the monitoring of running jobs, resources, and system vitals:

  - **Flink Dashboard**: The Flink Web UI offers a visual overview of running jobs, task managers, and metrics. It includes detailed visualizations that aid in understanding task execution flow, checkpointing status, and data throughput.

    This interface is accessible via the REST endpoint configured in the flink-conf.yaml file:

    ```
    rest.port: 8081
    ```

    The dashboard is crucial for real-time performance monitoring and provides intuitive navigation through job views, task pool usage, and more.

  - **Task Manager Logs**: Access task execution logs to glean insights into task-specific failures and performance issues. Logs offer granular details about task execution lifecycle, exceptions, and progression of streams.

261

```
tail -f log/flink--taskmanager-*.log
```

Logs can be configured for retention, verbosity, and rolling strategy depending on application needs:

```
log4j.rootLogger=INFO, file

log4j.appender.file=org.apache.log4j.RollingFileAppender
log4j.appender.file.File=log/taskmanager.log
```

- **Integrating Third-Party Monitoring Tools**

  The integration of external monitoring tools enhances observability with extended metrics and more advanced analytics:

  - **Prometheus and Grafana**: These tools offer powerful metric visualization and alerting capabilities that complement Flink's native monitoring.

    Start by integrating Flink's metric system with Prometheus:

    ```
    metrics.reporter.promgateway.class: org.apache.flink.metrics.
             prometheus.PrometheusPushGatewayReporter
    metrics.reporter.promgateway.port: 9091
    ```

    Configure Grafana dashboards using Prometheus as a data source to visualize performance across a range of custom and built-in metrics, such as task slot utilization, CPU usage, RAM consumption, and task latency.

  - **Elasticsearch-Logstash-Kibana (ELK Stack)**: Use ELK Stack to gather and analyze logs derived from Flink applications, offering search and analysis capabilities over large volumes of log data.

    Send Flink logs to Logstash for processing:

    ```
    log4j.appender.logstash=net.logstash.log4j.
             LogstashUdpSocketAppender
    log4j.appender.logstash.host=localhost
    log4j.appender.logstash.port=5000
    ```

  - **Apache Kafka**: Utilize Kafka for logging and metrics distribution, facilitating a scalable and durable data transport layer for operational insights and alerting strategies.

- **Advanced Profiling Techniques**

262

While monitoring provides a macroscopic view, profiling dives deeper into runtime characteristics and performance signatures:

- **Java Profiler Tools**: Tools like VisualVM, YourKit, and JProfiler can be employed to view real-time JVM properties, thread activity, memory allocation, and CPU usage.

  Attach a profiler to the running Flink task manager process for real-time insights:

  ```
  jvisualvm &
  ```

  Use these profiles to identify hotspots in CPU and memory usage, threading inefficiencies, or excessive object creation that might affect throughput and latency.

- **Flink's Backpressure Monitoring**: Backpressure can seriously influence latency and throughput. Flink provides backpressure monitoring capabilities accessible through the web dashboard, where subtask backpressure percentages aid in detecting bottlenecks:

  ```
  execution.backpressure.resampling.interval: 30000
  ```

  Address warranted backpressure by revisiting parallelism settings and reducing operators that block or buffer output substantially.

- **Best Practices for Monitoring Setup**

  To ensure that monitoring and profiling setups yield actionable insights, adhere to these best practices:

  - **Metric Granularity and Retention**: Define the granularity of metrics collected to balance between detail and storage/resource overhead. Consider aggregation of fine-grained data to longer-term trends for historical analysis purposes.

    ```
    metrics.scope.job: <job_name>
    ```

  - **Distributed Environment Configuration**: With cloud-native applications, ensure that metrics and log collection are distributed across geographical regions or fail-over zones to provide full observability regardless of node locations.

Implement geo-redundancy with multiple log/metric endpoints:

```
metrics.reporter.graphite.class: org.apache.flink.metrics.graphite.
    GraphiteReporter
metrics.reporter.graphite.host: graphite.mycompany.com
```

– **Automation with Alerts**: Automate alert systems based on thresholds of critical metrics, such as task errors or resource exhaustion, to immediately flag potential issues and enable rapid responsive strategies.

- **Utilizing Custom Metrics**

In addition to built-in metrics, custom metrics offer insights tailored to application-specific performance goals:

– **Custom Metric Sideloading**: Implement custom counters, gauges, or histograms within job logic to observe application-specific data flows or resource accesses.

```
final Counter customCounter = getRuntimeContext()
    .getMetricGroup()
    .counter("customCounter");

input.map(value -> {
    customCounter.inc();
    return value;
});
```

Use custom metrics to track events like processed records, API call frequencies, or specific data conditionals that might indicate processing anomalies.

- **Reactive Response Techniques**

Once the bottlenecks and inefficiencies are identified, deploying reactive response strategies becomes essential:

– **Dynamic Scaling Solutions**: Automatically scale Flink job resources based on metric triggers or workload trends. This can be achieved through integration with orchestration frameworks like Kubernetes or cloud-native scaling services:

264

```
kubectl autoscale deployment flink --cpu-percent=75 --min=1 --
max=10
```

- **Feedback Loop Systems**: Implement self-adjustments within applications to respond autonomously to inferred patterns from monitoring data (e.g., dynamically altering task parallelism based on input rate analyses).

In summary, the adoption of robust monitoring and profiling practices in Flink environments equips developers with the necessary tools to maintain application health effectively, refine performance, and address issues before they escalate, fostering an ecosystem of performant and resilient data processing applications.

10.6 Common Pitfalls and Solutions

In developing and deploying Apache Flink applications, practitioners often encounter numerous pitfalls that can impede performance, cause unexpected failures, or lead to inefficient resource usage. Understanding these common traps and their solutions can significantly enhance the robustness and efficiency of Flink applications. This section delves into typical challenges and provides practical solutions to overcome them.

Developers embarking on stream processing with Flink must navigate complex requirements, from ensuring data consistency to optimizing state management, all while maintaining high throughput and low latency. Anticipating common pitfalls and implementing effective solutions is crucial for successful deployment and operation.

Inefficient State Management

One frequent issue arises from suboptimal state management, which can lead to increased latency and memory pressure:

- **Excessive State Size**: When storing large amounts of state, improper management can quickly exhaust available memory, degrading performance.

Solution: Use state TTL (Time-to-Live) to limit the duration for which state is retained. This automatically purges obsolete data:

```
StateTtlConfig ttlConfig = StateTtlConfig
    .newBuilder(Time.hours(1))
    .setUpdateType(StateTtlConfig.UpdateType.OnCreateAndWrite)
    .setStateVisibility(StateTtlConfig.StateVisibility.
        ReturnExpiredIfNotCleanedUp)
    .build();

ValueStateDescriptor<String> stateDescriptor =
    new ValueStateDescriptor<>("keyedState", String.class);
stateDescriptor.enableTimeToLive(ttlConfig);
```

- **Improper State Backend Selection**: Choosing the wrong state backend can introduce unnecessary overhead.

  Solution: Ensure that the RocksDB state backend is used for large states entailing significant I/O operations. This allows using disk for state storage, freeing up in-memory resources.

  ```
  state.backend: rocksdb
  ```

Data Skew and Imbalanced Load

Data skew, where specific keys occur more frequently than others, can lead to an imbalanced distribution of workload among parallel tasks:

- **Inefficient Key Partitioning**: If the key distribution is uneven, certain nodes may handle significantly more data than others, leading to resource contention.

  Solution: Mitigate this by selecting a more evenly distributed partitioning key or implementing a composite key strategy based on combining multiple attributes.

  Consider creating a hash-based partitioner to ensure even data distribution:

  ```
  dataStream.keyBy(value -> value.getPartitionKey())
      .partitionCustom(new MyHashPartitioner(), value -> value)
      .process(new MyProcessFunction());
  ```

Excessive Backpressure

Backpressure occurs when downstream tasks cannot keep up with upstream data flow, leading to processing delays:

- **Under-provisioned Task Slots**: Insufficient task slots can cause backpressure due to bottlenecks in resource availability.

  Solution: Increase task slots relative to available cores or increase parallelism:

  ```
  taskmanager.numberOfTaskSlots: 8
  parallelism.default: 16
  ```

- **Blocking Operations**: Synchronous or blocking operations within stream processing create backpressure.

  Solution: Wherever feasible, convert blocking I/O operations to asynchronous alternatives. Using Flink's Async I/O API can offload potentially blocking operations to separate threads, thus maintaining stream throughput.

  ```
  AsyncDataStream.unorderedWait(dataStream, new MyAsyncFunction(),
      1000, TimeUnit.MILLISECONDS, 100);
  ```

Checkpoints and Latency

Incorrectly configured checkpoints can negatively impact latency and overall performance:

- **Frequent Checkpoints**: While enhancing fault tolerance, overly frequent checkpoints impose unnecessary I/O overhead.

  Solution: Set checkpoint intervals such that they balance state recovery speeds with processing performance.

  ```
  execution.checkpointing.interval: 30000
  execution.checkpointing.max-concurrent-checkpoints: 1
  ```

- **Synchronous Checkpointing**: Can increase processing pauses due to waiting processes during state snapshotting.

  Solution: Prefer asynchronous checkpointing to allow non-stop processing:

  ```
  env.enableCheckpointing(30000, CheckpointingMode.EXACTLY_ONCE);
  env.getCheckpointConfig().setCheckpointingMode(CheckpointingMode.
      ASYNC);
  ```

Inappropriate Time Characteristics

267

Misconfigurations related to event time handling can lead to unexpected results:

- **Underestimating Event Latency**: Skewed results can occur when calculations are performed against out-of-order events or insufficiently buffered event-time windows.

  Solution: Increase allowed lateness and use aligned watermarks for managing late events. Employ side outputs to retain late-arriving data for further analysis or reprocessing:

```
dataStream.assignTimestampsAndWatermarks(new
    BoundedOutOfOrdernessTimestampExtractor<MyType>(Time.
    seconds(10)) {
    @Override
    public long extractTimestamp(MyType element) {
        return element.getTimestamp();
    }
});
```

Mismanaged Resource Allocation

Resource misallocation can hinder job performance by leading to saturation or starvation of the processing elements:

- **Overcommitting Task Managers**: Allocating too many resources per task manager could degrade performance by causing resource wastage or increased context switching.

  Solution: Scale resources in correspondence with task load and complexity. Utilize resource managers and auto-scaling tools adapted for distributed Flink deployments (e.g., YARN or Kubernetes for dynamic resource management).

Coding Errors and Inefficient Practices

Even small coding mishaps can lead to inefficient Flink applications, which affect scalability and reliability:

- **Inefficient Data Transformations**: Non-optimized transformations can unnecessarily inflate processing times.

  Solution: Use map and filter operations instead of bulky loops, and prefer lazy transformations that defer execution until absolutely necessary.

```
DataStream<MyType> filteredStream = dataStream
    .filter(myType -> myType.isValid())
    .map(myType -> doSomethingComplex(myType));
```

- **Missed Optimization Opportunities**: Overlooking Flink-specific optimizations can hinder performance.

  Solution: Ensure task chaining—combining operators in one task—to minimize serialization/deserialization between operations:

  ```
  taskmanager.chain-tasks: true
  ```

Understanding these common pitfalls and integrating the requisite solutions into your Flink job designs can dramatically enhance application robustness and efficiency. By proactively identifying potential issues and applying strategic optimizations, developers can achieve robust and scalable Flink deployments that maximize the value derived from real-time streaming data.

www.ingramcontent.com/pod-product-compliance
Lightning Source LLC
LaVergne TN
LVHW051439050326
832903LV00030BD/3157